CW00644712

NIHILISM

A Philosophy Based In Nothingness And Eternity

BRETT STEVENS

WWW.MANTICORE.PRESS

Nihilism: A Philosophy Based In Nothingness And Eternity
Brett Stevens
© Brett Stevens, 2016

All rights reserved, no section of this book may be utilized without permission, including electronic reproductions without the permission of the author and publisher. Published in Australia.

BIC Classification:
HPX (Popular Philosophy), HPS (Social Philosophy), HPQ (Ethics)

978-0-9945958-3-6

MANTICORE PRESS
WWW.MANTICORE.PRESS

CONTENTS

INTRODUCTION

These texts took form during walks through the Texas wilderness in the transition between the last years of the previous century and the first decade of this one, with each column conceived as concept and outline in the safety of the woods. These were then transcribed late at night to be published on the fledgling dissident web.

Inspired by writings from the previous five years for an early e-zine, *The Undiscovered Country*, these writings developed further after the theoretical framework first expressed in the flier *Design Against Democracy*, a text now lost to time. They are written in a conscious homage to an ancient style by someone trained in not just writing, but postmodern writing, who found in the kenning and ring composition of older thinkers like Tacitus a better way to saturate the mind with ideas.

The thoughts that originated these writings began far earlier, in another patch of wilderness where the raw essence of reality and the transcendent possibilities of beauty both reared their contrasting but complementary heads. Let us turn to that scene:

A child arranges his wooden blocks to form a city unlike the one where he lives. He has bored of making houses and tanks like his friends, and instead is constructing an elaborate avenue with a stately building at its head and circular, recursive boulevards rising from it like wisps. The call comes from downstairs; it is time for school.

He ignores it at first, but then gets up to go. He looks at his creation one last time, knowing that when he returns the blocks will have been swept up and dumped into their box. All of the thought that went into that construction and all of the information it represents will be destroyed forever.

He gathers his books and gets into the car. The adult smell is there – a mixture of perfumes, paper, sweat and fear, which he knows from his own shivering at the thought of going to school or, worse, the dentist.

A short drive later, he is let loose on the steps of the school and the car peels out into traffic; he knows that jobs and other adults command the time his parents have. He cannot imagine growing up into that. He senses that something is hidden from him here, some large equation like the ones the bigger kids do in class. Sighing, he goes into the school.

In his classroom, the teacher begins with a lesson about civics. Susan and John are having a tussle over a toy, which interrupts the start of the lesson.

"Just give it to him," says the teacher.

"But I had it first!" says Susan.

"It doesn't matter," says the teacher. "It's important to share."

Then she turns to the other end of the classroom. Robert is on top of Roger, about to pound on him.

"Stop!" says the teacher. "No fighting."

"He hit me first," says Roger.

"He kept stomping on my clay people," says Robert, gesturing to a disordered pile of colored clay. "Now it's ruined. Like you do every day."

The boy who built the block city watches intensely. Robert has been nice to him. Roger he stays away from. His mother says Roger has a hard life at home. His mother lives in another city now.

"It doesn't matter," says the teacher. "You both know fighting is bad. Robert, you started it, so you go to the principal's office."

Order restored, the teacher turns around. "Why can't we all just get along?" she hums, as if it were a song she heard on the radio.

Now it is time for the lesson. The teacher begins by drawing two stick figures on the board. She takes out the red pen and draws a shiny apple in the hand of each.

"George has an apple, and David does not have one. David asks for a bite of George's apple. What should he do?"

The class pauses, then answers start coming:

"He should give him the apple."

"Yuck. I don't want his spit on my apple."

"He should tell him to get his own apple," says a familiar voice, and the child who built the block city is stunned to find he has spoken up.

The teacher stops, then takes two steps backward.

"But that isn't very polite," she says.

The boy speaks up again, unusual since he is a quiet child. "If he gives him the apple, George will have to find another apple. David will come back tomorrow and want an apple again. If he tells him to get his own, David will have to plant a tree and then both will have apples."

The teacher goes over to her desk, takes out her list of students, and makes a mark near one name. Susan flashes a victorious stare.

"George should give him a bite, and if he doesn't want spit on his apple, he can use a knife to cut the apple," says Susan.

The teacher smiles. "In half."

She walks to the area next to the door. "Isn't that fair, class? Now instead of one person being unhappy because he has no apple, both are happy."

She looks worriedly at the boy who built the city. He smells the scent of fear on her as well. The bell rings and escape occurs just in time.

On the way home, the boy has little to say. He spends most of his time staring out the window, waiting for other students and occasionally the teacher to catch up with what has been said. He hands the note that the teacher wrote to his mother, who clucks her tongue over it. "We'll see what happens when your Dad comes home," she says.

At home, he goes back upstairs. The blocks are neatly stacked in the box. "You always make work for me," says his mother. "You need to start cleaning up after yourself, so you can succeed in life like your father and I have."

His father comes home. He's had a few drinks after work. He and the mother retreat to another room and talk in angry whispers. The boy is worried at first. His parents are like most adults in his neighborhood very active in ensuring their children "turn out all right." This involves giving him little guidance, then punishing him when his guesses turn out wrong. Then they tell him what to do and if he refuses, throw out one of his toys. This was written in a magazine so it must be right. He shrugs and takes out a coloring book.

The bedroom door slams. It does this often. Then opens again, more cautious voices. The boy hides his face in the coloring book.

But when his parents come out, they say nothing. He asks his mother about the note from his teacher. "We'll talk about *that* later."

8

They sit down to dinner. It is the picture of normalcy: house in the suburb, good job, devoted mother, one boy and one girl sitting quietly at the table. His sister does not want to eat her Brussels sprouts. The parents are talking about an upcoming vacation. Something again is hidden.

"Boy, I need it," says the father. He and the mother pour more wine. The boy uses that moment to grab his sister's Brussels sprouts and yank them under the table where the dog eats them out of his hand.

"We should think about the Bahamas," says the mother, drinking.

"I told you already," says the father. "We can't afford that. Not and build up our retirement plan."

"Sod the retirement plan," says the mother. "When are we going to actually live? We spend all this time and money toward the future, and for what… we should enjoy ourselves now."

"That's *the* problem with you," says the father. "Always with your head in the clouds. It's why we never get anywhere."

"Fine, blame me," says the mother, throwing down her napkin and leaving.

The father turns to the children. "Never get married," he says. The dog wanders out from under the table and vomits green sludge onto the rug.

"Stupid dog," says the father, swatting it. It yelps and scoots from the room with its tail between its legs. "Why is it green—"

He inspects it more closely. "Brussels sprouts. At seven bucks a pound."

Horns sound insistently from the street, first a couple and then many, like angry voices shouting.

He turns to the kids. "And that's *the* problem with you," he begins. "We slave away and give you everything, and you can't even appreciate it. If you don't get yourself in line, mister, you're going to end up a garbageman."

The boy shrugs. It sounds kind of fun.

"I guess you haven't picked up on the fact that this world is a mess," says the father. "You either get on top, or you're nobody. That's not the kid I raised you to be. I want you to be like me, driven to get ahead, but skipping my mistakes. A little me with the options I never had. Instead I get a little miscreant."

The kids laugh at the word, which the father pronounces with a scowl. He throws down his napkin and storms out of the room. The bedroom door slams. They hear their father's voice come out clearly: "*And* a note from the teacher? Why did *we* get the defective kids? We did *everything* right. Everything *they* told us to. These kids are going to ruin it for us."

The children flee the dinner table.

When his mother comes to tuck him in, the boy asks what his father said. "Don't worry about it now, honey," she says sweetly. "But if it continues, we're going to have to take you out of school and send you to a military school. You'll stay there all year and if you misbehave, they'll take it out of your hide." Her voice has become dry. She snaps off the light with a violent motion.

The problem, the boy reflects. This night as usual he does not sleep much. His father watches television downstairs, the show with the angry voices about the war that still might be happening. His mother drinks more wine alone in the breakfast nook near the kitchen, reading a book about romantic experiences in a faraway land. Planes roar overhead and the car horns never quite stop.

A train passes in the night. Its horn stretches in Doppler-space into a plaintive call from far away, a hint of what might lie beyond the trees that block the horizon, a cold northern breeze bearing hints of a world beyond. There might be escape; but adults seem so odd.

He remembers a conversation his mother had with Mrs. Fitzgerald, the older lady at the end of the street who is important somehow to the neighborhood. His mother put on a really nice dress and the perfume she wore when going out at night. They were talking about Susan's mother.

"It's her birthday, poor dear," said Mrs. Fitzgerald. "She's nearly in tears."

The boy looked up, confused. She saw his face and said, "She's getting older."

"It's different when you grow up," said his mother. "Enjoy your young years while you can. It will never be this easy again."

"I remember them well," said Mrs. Fitzgerald. "Those were the easy days. Someone else paid for everything. No job, no mortgage, no bills and no – well, time is different then." He smells the fear on her as well, an ancient and dusty smell, like rooms where nothing good happened that have been abandoned in haste.

Both adults drank tea. The hidden thing took up the room like a shadow. He looked down and stays that way until it is time to go, the perfumes of the mothers mingling in a choking cloud.

"She means that Mrs. Kozlowski is upset because she is getting older," his mother explained in the car.

"Why is that sad?" said the boy.

"When you're older, you get old, and what are you closer to?" she asked. "You should think about these things because they are important when you grow up."

"When you die?" said the boy, after thinking for a moment.

"Don't worry about it now," said his mother. "Just put your head down, work hard and get ahead. It helps," she added, as they turned into their own driveway. "Then you can have a nice house like this one, and things to make you feel comfortable, and not be a garbageman who has to live in a city apartment."

Now in the middle of the night he feels it: death, a far-off concept. He remembers the goldfish they buried in the backyard. "It's just a goldfish," his father had said, and they never mentioned it again.

Like a flame on a candle, there for an instant, and then gone. Never really existing, but coming into form from heat, wick and air.

Now he feels in increasing panic the instants running away from him. His time, infinitely short, and taken up by school and after that, a job. No escape. He would be kept doing things for other people, that like his parents he would hate, until someday death took him away.

The train horn sounded again, a hollow distant sound like time itself.

The next morning he got up early. He walked past the blocks in their box and got himself some cereal. Eating, he stared straight ahead. It was Saturday and his sister was watching cartoons. He walked past. The flame would eat them, too, but even more quickly. He went outside.

Their backyard abutted a drainage path for the neighborhood. He would see the rain growing deep and flowing into it from the puddles that formed on the concrete around the neighborhood. The water had nowhere to go so it ran in circles until there was too much, then it spilled into the drainage. There were no fish – he always checked.

He kept walking until he reached the forest. This was the end of the neighborhood and because they were in something called "the suburbs," the limit of the city. Cooler air beckoned from the darkness within. He ran in with a small gasp.

Under a tree he looked around him. Leaves covered the floor, some decayed so that their fine skeletons of veins were all that remained. Birds called from hidden areas in the leaves. He walked through the gentle hills and over small streams. At one point he found the skeleton of a squirrel, and recoiled from the smell of death. But it melded with the smell of leaves and soon, he had forgotten it. He walked on.

In a small clearing, surrounded by strange plants with large leaves, he sat. Nothing was here, and everything. It all made sense: the trees dropping leaves that made the dirt rich and full, the sun caught in treetops and making them grow big, the squirrels and birds eating fruit and each other, sometimes. All is the flame, untouchable yet recurring. He had found what had been hidden from him.

In that clearing, which would soon be bulldozed flat to make room for more houses, he made a pact with himself: he would see things as they were here, always, no matter what the adults said. But he feared the day when he would become an adult, too, and worried that the hidden thing inside of people would take him, too.

These essays reflect a denied truth: unless we get control of ourselves as a species, the bulldozer is coming for every forest. Misery will infect every soul. Ugliness will beat out beauty, and we will live in a Hell of our own creation. The root of this confusion is a denial of reality and its substitution with feelings, judgments and desires that reflect our personal emotional intentions toward what the world *should* be, not what it is.

Humanity should fear the future, but also loathe the present. Jobs are jails where 90% of the activity exists only to demonstrate the importance of the people involved, cities are utilitarian catacombs of mutual revulsion, schools are rose-scented concentration camps, commuting and bureaucracy waste our time, and our general outlook on ourselves is bad because we know our world is ugly and expanding to export that ugliness everywhere it can touch. We hate ourselves for living in misery and tolerating insanity and stupidity all around us in addition to our ongoing wholesale destruction of our natural world. We breed like yeast and every person wants a suburban home, two cars, large-screen television and three meals a day. The problem is not space for housing people, but for the infrastructure required to support them: farms, hospitals, schools, streets, parking, malls, workplaces, gas stations, restaurants and stores. This is the root of our crisis both as a society and as an ecocidal species out of control. We expand, and this marginalizes nature, crushing ecosystems and replacing them with parks and wasteland in which only adaptive generalists like squirrels, sparrows, rats and cockroaches thrive. There is no plan, except for more of us living in the same way, and we are not certain we like what we have become.

When a choice leads to a gradual intensification of the same symptoms, it is time to change that choice, starting with the reasoning that led us there. For humans, that reasoning is the validation of illusion because individuals choose to believe it is true and it becomes popular. Changing direction requires crossing the taboo line and denying the union of individualism and collectivism that takes form in the egalitarian, altruistic and democratic order of our current time. This requires some direction other than further into individual desires, a change which in turn demands we pay attention to larger concerns than ourselves and find purpose in doing so.

The *Design Against Democracy* flier clarified these issues. It described the difference between *structure*, or the invisible interrelationship of things, and *appearance*, or the surface that humans see and confuse for the real thing. We either choose knowledge and structure, or we live in a world of self-referential illusion where we deny how wrong we are before we even see the outcome. As nihilists, we look toward particularized solutions through structure instead of social responses through appearance. There is no single universal truth, or ideology, which can guide us. We need instead quality of decision-making at every level which is a function of the quality of people and degree of their mental and moral acuity instead of a political or social system. This is a struggle for survival against our own bad impulses and illusions, and how in groups we turn those into pleasant-sound, socially acceptable insanity.

These writings describe nihilism as a philosophical gateway more than end result. Nihilism is a psychological and analytical tool for deconstructing human deconstruction, which consists of dividing reality into tiny mental objects so it can be analyzed independent of context and consequences. This allows us to continue the illusion in self-congratulatory "scientific" and "moral" impulses of justification, missing the point that the results we obtain are the ones we are accountable for. The Nuremberg defense – "I was just following orders" – will not save us from the results that may not be of our personal choice, but are our personal responsibility to avoid. We are in the driver's seat, both as individuals and as a species, and we need to steer this car toward sanity instead of its present path.

None of this is popular knowledge. Nihilism is the opposite of popularity; it requires the individual to look deep within his inner self and understand that core as a means of perceiving the world, and through that, to recognize how to adapt to that world without sacrificing it to human pretense. This in turn forces humility on ourselves as we realize our limitations and, often, the animal nature of our desires. But like all philosophy, the distillation of wisdom pushes us to further knowledge and in doing so, abandons the answers that took us only halfway. Nihilism opens the door and the rest is up to us.

NIHILISM

The bomber approaches Haiphong, furtively hugging the ground in the shadows of radar fields. The pilot reviews the checklist on his knee; he flips each switch carefully, taking pleasure in the task for the sense of both security and strength it conveys. Power rushes through the aircraft as its engines blast fire into the clouds. He knows that each choice he makes, even a millimeter of difference in his hand on the stick, will determine success or death. He reflects that every moment in life is like walking on the edge of a knife, but here, the SAMs and MiGs make the lurking menace tangible. He feels mortality on his face like a cold northern breeze. And then he reaches forward, and guides his aircraft toward the target.

Nihilism grows from a conceptual seed: neither universal truth nor subjectivity exists. Both are human constructions designed to remove the fear of unknowns in our world. All we have is reality and our ability to adapt to it.

This philosophy does not give us the comforts of materialism, which says that the physical world is all that exists, as if demanding license to indulge in personal comfort at the expense of all else. Nor does it give the assurances of dualism, which states that only a metaphysical world is real and our physical world is secondary, where the primary world suspiciously resembles human hopes contrary to reality. Nihilism leaves us with life as mostly mystery and reveals the emptiness of our own attempts to conquer this.

As an extreme form of realism, nihilism reverses the human tendency toward backward perception of the world. Humans obscure unknowns by creating hypotheses about what is real, selectively choosing a subset of the data present to justify each hypothesis as reality through a process called *rationalism*. Our hypotheses are necessarily narrower than the world at large, and can be true without reflecting reality, so we are always finding answers that match our questions. These hypotheses flatter our notion of being in control of our destinies, which pleases the individual and the group. Society uses intermediaries – laws, rules, politeness, economies – to impose these hypotheses as replacement for noticing reality itself, and making decisions based on particular situations. We often talk about whether an action taken by someone that had bad consequences was legal or not, but that concerns the intermediary, not the results. Intermediaries are designed to conceal results behind interpretation, especially of intent.

We use group consensus of to create an alternative reality from those hypotheses, like a collective consensual hallucination, which allows us to control others, forcing them to conform to our new notions in order to avoid seeing the whole picture. This process deteriorates shared values and causes society to seek instead *validity*, or the obligation to bestow equal social acceptance on all people. This egalitarian and altruistic appearance conceals an ambition for power. As the official story conflicts with noticed reality, people fear for a lack of validity and, instead of acknowledging their own incorrect perception, *scapegoat* reality itself and portray life as negative and pointless. The primitive man curses the sky and presumes the gods must be angry, where the advanced man cooks up a scientific study or book of philosophy to explain failure as success through a positive, "humanistic" and Utopian view of it as "progress."

Humans justify this illusion with the mentally convenient process of social control, which takes the form of *utilitarianism*, or deciding that what most people think is "good" – not real – is best. Like kindergarten teachers who prioritize having everyone get along over finding the correct answer, our societies control us through the utilitarian methods of (1) democratic voting, (2) consumer purchases including of media, and (3) social popularity itself where the idea that flatters most people in the room is victorious. At that point, society has become entirely self-referential and circular like its logical process, declaring that what most of its people desire is true and arguing for it with a highly selective, filtered, and social view of reality. This subverts all fact and language because those are quickly re-interpreted in order to support the narrative. That act creates an enduring tension between the official story and the reality that keeps peeking through, gradually consuming all of civilization with the debate and tearing it apart with internal friction as happened in ancient Rome and Athens.

Convention dictates that nihilism denies truth, values and the possibility of communication. In actuality, nihilism denies inherent truth because truth is particular to a hypothesis and the persons perceiving it, and so is neither universal nor subjective. Nor are values universal, but reflect the agreement between people on what is important, which is in turn contingent on what they recognize as real. Like truth, values are discovered through a philosophical process called *esotericism* which states that truth is revealed only to those with the cumulative knowledge to understand it. This in turn – very politically incorrectly – is regulated by our innate abilities, including intelligence and moral character, through something called the Dunning-Kruger effect:

> *People tend to hold overly favorable views of their abilities in many social and intellectual domains. The authors suggest that this overestimation occurs, in part, because people who are unskilled in these domains suffer a dual burden: Not only do these people reach erroneous conclusions and make unfortunate choices, but their incompetence robs them of the metacognitive ability to realize it.*[1]

We are revealed by our choices, which are not subjective but reflective of what we know and intend. Communication itself is not universal

---

[1] J Kruger and D Dunning, "Unskilled and unaware of it: how difficulties in recognizing one's own incompetence lead to inflated self-assessments," *Journal of Personality and Social Psychology* (1999).

either. Nietzsche illustrates[2] that tokens only work when both parties share the same meaning, which is dependent upon our "subjective" different IQs, character, experience and basic moral outlook. There are no universal truths except reality, and it is not universal – capable of being summed up in simple postulates that apply in every situation which everyone in the crowd can understand – but highly particularized, with specific local context and situational factors heavily influencing outcome. Our society relies on these universal symbols to control its population, but spends most of its time debating them in a futile attempt to preserve order. Whatever nihilism denies was never to be relied on in the first place.

Only one solution exists for illusion: (1) a gnarly realism to carve under it and get to a representative view of the way the world around us works, and (2) a transcendent goal which takes us past the trivial activities of a dying civilization toward something more rewarding. In a dying civilization, most activities consist of gift-giving through expansion of an altruistic/egalitarian franchise, pursuit of trivial commercial success, and self-aggrandizement through social activity. The latter is important because without an ongoing goal that we can never achieve, we relapse into backward-looking pursuits of social success, or pleasing others with actions that because they do not correspond to reality, seem inspirational or hopeful to others.

Nihilism represents an option to the decay of civilizations, not by finding "higher" values but by rejecting all values and instead looking at plain cause-to-effect logic. Our pretense of "higher" values justifies itself through a morality of universal acceptance and universal truths, which nihilism then deconstructs and replaces with the question of results in reality. This finally restores to humanity the Darwinian goal of all species: adapt to reality, and then maximize your position within it. The crowd fears *any* goal because social standards such as goals mean that individuals can fall short, therefore social hierarchy will occur as some rise above others. Utilitarianism preys on that fear by demanding universal truths and equal inclusion for all people, but that reduces the quality

---

[2] Friedrich Nietzsche, "On Truth and Lying in a Non-Moral Sense," *The birth of tragedy and other writings*, Cambridge University Press (1999).

of those people by reducing competition for higher traits. Nihilism recognizes reality as immutable and hopes to improve the quality of human thinking instead so we can more elegantly adapt to reality, starting by showing us the transcendent value of a world where we can distinguish ourselves based on our inner characteristics of intelligence, moral goodness and strength of character.

With this transcendental path, nihilism unleashes a sense of wonder and adventure that is conditioned upon the necessary darkness, violence and instability of nature which provides the opportunity for epic contrasts to emerge, allowing us to make choices that define us, and through those produce meaning. Nihilism says that there is no one right path to give life order, but the lack of such a path does not mean emptiness, only a need to understand our world and see where it and our inner selves overlap, and then to learn to like ourselves by rising to meet the challenge. This heroic attitude places principle above personal convenience, and wisdom above popularity, which makes it hard to control but gives us a sense of purpose and worth to our existence. Only in that do we surpass negativity, reconnect with life in a unitive sense and, for the first time, realize that we adore existence and want to honor it with our actions.

The pilot runs down the checklist one more time. His survival depends not just on this second but on every moment, and he knows that the calming sounds of rushing air and throbbing engines mask the possibility of death invisibly rushing at him. Yet the sensation of agility as he cuts through the atmosphere instills in him a belief in life like a form of love or religion where he sees existence as logical and possessing a beauty far greater than what any individual can achieve. As he selects his targets and arms his weapons, he feels an intense sense of thankfulness for the opportunity to be this incarnate being with these mortal struggles that create in him an urge to be responsible for improving his world. With that thought, he nudges the stick and without regard for those who will die below, unleashes his weapons.

LOVE AND NIHILISM: A PARALLELISM PRIMER

As social animals, we get our information from others. This includes morality, or a group behavioral code based on a sense of value and purpose inherent to individual lives.

In contrast, nihilism denies value and purpose, and in turn denies any special role to humanity. Like emotions, value and purpose are human judgments which do not exist in the outside world.

By denying the human-centric view of the world, nihilism forces us see physical reality as a mechanical process in which our part is small. When we are walking in winter, falling snow appears to be coming toward us, but in reality we are moving forward as it falls.

Where morality deals with how things appear to us, nihilism addresses reality as a design and encourages us to learn how to adapt to it. Morality is withdrawal from natural selection; nihilism embraces it, and describes the world as a complex ongoing calculation that produces good results through sorting: better ideas above worse, stronger above weaker, beautiful above ugly.

Nihilism

We frequently talk about "human nature." It is more sensible to talk about the challenges facing any animal with higher intelligence. Any smart animal will face the same challenges and use roughly the same methods to adapt.

While having a big brain is an asset, it is also a liability, in that if a big brain has to re-analyze its surroundings, it will move very slowly. Instead, big brained animals analyze once, create a mental "map" of their world, and update as needed.

In theory, we update our maps when new data comes about. But if this data is incorrect, our knowledge of the world gets corrupted. We act expecting certain outcomes and are stunned when things do not go as planned.

What corrupts our minds is when we reverse the causal process of understanding. Instead of looking to the world, making conclusions and updating our maps, we update our maps based on what we wish were happening – or what others tell us.

When our maps become solipsistic – based on human desires for the world, not the world as it is – we lose the ability to predict the results of our actions. We intend certain results, but if our actions are based on illusory assumptions, they will have unintended consequences.

Corruption

Values and purpose are human inventions designed to be shared between us. Like language, values and purpose only work if we all know and agree on what they mean. They are easily manipulated by changing meaning without changing the symbol for it.

The world around us is consistent and non-judgmental. It functions and leaves thinking to us. If we do not make sense of it, the response will be bad. If we adapt to it, the response will be good.

Individuals using goodwill as a cover story have re-defined our values and purpose. They do this to benefit themselves, but as a result, *corrupt* the mental maps of society around them. This process takes centuries to fully show itself.

We cannot see evidence of our corruption in a single fact, but can measure it from multiple points of view and find what they have in common, like we triangulate to find radio signals. Our measurements are:

- *Ecocide.* Our inability to constrain our numbers and our desires has resulted in human expansion which eliminates natural habitats, and both pollutes the environment and takes resources from it beyond what it can replenish.

- *Boredom.* Society and jobs cater to the lowest common denominator, and so lapse into a utilitarian modernism that produces ugly architecture, mind-numbingly micromanaged tasks, disorder and dysfunction.

- *Selfishness.* A culture based on individual desires makes it easy to manipulate one another, but produces no great art, and leaves us with commerce and political dogma that constrain not liberate us.

- *Neurosis.* Value and purpose, when used to convince others that we are altruistic, good people, create a social reality that steadily drifts farther from the many factors of reality into a single, social or commercial factor. Our minds split between social reality and physical reality.

- *Depression.* We compensate for a failing civilization through surrogate activities. These are ineffectual symbolic acts that we do not expect to make change, but they "uplift" us for a few moments so we feel better about ourselves.

2400 years ago Socrates recognized that individuals prefer how things appear – or can be made to appear – to their intelligible form, which requires knowledge of their context and consequences. Appearance is tangible and public but knowledge, like goodness, is intangible and silent.

The Civilization Cycle

Civilizations have a life cycle from birth to death. Each stage in this cycle has a distinct philosophy and psychology which corresponds to the type of government people in that time believe is best. These patterns taken together form "civilizational designs."

From the day a civilization is founded, it slowly drifts farther from reality and further into the world of appearance. People manipulate each other to get ahead, and the side effect is a corrupted image of reality.

People use wishful thinking to manipulate each other. Wishful thinking pretends that humans are omniscient and not part of nature; that our intent is more important than the outcome of our actions. It avoids all mention of death, conflict, unequal abilities and eventually, reality itself.

In a new civilization, wishful thinking is kept in check by the need to interact with the natural world. As a society grows, more intermediaries like law, economics and morals serve to interpret nature for it. These interpretations reflect their interpreters more than their subject, which causes a gradual growth of illusion.

At the end of civilization, the illusion has entirely replaced any notion of reality and only those who vigorously uphold the illusion, now called ideology, are rewarded. When collapse comes, it surprises everyone inside the civilization, but outsiders can see it coming.

Modernism

Modernism occurs when a society selects the philosophy of linear logic ("rationalism") and the belief in technological progress overcoming nature. This happens to civilizations when they are nearing the end of their life cycles.

The last thousand years of Western civilization have been defined by a steadily-increasing modernism, and the previous thousand were expended on conflict allowing that modernism to happen. During the past two centuries, the process has accelerated into the final stage.

Rationalism

The philosophy that came to be called rationalism emerged from our use of tools. Where previously we had to seek out a situation that matched our needs, now we needed only a single factor: the tool.

Normally, we think from cause to effect: Each time it rains (cause) the sidewalk is wet (effect). But this equation cannot be reversed because when the sidewalk is wet, a cause other than rain may be responsible.

Rationalism arose through the logic of tools. A single factor produces the effect as a method, and not a cause in itself. With the logic of rationalism, we filter out other factors as "irrelevant."

This results in us assigning cause to the tool, which we assume is the intent, forgetting that what we see as effect may be a cause to another effect. For example, someone wets a sidewalk not to make it wet as an effect *in itself*, but to ready it for cleaning.

In social circumstances, this makes us think of methods as causes, and impels us to limit methods as a means of regulating intent. This removes cause from the equation, reducing it to *effect = intent*, which creates a solipsistic world where only intent matters.

In this narrow view, we deny that cause (intent) cannot be inferred from method (effect). This creates a mentality of *control*, or the idea that by limiting methods, we can change cause and through it intent, manipulating the minds of others.

Externalization

We externalize ourselves by relying on the idea of methods and intent being the same. This in turn makes us rely on the method of appearance, or what others agreed was good.

This causes conflict because often, methods seen as bad were necessary to produce good results. Not everyone can understand that, which results in a standardization of morality to methods regarded as safe.

External control arises from this standardization. It results in a utilitarian order with three prongs: what makes profit, what people vote for, and what is popular.

Socialization

As part of the process of specialization of labor, we must make it known why our needs are important so that others collaborate with us without resentment. In order to convince them, we use the appearance of *altruism* to make ourselves look good.

We demand the same rights for others as ourselves to convince everyone of our goodness. When you must convince others that you ought to be helped, you need to first show them that you have goodwill toward them – without judging them.

The best way to do this is to suggest that the human form, and not the unique abilities of the human, makes this person entitled to being treated well. This way, no matter what they think of you, they will feel good for helping you.

We achieve this false goodwill through universal inclusion, or equality. It purports to achieve a society where all are welcomed despite their faults and will not be ranked according to ability, moral character or aptitude.

This process shows rationalism in action. We use appearance as a tool to control others. This takes several forms:

- Equality of all humans (or, universal inclusion)
- Ability for anyone to do whatever they want
- Peace, nonviolence, tolerance are good
- Freedom from criticism on the basis of reality

In a rationalistic outlook, if social instability is bad, then social stability must be achieved by regulating methods regardless of context or consequence. As a result, we make aggressive behavior taboo and reward those who avoid conflict.

To avoid conflict, we must compromise any idea where others will object to it. We ignore the consequences of our actions and focus instead on showing goodwill, which eliminates the visible conflict but prevents resolution of what caused it.

Since these compromises must avoid that which will cause offense or fear to any one person, we create a *lowest common denominator* response to reality made of the inoffensive, benevolent-sounding, and easy. This enables us to ignore reality because we have a consensual substitute.

Individualism

Since linear logic convinces us to pick one factor of many in our thinking, when approaching the question of life itself we pick a single factor: ourselves.

In order to make ourselves more powerful, we act so we appear altruistic, but we also perform so that we appear independent and unique in order to attract others to our personalities. This causes us to act entirely through social thinking.

Through this method, individualism creates a "social reality" or a tacit conspiracy between people to manage reality with social factors. Since we need others, thanks to specialization of labor, we use this more than reality itself.

This has two effects: first, we become neurotic because we see reality in the details but are encouraged to ignore it; second, since social reality ignores secondary effects, disorder spreads and the cost is passed on to us.

This in turn encourages us to try to break away from social obligation, since we feel it is parasitic to us, and so we use individualism as an argument to reduce obligations to others. This does not work, so we turn to our leaders and ask for more control.

Control is the external imposition of what some people agree is true. Unlike an organic order, or one arriving from agreement and cooperation among people, it requires force against non-conformists and small rewards for conformists in order to function.

In this way, we can see how individualism leads to disorder which requires more control, in a cyclical process or "death spiral" that gains intensity over time, causing civilization to collapse.

Utilitarianism

The public display of altruism is a powerful tool. It could get you elected, or make others follow you as a leader, or make them work for less money. It can get you ahead at the expense of others.

Civilization through its wealth makes it possible for us to be far enough removed from nature that we pretend there is no reality except human reality. We withdraw, and we do so in a group which defends itself against critique.

Because the civilization is based on the idea of individualism, or each person being able to do whatever they think is right, it soon becomes *utilitarian*. "What most people think is best is best" defines utilitarianism.

At this point, the tail wags the dog. We no longer do things because they are realistic actions. We do them to make ourselves look good, so that we can leverage services out of others with our perceived altruism.

This triumph of unreality brings consequences but because it is antisocial to mention them, those who speak of them are ostracized and kept out of jobs, relationships, friendships and public favor. The dogma overrides reality.

Like a society of drunks, civilization becomes dysfunctional but it is not permitted to notice. Behavior is disorganized, and the only plan is one based on a form of linear logic that involves removing the "bad" and assuming that what is left is the good.

The only things people can agree on are that they want to be able to earn money, and that they do not want other people interrupting them. They call these agreements "freedom," "equality" and "justice" and crush any who oppose them.

Totalitarianism

We are all acquainted with centralized authoritarianism. More terrifying is the tendency of crowds, through constant rebellions for more "freedom" which cause negative social consequences and thus require more control, to create camouflaged totalitarian states.

The first part of this process is *decentralized* totalitarianism, or the tendency of crowds to enforce dogma by ostracizing those who do not repeat the illusion so that they are deprived of the benefits of specialized labor.

In this stage, individuals gain power by pandering to the desire of the crowd to see appearance triumph over reality. Individuals can find others lacking in altruism, point it out, and be rewarded with higher social status.

The second, when disorder rises enough at the same time the civilization becomes more disorganized, occurs when the powerful who have profited from its decline choose a tyrant to enforce a brutal, simplistic and effective order because on their own the people are too chaotic to behave.

This is how freedom, equality and justice create tyranny through control. Because they are imposed orders, derived from linear logic which picks one factor of many to be absolute, they conflict with reality and require more not less control as time goes on.

Parallelism

Reversing this process of decay is surprisingly easy. We need to change our assumptions and method of thinking. Nihilism changes our unrealistic thinking and leads us to another philosophy called *parallelism*.

Parallelism replaces linear logic. Where linear logic says to pick one factor of many, parallelism says we consider all factors at once and look at how they regulate one another. Then we assess our actions by their impact on these non-linear patterns, such as ecosystems, economies and social hierarchies.

In parallelism, instead of killing a buffalo for clothing, we determine how many buffalo we can take without destroying the herd or interfering with the factors required for more buffalo, such as open land, clean seas, healthy predators and the food supply for the buffalo.

Holism

Most political control structures create a partial truth of reality, define obedience to it as good/evil, and rapidly control people using that. The dogma of equality, freedom, peace, tolerance and nonviolence is no different.

Parallelism reverses this pattern by forcing a description of reality as a whole, and then pointing out what actions will bring negative consequences from reality itself – with no need for the evil/not-evil artificial reality of control. Parallelism measures by results in whole, not the single factor of methods.

Unlike idealistic and utopian systems, parallelism recognizes that there is no way to avoid tragedy, conflict, horror and decay, but that they can produce positive results if people are vigilant about keeping each other on track toward reality.

Where most political systems define what is bad, and assume the rest to be good, parallelism defines a goal and strives toward it through whatever methods work. We call it a "whole" philosophy since it does not divide the world into bad and good but accepts both as means to an end.

Beyond Good and Evil

Parallelism recognizes that bad and good do not exist, but are our judgments of outcomes. It also recognizes that the ultimate outcome of life, its perpetuation, requires both good and evil, so we call it "meta-good."

Once we see reality as meta-good, we do not need false positivity and false inherency as offered by other "worlds" created through human judgment. Whether secular (social reality) or religious (heaven), these other worlds corrupt us.

Denying inherent value and purpose removes this false positivity and with it the means of mental control of individuals that in turn empowers the control of the state. When the good symbol appears, people rush toward it much as they flee the bad symbol when it appears.

When the thought process of justification is reversed, people stop looking for inherent or social reality proof, and instead turn to the scientific method – observing reality, and testing their knowledge of it, to see what patterns emerge.

Immanent

By denying the inherency of truth, nihilism orients itself toward patterns that emerge from specific situations formed of the intersection between natural laws, objects and human acts. This moves away from *universal* or absolute truths.

Where linear logic and control structures demand a single absolute path, in parallelism, nothing is universal. Objects and situations do not have inherent, fixed properties. Instead, non-linear patterns "emerge" through the intersection of multiple factors.

Every time certain conditions are met, patterns appear. These have a logical basis, and can occur in the forms of matter, energy and thought alike. Philosophers describe emergent properties as "immanent," or distilling out of a situation rather than being inherent to one of its parts.

We can describe immanent properties as "organic," because like life itself, they grow from a few conditions into a diversity of objects formed from similar patterns under slightly different circumstances. Control – as is required for "inherent" truth – must be imposed.

Transcendent

Because nihilists believe neither in religious other worlds (heaven) or secular other worlds (morality), we are independent from the principle of absolute and universal dogma that denies the importance of reality.

Values and purpose are things we impose based on our observations of what will succeed in adapting to reality, and yet also give us a sense of *meaning*. Meaning is interpreted by the individual but derived from reality, so realistic individuals have similar ideas of what is important.

Philosophers call this *transcendental*, from the Latin "climb over," because it encourages us to accept reality including its negative aspects. Instead of denying the negative, we find a greater positive goal in the possibilities of reality itself, the "meta-good."

When we transcend, we no longer need false absolutes. Instead, we delight in reality because it is a space of potential. Good and bad are methods we can use to realize that potential; morality is measured by results, not methods or intentions.

Science

Since nihilism is ultimately an affirmation of the scientific method in non-linear form, we can look through history to see what designs of civilizations have worked best in the past. We can choose the best for our own.

We do not have to like the answers we find. These are not arbitrary choices, preferences, or beliefs; they are deductions from using our logical skills. They are too complex to be "proved" by experiments, but our sense of logic can help us see truth in them.

Organic Society

Every civilization needs a narrative. This consensus describes the origins of the civilization, its ongoing but unattainable goals, and what its values and methods it can use to achieve that.

The best goals are not tangible ones, but goals that can grow over time, much as we compete against ourselves to exceed our past achievements. For most, the goal is tied to a land, a worldview, a values system and people like themselves. Eventually these expand to *transcendentals*, or abstract goals like the simultaneous realization of the good, the beautiful and the true.

Immanent goals are patterns which naturally make sense given a certain situation. These do not change over time because humans do not change. When these occur as a part of the growth of a civilization, we call them "organic" goals.

> *Organic, adj. Having an organization similar in its complexity to that of living things.*[3]

Organic societies are logical responses to their environments. They exist on a "whole" level, or one that considers all factors at once. They are the opposite of rationalist societies, which consider only one factor at a time.

Where control societies encourage us to think in terms of one condition being true at a time (logical OR), parallelism encourages us to see how many can be true at once (logical AND). Organic societies are cooperation, not control, based. They are able to be this way by having a goal toward which people work together.

Parallelism tells us there is no one way all people should live, but that different societies should use different methods toward the same goals. Those that adapt to reality using their specific method will thrive over time.

Further, parallelism does not attempt to repeat the past nor does it throw away learning. History is our laboratory and science is our method. Parallelism encourages us to accept modern technology, industry and knowledge – and use them wisely.

---

[3] "Organic," Random House Dictionary, retrieved from http://dictionary.reference.com/browse/organic.

Principles

As parallelists, we believe that we can establish a handful of principles that modify our current liberal democratic consumerist society, and that these will "organically" grow into a whole concept:

1. *Localization.* We do not need to live in big cities, and are happier in small communities. These can manage their own affairs, and an overlapping hierarchy of county, state and national leaders can address bigger issues.

2. *Culture before commerce.* If we change our outlook to think in terms of cultural demands which commerce should serve, instead of the other way around, our society will possess a greater degree of consensus.

3. *Organic, whole society.* In everything that we do, we consider whole factors. It may benefit a few factors to have another fast food restaurant on a busy street corner, but we must think of all factors and make decisions accordingly.

4. *Affirmative values.* We have a clear consensus and everything else is permitted. We can approach values two ways:

    a. use negative logic and try to avoid evil, which implies that everything else is good, leading to lack of direction;

    b. use positive logic and try to achieve good, which implies that all not leading to that goal is not useful.

    We should approach values through method (b), as it means that more things are permitted.

5. *Constructive goals.* We can spend our time, money and effort on fears, or we can build up the best hopes we have. We should do the latter.

These attitudinal changes alone will produce a parallelist society from our current ruin. They require only the agreement of minority of people in society who are natural leaders in their communities.

Manifestation

The possibility of action confounds the modern person when looking at the vast delusional herd. How to change a society dedicated to distraction?

Among us, there are 2-5% of people in our society who are leaders in a practical sense. This means that whether they have an official title or not, they lead the community in the areas of business, spirituality, community, and agriculture.

These are the people that your average person trusts. They rely on information from these people more than from the government, their televisions, or casual friends. They respect the judgment abilities of these people.

Our goal is to inform these leaders of our values, get them to form consensus that these should be adopted, and then send them forth to implement these values in all that they do and to demand them from politicians.

This occurs in three steps:

I.   Identify, brand and promote an ideology via the internet.
II. Bring the discussion of this ideology to mainstream media.
III. Unite the people who find it meaningful to aggressively push it to others.

In modern societies, having a large number of vocal supporters is important but you do not need "most" of the population or anywhere near it. Successful revolutions are generally championed by 1-2% of a population.

Parallelism offers a better form of life that can be "sold" to other people like high-performance cars, luxury housing or exceptional music. Perceiving its value requires intelligence and bravery, and the world it delivers, while not for mass consumption, appeals to the restless existential soul in us all. Others emulate those whose acts and opinions they respect, causing a "trickle down" effect.

As we approach step III, it makes the most sense for us to find candidates to take local offices and implement parallelist ideas, demonstrating that these ideas produce a higher quality of life than the mass product existence offered by our current system. Ours is not a revolution but a deliberate transition.

You can help by joining us, and convincing others who are leaders in thought in your community to take a look at what we have to offer.

A NIHILIST PARABLE

Arminass stepped out of his ship. Unfortunately it was ruined. He set the self-destruct mechanism and walked toward the break in the trees as fire clasped the sky behind him.

The people of the village found him very strange, but eventually came to accept him. In his third week there, the entire village went into an uproar. A girl was pregnant with a young child that had no father.

"Kill it," said Arminass. "Don't make the mother a slave to it, or it a slave to life."

"You're insane!" said the Priest. "Its life is precious too."

Arminass pulled back his sleeve and sliced open his arm. Blood flowed freely. "Material is the means, not the end," he said. Then he asked for a glass, and holding it with his bleeding arm, urinated in it.

Then he drank the urine.

"The world is one continuous thing," he said. "My urine is not poison, nor is my life the only one. Truth is a way we describe accurate predictions or observations of this world. An unwanted baby is extra flesh. I am not concerned with the individuals, but the whole."

The town hipster sauntered over. "Well why don't you kill yourself then?"

Arminass sliced the hipster's head from his shoulders. "I would rather kill you," he said. "I can do useful things besides dying."

Two days later the town was attacked by bandits. The town elders said a defense had to be raised. "I can't do it," said a young man. "I can't kill."

"You are not killing," said Arminass. "You are pruning leaves from a tree, and the tree still lives."

An old man tottered over. "I am so afraid to die," he said. "It hides on my shoulder like a vulture."

"It is better to die for something, than simply to die. And what has your life meant?" said Arminass.

"I've been the head rear-left-screw-tightener at the factory for 41 years."

Arminass handed the man a sword. "All your life people have told you what to do. Now you must tell yourself what you care about enough to die for."

The bandits were beaten back and the dead buried. The Priest was drenched in tears at the sight of so many coffins. "Oh, what a tragedy is war!"

Arminass stabbed the Priest and let blood flow freely. "Without war, we never would have defeated the bandits, but they would have lived among us like parasites. With war, the town is healthier, we survive and move on! More will be born to replace those lost."

Sure enough, in some years there were more born.

Arminass worked at the library shelving books. People said scornful things to him because he did not earn much money.

One day there was a nuclear war. The banks collapsed, the government went away and anarchy reigned over the land. "Now I earn as much money as any of you," said Arminass, laughing.

When bandits attacked again, he told the town elders: "A gun makes any man likely to be victor, because if he shoots enough, he will hit someone. When they come with swords, let us fight with swords!"

In the next battle over half of the town was killed. "What ill advice he has given," murmured one woman, her face hidden behind a veil.

"You won't know that until you see what the future holds," said Arminass. "We have lost those who could not figure out how to fight off starving, illiterate, not-very-bright bandits. The half we have left is the better half."

The people of the town came to trust Arminass more and more. He told them when to plant, what to plant, and stopped them from giving away food to wandering mendicants. He made sure they killed all of the people who lived nearby who could not make a town as well functioning as their own town. Some of the women cried, but others looked at Arminass and said, "This is a Man."

The next generation of the town was fruitful, and two decades later Arminass faced the best army in the country.

"We are so powerful, we do not have to engage the others," said one man.

"But we will," said Arminass.

"Why?" cried the daughter of the Priest.

"Because we represent a better order. Look at these people. They strip the trees bare, they live in filth, they have no letters or music to speak of."

"But that's how they want to live," she shot back.

"It's not how I want this country to be," said Arminass. "And since I trust myself, I will do everything I can to crush them."

The people of the town waged a brutal war against the enemy, and when it was over with, there were many casualties but the town controlled the country.

"What do we do now, Arminass?" said the people of the country.

They fixed everything as it was, and got the machines running again and sent people to work. Soon most people had food, shelter and some money left over for entertainment. They began to grow complacent.

"Now it is time for war," said Arminass.

"War against whom?" said the grandson of the Priest.

"War against ourselves," said Arminass. "Modern society has brought you no happiness. We were told the machines would make it so we have to work only three hours a day, but instead we work ten. We were told having a big society with people from all over the world would bring us interesting other cultures, but most are happy with our own. We shall wage war against this stupid system."

"But it is a just system!" said the daughter of the Priest.

"Kill her," said Arminius. "Justice accomplishes nothing. War and planting-time accomplishes something, and if it is not just, the world keeps turning. But we are frozen in time when we worry too much about whether our actions are just."

"We will work with you toward a solution," said the bureaucrats. Arminass had them killed.

"We will work with you toward a solution," said the politicians. Arminass had them killed.

"Together we can make a change," said the religious leaders, shortly before they were killed.

Arminass called the working people together. "The old way does not work anymore. We do not need a society where we fight each other for the privilege of wealth. Our bureaucrats make sure we all have 'justice,' but the price is that we spend longer at work while people fill out paper."

The bureaucrats were all fired and sent to work on the farms. Most died of exhaustion, heat prostration, or medical ailments they did not know they had. Arminass lined them up and asked who had complaints. They all did, except for a handful of people who were suntanned and happy. Arminass had the rest killed.

They took the machines to one part of the center city. Those machines ran all day and all night, with people working four-hour shifts and then going home. "Get to know your families," said Arminass. "None of us knows how much time he has left."

He took all of the costumes, novelties, finery, and entertainment products to the town dump, and burned them. "We do not need these things," said Arminass.

He and his disciples went to those who sold things and destroyed all the products which did not have a survival function. "Meaning is not found in coins and what they can buy," said Arminass.

The disciples went far and wide through the land and counted the people. "We have many people now, Arminass," they said.

"How many are smart enough to understand what we must do?" he said.

"Only about one for every ten," they said.

"Take this knife," he said to each disciple. "Go to those who do not understand and promise them free beer for the rest of their lives if they will let you sterilize them so they cannot breed. Take the chronically poor, the criminal, the drug addicts, the priests and the perverts and drown them in the swamp."

They smashed every television and cash register, and took the plastic toys away from the children. All empty buildings were destroyed, and any roads that were not necessary were replanted with trees.

"Our government is nearly bankrupt," cried the elders.

"Good," said Arminass. "We do not need an economy. From now on, we do things because they must be done to keep our society going."

"But what will we do with our time?" said the people. "There is no structure to our social lives."

"You will do whatever you need to," said Arminass. "You will meet some people, and you will find friends. But ultimately you should realize that you are alone in this life, and socializing will not substitute for having something that makes you feel your life is worth living."

Arminass fixed the people with a fierce stare, and suddenly they fell into a trance.

A warrior was standing nearby. "You are a warrior," said Arminass. "What do you enjoy?"

"I like to climb trees," said the warrior. "I like to walk on the beach with my wife. I like to play with my children, and build furniture for my neighbors. And I like to be a good fighter."

Behind him was a grocer. "What do you enjoy?" said Arminass.

"I like to know what is good meat and what is bad. I like to pick out the good vegetables and throw away the rotten. I like to make sure that the people who come to my store go home with good food. I like to walk among the hills, and tend to my garden."

Next to him was a leader. "What do you enjoy?" said Arminass.

"I like to know the reasons why things turn out the way they do. I like to find out why people act the way they do. I like to solve problems, and have people come to me when they need me to do that. I like to play music, and take my family to the forest where we camp and look up at the eternal stars."

Arminass looked over the people. "As these are, so are you all. What you do for all of us is part of what you do for yourselves. That makes sense, since you are part of the group that is all of us. I want you do to what you enjoy, and thus not require money or my sword to motivate you."

The people went back to their homes, stores, fields, pubs and posts. Except one.

"And what do I do?" said the surly voice of the small man. He was short and stout, was not very smart, not very good looking, not very good at anything, so he did odd jobs around the town square.

Arminass poured two beers. He handed one to the surly small man. "You work odd jobs, and do what others tell you to do, and do not worry about the problems of this town," said Arminass.

"That's what I always did," said the small man. "You're just like the rest of them, keeping me down. If it weren't for you, I would be rich."

Arminass pointed across the square. "That grocer was an orphan who had no money, but now he has a store. Did you have two parents?"

"Yes," said the small man.

Arminass waved to the town policeman. "That man started out life as a small baby, fighting for life, blue in the face. Were you born normally?"

"Well, yes I was," said the man.

Arminass thought, told the man to drink his beer, and then pointed to a woman who was tending small children. "Her husband died and left her with no money, but now she has her own store and a healthy family. Is your wife alive?"

"Why, yes she is," said the man.

Arminass turned to him and said, "You can see there is a reason why you are what you are, and it is not that I kept you down, or anyone else did. You are at the position life has selected for you. What you should do is rejoice in your freedom from having to worry about the complications of life, and spend your time enjoying it. In fact, I suggest you drink and be merry."

The man drank. "Why are you not drinking?" he asked.

"I must consider the safety of the town," said Arminass. "If tigers show up and I am drunk, I cannot slay them. If a fire breaks out and

I am drunk, I cannot smother it. If bandits appear and I am drunk, I cannot fight. This is why you should be glad not to have to serve as I do."

The man considered Arminass. "But isn't that boring?"

"No. It is what life made me to do, and I find that while I would like to be drunk sometimes, I feel better if I am doing what I am made to do, so that my life may have meaning."

The grandson of the Priest came up to Arminass. "You are right on time," said Arminass.

"Why is that?" said the grandson.

"There is no perfect town, nor would we want there to be," said Arminass. "A healthy town needs no Priests, but it needs for there to be error at every step. When the town ceases to be healthy, that error rears its ugly head, and the generation at the time takes care of it. If at some point the people are too weak to overcome it, the town has reached old age and must die."

"That's a lie," said the grandson. "There could be a perfect town."

"There could," said Arminass. "But then it would fall apart inward, since there would be nothing to strive for, no reason for exchange of blows or leaders."

The grandson stabbed him and Arminass coughed blood. "That is your purpose here. It is now time for me to die," said Arminass.

"But what are we to do for a leader?" said a town elder.

"One will come along," said Arminass. "And if he does not, the town is old, and like me, must die."

Arminass died.

BELIEF IN NOTHING

Nihilism confuses people. "How can you care about anything, or strive for anything, if you believe nothing means anything?" they ask.

In return, nihilists point to the assumption of inherent meaning and question that assumption. Do we need existence to mean anything? After all, existence stays out there no matter what we think of it. We can do with it what we will. Some of us will desire more beauty, more efficiency, more function or more truth – and others will not. People of different abilities need different things. Conflict results.

Nihilists who aren't of the kiddie anarchist variety tend to draw a distinction between nihilism and fatalism. Nihilism says that nothing has meaning. Fatalists say that nothing has meaning, so nothing will have meaning for them personally. It's the difference between having no authority figure to tell you what's right, and giving up on the idea of doing anything since no one will affirm that what you've done is right. You reject authority, which is a proxy for results in reality, and defer to reality itself. We have 6,000 years of recorded history to show us what works, and only need to translate that to the particularized circumstances of each new problem. Authority is found in results, and anti-authority is a case of rejecting the method to avoid taking on the actual burden. None of this fatalism applies to you any longer.

What is Nihilism?

As a nihilist, I recognize that meaning does not exist. If we exterminate ourselves as a species, and vaporize our beautiful world, the universe will not cry with us (human anticipation of this result is a condition called the *pathetic fallacy*). No gods will intervene. It will just happen and then – and then the universe will go on. We will not be remembered. We will simply not be.

In the same way, I accept that when I die, the most likely outcome will be a cessation of being. I will at that moment cease to be the source of my thoughts and feelings. Those feelings having only existed inside of me, never did "exist" except as electro-chemical impulses, and will no longer be found when I am gone. I also accept that it is possible I will experience something else. Life is mostly mystery, and a nihilist does not cast aside ambiguity by falsely projecting stolidity. We simply do not know the answers to questions of our origin and future after death; agnosticism is a sensible response, where atheism and dualism are broken ones.

Even further, I recognize that there is no golden standard for life. If I note that living in a polluted wasteland is stupid and pointless, others may not see this. They may kill me when I mention it. And then they will go on, and I will not. Insensitive to their polluted wasteworld, they will keep living in it and suffering under it, oblivious to the existence of an option.

A tree falling in a forest unobserved makes a sound. The forest may not recognize this as a sound because a forest is many life forms interacting, not organized by some central principle or consciousness. They just do what they do. In the same way, playing Beethoven's *Ninth Symphony* to a bowl of yeast will not elicit a response. The insensate remain unobservant, much like the universe itself.

Many people "feel" marginalized when they think of this. Where is the Great Father who will hear their thoughts, validate their emotions, and tell them with certainty what is true and what is not? Where is the writing on the wall, the final proof, the word of God? How do we know for certain that anything is true, and if it is true, that it's important?

Meaning is the human attempt to mold the world in our own image. We need some meaning to our existence, but feel doubt when we try to proclaim it as a creation of ourselves. So we look for some external meaning that we can show others and have them agree that it exists. This forces us to start judging every idea we encounter as threatening or affirming of our projected external meaning.

This distanced mentality further affirms our tendency to find the world alienating to our consciousness. In our minds, cause and effect are the same; we use our will to formulate an idea and it is there, in symbolic form. When we take that idea to the world and try to implement it, however, we can estimate how the world will react but we are frequently wrong, and this causes us doubt.

As a result, we like to separate the world from our minds and live in a world created by our minds. In this humanist view, every human is important. Every human emotion is sacred. Every human preference needs to be respected. It is us against the world, trying to assert our projected reality where we can because we fear the lack of human-ness in the world at large.

Nihilism reverses this process. It replaces externalized meaning with two important viewpoints. The first is pragmatism; what matters are the consequences in physical reality, and if there is a spiritual realm, it must operate in parallel with physical reality. The second is preferentialism; instead of trying to "prove" meaning, we pick what appeals to us – and acknowledge that who we are biologically determines what we seek.

In rejecting anthropomorphic pathetic fallacies such as inherent "meaning," nihilism allows us to toss out anthropomorphism. The idea of an absolute morality, or any value to human life, is discarded. What matters are consequences. Consequences are not measured by their impact on humans, but by their impact on reality as a whole. If a tree falls in a forest, it makes a sound; if I exterminate a species and no human sees it, it happened anyway.

Your dictionary[4] will tell you that nihilism is "a doctrine that denies any objective ground of truth and especially of moral truths." It's not a doctrine; it's a method, like the scientific method, which starts by crawling out of the ghetto of our own minds. It is a quieting of the parts of our minds that want to insist that our human perspective is the only real one, and the universe must adapt to us, instead of the sane alternative of adapting to our universe.

---

[4] "Nihilism," Merriam-Webster online dictionary, retrieved from http://www.merriam-webster.com/dictionary/nihilism.

In this view, nihilism is a gateway and an underpinning to philosophy, not a philosophy in itself. It is an end to anthropomorphism, narcissism and solipsism. It is humans finally fully evolving and getting control of their own minds. As such, it is a starting point from which we can return to philosophy and re-analyze it all, knowing that our perspective is closer to that of the reality outside our minds.

Spiritual Nihilism

Although many interpret nihilism to negate spirituality, the only coherent statement of nihilism is that there is a lack of inherent meaning. This does not preclude spirituality, only a sense of calling it inherent. This means that nihilist spirituality is exclusively transcendentalist, meaning that by observing the world and finding beauty in it, we discover a spirituality emerging from it; we don't require a separate spiritual authority or lack thereof.

It is incorrect to say that nihilism is atheistic or agnostic. Atheism is incoherent: claiming an inherent meaning to the negation of God is a false objectivity just like claiming we can prove there is a God. Agnosticism makes spirituality revolve around the concept of uncertainty over the idea of God. Secular humanism replaces God with an idealized individual. These are all pointless to a nihilist.

In the nihilist view, any divine beings would exist like the wind – a force of nature, without moral balance, without any inherent meaning to its existence. A nihilist could note the existence of a god, and then shrug and move on. Many things exist, after all. What is more important to a nihilist is not inherent meaning, but the design, patterns and interconnected elements of the universe. By observing these, we find a way to discover meaning through our interpretation.

This in turn enables us to make unforced moral choices. If we are relying on another world to reward us where we don't get rewarded here, we are not making a sacrifice. If we believe that a god outside of the world must exist in order for it to be good, we are slandering the world. Even if we think there is an inherent right way of doing things, and that we may get rewarded for it, we are not making moral choices.

Moral choices occur when we realize there is no compelling force on us to make that decision except our inclination to care about the consequences. That in turn is contingent upon us being hardwired with enough intelligence to revere nature, the cosmos and all that has brought us consciousness. Indeed, the only way we will have such respect for the world is if we view consciousness and life as a gift, and therefore choose to enhance and complement the order of nature.

In a nihilist worldview, whether we live or die as a species has no inherent value. We could stay, or blow away like a dead leaf, and the universe doesn't care a bit. Here we must separate judgment, or caring about consequences, from the consequences themselves. If I fire a gun at someone and he dies, the consequence is his death. If I have no judgment of it, that means nothing more than his permanent absence.

If the universe has the same absence of judgment, there is nothing more than his absence. No cosmic conclusions, no judging by gods (even if we choose to believe they exist), and no emotion shared by everyone. It is the event and nothing more, like a tree falling in a forest when no one is around to hear its crash.

Since there are no inherent judgments in our universe, and no absolute and objective sense of judgment, what matters is our preference regarding consequences. We may choose not to survive as a species, in which case insanity and sanity have the same value level, since survival no longer has a position of value for us. Our survival is not inherently judged to be good; it's up to us to do that.

In nihilism, as in every sufficiently advanced philosophy, the ultimate goal is to make "everything just what it is," or to decipher enough of our consciousness that we do not confuse the instrument (our minds) with its object (our world). To a nihilist, the greatest human problem is *solipsism*, or a confusion of the mind with the world; our solution is to point out that the human values we consider "objective" and "inherent" are only pretense.

Nihilism conditions us instead to actualize ourselves. It denies nothing of the lack of inherent meaning to existence, and does not create a false "objective" reality based on our perceptions of what we wish did exist. Instead, it charges us to choose what we wish existed, and to work toward making it occur in reality.

The fully actualized human is able to say: I studied how the world works; I know how to predict its responses with reasonable success; I know what cause will create what effect. As a result, we can say, I am going to pick a certain effect I desire that is coherent with the organization of our world, so it will succeed.

This returns us to the question of whether beauty is discovered, or invented; some suggest that beauty is inherent to certain approaches to organization of form, while others think we can invent it of our own accord. A nihilist would say that the patterns that define beauty are not arbitrary, therefore have a precedent in the extra-human cosmos, and that our artists create beauty by perceiving the organization of our world and then transposing it to a new, human form.

Through the embrace of "ultimate reality" – or physical reality and the abstractions that directly describe its organization, in contrast to opinions and judgments – as the only inherent constant to life, nihilism forces humans to make the ultimate moral decision. In a world that requires both good and bad for survival, do we choose to strive for what's good, even knowing that it may require us to use bad methods and face bad consequences?

The final test of spirituality in nature is not whether we can proclaim universal love for all human beings, or declare ourselves pacifists. It is whether we can do what is necessary for survival and improvement of ourselves, as this is the only way to approach our world with a truly reverent attitude: to adopt its methods, and through an unforced moral preference, choose to rise and not descend.

We must make the leap of faith and choose to believe not in the existence of the divine, but in its possibility through the merging of our imagination with our knowledge of reality. Finding divinity in the venal and material world requires an epic transcendental viewpoint that finds in the working of an order a holiness, because that order provides the grounding that grants us our own consciousness. If we love life, we find it to be holy and become reverent to it, and thus as nihilists can rapidly discover transcendental mysticism and transcendental idealism.

From this viewpoint, it's easy to see how nihilism can be compatible with any faith, including Christianity. As long as we do not confuse our interpretation of reality ("God") with reality itself, we are transcendentalists who find our source of spiritualism in the organization of the physical world around us and our mental state, which we can see as having parallel and similar function. When people talk about God, a nihilist thinks of the patterns of trees.

Practical Nihilism

How does a nihilist, or one who is beyond morality and the sanctity of human life and illusions, apply these principles in everyday life? The short answer is "very carefully." Human history provides one story after another of how a few smart people started something good, then parasites encrusted it, and eventually formed a political movement to murder those who knew better, thus plunging that something good into disrepair.

The essence of nihilism is transcendence through eliminating a false "inherent" meaning that is a projection of our minds. When we have cleared away the illusion, and can look at reality as a continuum of cause and effect relationships, we can know how to adapt to that reality. This gets us over the fear of reality that causes us to retreat into our own minds, a condition known as solipsism.

This in turn leads to a kind of primal realism that rejects everything but the methods of nature. These are inherent to not only biology, but physics and the patterns of our own thoughts. We need no inherent meaning; we need only to adapt to our world and, from the palette of options offered, choose what we desire. Do we want to live in mud huts, or like the ancient Greeks and Romans strive for a society of advanced learning?

Most people confuse fatalism with nihilism. Fatalism, or the idea that things are as they are and will not change, relies on an inherent "meaning" being denied for its emotional power. Fatalism is a shrug and a wish that things could be different, but since they are not, we will ignore them. Nihilism is the opposite principle: a reverent acceptance of nature as functional and in fact genius, and a determination to master it.

This is not a philosophy for the weak of heart, mind or body. It demands that we look clear-eyed at truths that most find upsetting, and then force ourselves past them as a means of disciplining ourselves toward self-actualization. Much as nihilism removes false inherent meaning, self-actualization removes the drama of the externalized self and replaces it with a sense of purpose: what quest makes meaning out of my life?

Unlike Christianity and Buddhism which seek to destroy the ego, nihilism seeks to remove the groundwork that makes the ego seem like all we have. It negates both materialism, or living for physical comfort, and dualism, or living for a moral god in another world that does not parallel our own in function. Any spiritual realm will parallel this one, because since matter, energy and thoughts show parallel mechanisms in their patterning, any other force would do the same.

Further, ego-negation is a false form of inherent meaning. A meaning defined in negative terms flatters the object as much as its positive counterpart; to say I'm anti-vole is to affirm the need for voles. The only true freedom from the ego consists in finding a replacement object, or *ur*-consciousnessness to reality, to replace the voice of personality which we often mistake for the world.

Our human problems on earth do not distill to simplifications like the narratives offered by the press because they are popular: we the people are exceptional, except when oppressed by kings, government, corporations or the beautiful people. Our human problems begin and end in our inability to recognize reality and enforce it upon ourselves; we instead opt for pleasant illusions, and generate the negative consequences one might expect.

If we do not get rid of our fears, they rule us. If we have created a false antidote to our fears, like a false sense of inherent meaning, we have doubly enslaved ourselves to those fears: first, the fears persist because we have no logical answer to them, and second, we are now indebted to the dogma that supposedly dispels them. This is why human problems have remained relatively unchanged for centuries.

As a philosophical groundwork, nihilism gives us a tool with which to approach all parts of life and make sense of them. Unlike merely political or religious solutions, it underlies all of our thinking, and by removing false hope, gives us a hope in the work of our own two hands. Where others rage against the world, we rage for it – and in doing so, provide a saner future.

March 23, 2010

HOW DOES A NIHILIST LIVE?

I'm thankful for the thoughtful emails I get. Most people want a handout (please review my mediocre, undistinguished, pathetic metal band) or want to attack me in the guise of posing questions to me (how can you claim you know anything when you don't believe in anything?). The latter think their cleverness consists of passively-aggressively humiliating someone above them, and that makes them happy, since deep inside they know they're mediocre. The former are just charity cases in disguise, and deep inside they know that the reason they're not getting anywhere is that they have not produced something of note.

However, some thoughtful questions really cut to the chase and point out that people have questions about things that are second nature to me now. Such a question arrived today: How does a nihilist live? I'll try to answer that in a conversational form so that we don't get lost in the intricacies of philosophy, because the pragmatic effects of nihilist belief are more important than detailed philosophical "proofs."

First, you do not ask others how you should live. All of the answers are before you.

Nihilism is discerning what is real from what is unreal. We do exist in reality. In it, some things actually exist and others are phantoms of our mind. Strip away the latter and focus on the former. If you have trouble figuring it out, go spend time in a forest. Buddha meditated under a tree, Jesus had his woods for 40 days, Nietzsche had his mystical trances and Arthur Schopenhauer had long nights ignored by his family. Take advantage of boredom, and natural surroundings, to decipher your world.

Truth doesn't exist. Truth is our perception of what does exist; our assessment of it. You will have to find the truth that's appropriate to your own life and also exists in reality. Note that I did not say "your own truth." Individualism is the greatest con job ever. You are the product of those who came before you in your bloodline, and the factors of your life. You do not exist separately from the world and you cannot escape this state. Furthermore, there's no point. Pursue truth as it is evident to you. If you're insane, your role in the universe is to be the insane failure that others mock and later, kill.

Not everyone can do this. In my view, there's no shame in saying "Look, I'm not a leader – show me a right path and I'll get to work." Even that however requires an evaluation of reality and acceptance of some of its basic traits. Your bloodline will be serving the commands of others until it evolves otherwise. I've accepted that I'll never be a Brad Pitt or Andres Segovia, but I'm not really bothered by that; I'm too busy being what I am. For that reason, I've got some general suggestions here.

The single most powerful weapon you have is your own preference. People can force all sorts of shit on you, but they can't make you accept certain things except as necessary in actual reality and not merely social judgment. For example, if the government decrees that everyone must have a morning enema on pain of death, you'll submit to it to avoid arrest, but even if every other person you know then chooses to have an afternoon enema as well in order to show their patriotism and signal social virtue, *you can reject that behavior* by not doing it. You'll stand out in a crowd. Big deal. It's not like these drones are paying attention to anything.

You will have to have some kind of work. Pick something that's inoffensive where you can rise through competence. There are plenty of good jobs, for example, in environmental, animal rights, politics and public service. Apply and rise. You won't get the same salary or public respect, but you're a nihilist now, and you recognize that public respect is as meaningless as it is fickle. Create a life for yourself instead and don't commit the same transgressions that make society odious. Affirm reality. Cease destruction of nature. Nurture your own culture. Reject modernity.

As becomes obvious, the people around you are tools; that is to say, they are grateful followers who passively lap up the rancid semen of industrial society and are grateful for the "opportunity." While in a just world they'd get a hollow-point to the forehead, that's not going to happen for a few decades, so content yourself with this: create a better example of humanity and leave them in your dust.

Most of your toolish coworkers, neighbors, people you meet on the street, etc. are capable of two modes of conversation: entertainment and personal situation. They'll discuss endlessly the "important" movies and television they see, not noticing that these repeat themselves on a three-year cycle, and they'll talk about the weather or their fuchsia hemorrhoids or other "important" issues of personal comfort. They cannot talk about ideas. Therefore, reserve ideas as the grounds on which the few smart people meet.

If you talk to normals, talk about basic aspects of life, namely events in our time. You don't have to take a side as long as you express an intelligent opinion. Be honest and when prompted, say you don't watch TV or movies. Talk about the good things you see in life, like something great a person did, or something you observed in nature or perceived about life itself. But don't fall into their trap. *Seinfeld* and *Friends* and *ER* are transient garbage that will not matter at all, and these fools are wasting their lives on this stuff. Don't let them pull you into the same mental morass.

Normals also have a tendency to express group-think sentiments, and then test others with them. Such things as "Isn't it terrible about that genocide in Darfur?" are probes to get you to either conform or be identified as a lone wolf. If you respond with "I think it's funny" or "We need fewer people" the wailing and lashing out by the crowd, which *hates* lone wolves, begins (the lone wolf has what the crowd never will: integrity, and for this reason, they hate it). The best response is indifference. "I didn't hear about that" will get you a lecture, but "I think politics is made-up crazy stuff" will leave them baffled. They ask you about something "serious" in their world; show them it's not serious in yours. Don't even take the issue itself seriously.

Normal: Did you hear how Bush stole the election?

Nihilist: Oh, they're stealing elections now. How funny. Did you know bell peppers are a good source of vitamin C?

Normal: OMFG I heard Al-Qaeda is planning to attack us!

Nihilist: You know, van Gogh really captured the essence of suspense in his surrealistic paintings. Might be a good time to check them out.

Normal: Gasoline is totally expensive these days.

Nihilist: Money everywhere. I made an interpretive sculpture out of my compost heap.

This drives normals nuts because it plays into their basic fear, namely that someone else knows something they don't know and thus is not subject to the laws of the crowd. However, if you do this without being aggressive, they have no way to justify lashing out at you and no way to handle what you've said. Let them keep discussing their "entertaining" TV (entertainment is for people who cannot find a purpose of their own in life; it's like slavery, but it's "fun") while you spend your time on more interesting things. Their unease will grow as they watch you, and it will help destroy them.

Be careful with your money. Some idiot comes around the office asking for birthday donations, or money to help the children in Sudan or whatever – blow it off. "No thanks," is all you need to say, and if they start asking more questions, they're in the wrong socially and nonsense replies are appropriate. "I'm saving up to buy a nuclear submarine" or "The price of ice cream and motor oil just went up" is an appropriate response. If you feel like you're talking to kindergartners, well, you are. These people are mentally immature and should be treated accordingly.

When you shop, don't buy garbage. You will be tempted because who isn't? But recognize what's crap and avoid it. You may have to pay $2 more for the metal version of some everyday object over the plastic one, but then you won't need to replace it for thirty years. Morons fear people with this kind of wisdom, because it reveals morons in contrast as unable to make such decisions. Don't spend your money on idiotic entertainment, flashy cars, or houses in trendy neighborhoods. Pick a good place and live independently. You don't need any of that posturing (if you're a nihilist).

Finally, don't accept their view of reality. They'll blather on about "progress" and other inventions of the human mental phantasm, but if you recognize these ideas are basically junk food for the mind, you can bypass it and focus on other things. If after two years have passed, you've learned a language and an instrument while they're still watching TV, they'll start to revere you. Then, profit from their idiocy and put the money to a good use, like buying up the remaining free forest land out there or translating Pentti Linkola into English. Nihilists bypass illusion and work on reality, and from it they get stronger while the herd stagnates. Most importantly, they laugh while doing this. And who wouldn't?

November 14, 2004

DUALISM VS. MONISM IN A NIHILIST CONTEXT

Could you enlighten me as to why you prefer monism to dualism?

This world may be a simulation. We may be figments of the imagination of a daydreaming god. We may be pure mathematics, or data in some cosmic computer. Or we could be physical beings, or some combination of the above. However, if this world has one characteristic to rely on, it's this: *Consistency.* It creates the same response to the same stimulus every time.

That means if you pick up a ball and hold your arm up away from your body and drop the ball, it will fall – every time. Even if a friend sneaks a hand in there to catch it, it will begin falling first. If you put a support table under your hand so the ball doesn't drop, the effect can be observed that the instant the table is removed the ball drops. The principle is consistent. Causality is consistent (although in multicausal cases there is some variability due to chaos and the inability to have consistent conditions like wind, uniformity of matter and the like).

Dualism

Dualism posits that there is another world where there are pure rules that differ from the rules in this world. In other words, this world is a put-on, but it's not the result of that other world, rather an inferior and unrelated copy to it. This breaks the principle of consistency. In addition, it rebukes the design brilliance of this world and encourages us to de-sacralize it. Further, it creates an arbitrary claim that can be manipulated by those for whom truth is a distant secondary concern to immediate reward through the work of others.

In my view, this world represents something utterly consistent with the logic that we have in our minds by intuition or can derive from experiments in the world, or even in our minds using arbitrary data. In fact, this world represents an *optimization* of design to take advantage of logic. A simple example is the sheer efficiency of trees: they are resilient, efficient, and highly effective at propagating themselves without wiping themselves out through over-breeding.

One interesting aspect of this logicality is that it does not aim for perfection. It shoots instead for things that work in every situation and, even if it takes many steps to get there, always get to an increasingly complex result. This means that if there are 100 seeds, nature does not guarantee that every one sprouts; it guarantees that absent truly blighted conditions, at least one will survive. Even more, it guarantees that in truly blighted conditions, *something* – if even bacteria or fungus – will survive, and begin the process of evolving until three billion years later it's a human. That is the genius of nature's design!

For this reason, I see our world as a logical optimum, and see it as unlikely and even laughable to posit a division between this and another perfect world. Especially when the other perfect world sounds like human wish fulfilment, such as the idea that judgment will occur over the bad and the good will be rewarded. Even more when it is suggested that, as in Heaven and Hell, this other world involves an eternity of doing the same stuff over and over again. It is discontiguous with the logic of this world and with logic itself that this world exists in that form, and that its activities are as described.

However, this is the nature of our thinking when pointing toward any world that is a *correction* to this one. We immediately turn to human ideas and judgments, desires and feelings. We shape it after what we wish were true, because after all it's a correction. But that requires us to abandon logic and causality and instead focus on a world that seems like the creation of a personality itself, even though nothing else works this way.

Materialism

On the opposite end of the spectrum, there's materialism, or the idea that matter is all that exists. Since the organization of things follows logic, and thoughts follow logic, and logic stands both intuitively and as a self-referential architectonic whole, it seems to me that logic comes before matter. Meaning: the organization of matter is a product of logic, not the other way around. Thus materialism itself is nonsense and there is clearly an underlying thought-like logical order to existence. I think it more likely that we find something like a simulation, where we are logical aspects of some larger logical entity, than a standalone system regulated by matter; if anything, we probably exist in a universe which is so logical that the concept of nothingness had to be created, which in turn required the concept of somethingness, which in turn created what we know of today as matter.

Thus we have both dualism and materialism negated, which leaves us with monism, a system where matter and idea are part of the same continuum, and any perfection is found in this world and any additional "metaphysics" would be part of the same logical system. In this the whole is logically consistent, which fits with the principle of consistency seen in all things observed so far. However, this leaves us with a question: how is monism different from some form of idealistic materialism?

The best answer is found in the work of Immanuel Kant, who perceived that our minds "filter" a raw reality and come up with a limited version of that which our physical bodies can perceive and serve that up to us. We know that our minds will remove from our perception the anomalous and incomprehensible in everyday life, and that we navigate the world through memory and basically confirm our memory instead of perceiving anew. How much else is filtered out? How much is invisible to us because it is not physical in the sense that we commonly recognize?

Monism

Monism suggests to us that instead of a world made of personality and the judgment of that personality, like the Heaven/Hell dualistic world, we exist in a single continuum of which the visible physical world is but a small part. Thus what we see is logically consistent with all that is, but is only part of the story. The end result there is that we can posit additional layers or dimensions to our world without them being dualistic, in that they will obey the same logical rules that we see here and will be similar. They may be interwoven with what we know of as reality. Even more, without the imposition of time, there may be other *directions* in which we can travel through this raw reality-space.

This might explain why monism is not as popular as dualism. It's harder to grasp, and although it's more consistent, it's less certain. It is also less satisfying than the idea of final judgment and slotting of people in Heaven or Hell, an image that I find comforting whenever I run into someone with bad or excessively selfish intent. But ultimately it is the only explanation that is logical and consistent, without which we are forced to consider our world as nonsense and treat it correspondingly badly, while leaving our futures in the hands of near-arbitrary conjecture, and denying the causal/logical idealism underlying all of existence.

How is this in any way compatible with nihilism?

Most people view nihilism as a form of hyper-materialism, or denial of all but the immediate and tangible. In my experience, what nihilism is in a sensible interpretation is a denial of human projection, and thus a focus on reality as it is. This then includes the aspects of it which we do not understand and are not easily grasped by humans. Both materialism and dualism make no sense under nihilism because they are impositions of the human perspective, e.g. touch and emotion respectively, and not a logical observational path from reality to the human. A sensible path is that we see reality, analyze it and understand it; projection is where we figure out what we want to be, find an example that supports this vision, ignore the context and anomalous examples, and hold up that one example to represent the whole. Both dualistic religion and the negation of it fall into this category.

Fatalism and Rationalism

While nihilism is a rejection of anything other than the individual and its immediate desires, needs, emotions, feelings, judgments and autonomy, most people see nihilism as a rejection of all choice and purpose in itself, like a form of mental heat-death.

I see this philosophy as something that can be called "fatalism" because it has given up on anything larger than the individual, including society, truth, creativity, and the world as something outside of the human mental construction. It believes that human efforts at improvement are ineffectual or doomed. A more sensible version of nihilism is that it is a rejection of everything other than what exists. It is not concerned with emotions, judgments, feelings and/or desires, but instead is concerned with how the world works and how it can be interacted with. Where most people think of themselves first, and see the world as a manifestation of their will, the nihilist sees us as a manifestation of the world's properties.

However, this does not imply a need to limit ourselves to the material, because since the world is a logical place defined by its consistency above all else, the only limit that matters is what is logical according to the order of this world. As logicality precedes materiality, the logicality is more important, and this implies layers of existence outside of the material which must also be considered. It is not sensible to call these "metaphysical" as they are part of the same spectrum of physicality, much like different colors are part of the same spectrum, including invisible colors that are outside the parts of the spectrum we can perceive.

In fact, this philosophy affirms nihilism by showing us the truth of the triad of traits normally associated with nihilism: nothing is true, nothing is communicated and nothing is known. That is because in this world, the option of truth is a choice and not inherent to people; many choose to avoid truth, in fact most do. Similarly, people must be receptive to have communication occur, and must be able to recognize knowledge for it to do its work as knowledge. The grim fact of life is that truth only exists to those who know how to locate it, communication only occurs between similarly situated parties, and wisdom is only visible to the wise. But even that fact will be disputed by people who wish to believe otherwise.

While wildly misunderstood, nihilism in its only sensible form is a rejection of human projection. That requires that we pay attention to the world and its function, rather than our emotions, desires and judgments regarding it or what we wish it were like. This does not limit us to the visible world, or even only the tangible world, since we need to use logical thought to even construct those fully. Rather, we instead may even reject appearances and tangibility in favor of those logical constructions which fully explain the world, which is part of a consistent trend since the earliest evolution of humanity toward more use of mind and less reliance on appearance.

Dualism is an enhancement of the differences between appearance and structure. By creating a world of inconsistent structure in addition to this one, dualism posits that this world is entirely appearance, and the other world is entirely structure. In fact, both appearance and structure exist in this world, and if the other world is inconsistent with them, it is likely a world of appearance and not structure.

This creates the troubling implication that it is human projection and thus an affirmation of it would be a rejection of nihilism. On the other hand, materialism suggests no possibility of structure beyond the material, which creates clashes with the underlying idealism of the cosmos, creating a disconnect between appearance and structure which makes appearance seem to be an independent and important measure.

A nihilist of the Hollywood type is basically an extremely self-focused anarchist. This person's justification is that they believe in nothing, thus they limit their concerns to what they know is "real," namely themselves and their immediate desires only. Further, in theory this person is possessed by an urge to destroy, which makes no sense as that requires a positive valuation. It seems more like a description of a person having a mental health issue than thinking their way through nihilism. This approach also ignores that all meaning comes from interaction with the world, and sacrifice of self for the ideals one wants to make incarnate.

Nihilism reduces itself from negation of everything because nihilism is in itself an affirmative act, a valuation of the world and a separation of what is actual from what is not. Thus even someone who tried to act out the Hollywood ideal and reject everything would soon find themselves both affirming some facts of the world, and rejecting some illusions of the self being absolute and separate from the world. A nihilist in the first seconds of nihilism might wander down the anarchist path, but within an hour of thought would be headed in a different direction.

Through this nihilism rejects another kind of dualism, which is the separation between human preference and reality. In this vision, which occurs exclusively in materialist thought, the human choice is somehow absolute and universal, where the natural world is viewed as random and/or illogical. This mirrors the projection of human thought onto a dualistic perfect world, which resembles human feeling and desires, as separate from a world where human feelings come secondary which is thus seen as appearance because it does not represent the "true" world of the personality. This dualism exists both in materialism and in metaphysical conditions.

For this reason, nihilism is not only compatible with monism, but is compatible *only* with monism. The false dualities of materialism and metaphysical dualism together represent the antithesis of nihilism, which is human projection. Further, to a realist, both dualism and materialism fail to deliver what is necessary for a logical view of reality and also show the influence of human projection, which means it is wisest to reject them and move on to something that is more representative of reality, even if it does not "appear" to be so.

February 2, 2014

REALITY IS NIHILISM

It is hard to define nihilism because the term is abused so commonly. People misuse the term nihilism because "nihilism" sounds cool like heavy metal, whiskey, shotguns and motorcycles. Cool is whatever isn't the norm; in a herd of sheep, you want to be the one doing something *different*. And for most people, you don't want to get that way the old fashioned way, which is to pick a discipline and work hard at it so that someday, you're known as the guy who invented the anal extractor or a cure for cancer.

Because they don't believe they're going to succeed at anything real, and because they lack the will to do so and so are correct in that first estimation, most people choose instead to adopt a surrogate: social status, or how many people like them; money, or how much power they have over others; popularity, or how many friends they have in the mainstream or a niche; morality, or how they can feel superior for doing a human-centric "right thing" by individuals, instead of addressing the problem that includes all individuals, namely the fortunes of human civilization.

In this environment, picking a radical belief that doesn't entail radical results is a clear winner. It lets you be "different" and rise above the pack, but you don't actually have to pay the price of taking a controversial position. Why be a real revolutionary, who might die or kill others (which is unpopular)? Instead be popular by being an armchair revolutionary. Preach some radical belief you don't believe, and fool others, who will then make themselves accessible to you as friends, sexual partners, business associates and so on.

Nihilism isn't a philosophy to most people. It's marketing. When a brand says "Better value for less money!" that's not their philosophy; it's their marketing. As they say about human beings, don't listen to what they say – look at what they do. Does the product actually offer better value for the money? Sometimes but not necessarily. In the same way, do people who are nihilists generally live that way? No, a thousand times no. They live like any other hipster, scenester, socialite, hanger-on, toady or one of the crowd. They're there to socialize.

In theory, nihilism could even be used to sell products, but only of the entertainment type. "This is the most nihilistic vacuum cleaner on the market!" somehow fails a basic test of credibility. But a rock band? We believe in nothing. A radical? Our belief is that nothing exists. A politician? Those nihilists are going to come and hate our freedom, or be racist like al-Qaeda. As with rock music, the news is entertainment, as is politics. It's keeping the proles entertained and giving them very simple symbols to use as "reasons" for them doing whatever they do, or what you want them to do.

And at the end of the day, the most public "nihilists" are the ones most likely to be lower-case-c conservative: they sell a product, they make a ton of money, and they retire to gated communities where they spend their time golfing. Nihilism, or just good marketing?

What's not Nihilism

The marketing/social-friendly "nihilism" could more accurately be described as the intersection of fatalism, or believing that we have no control over the outcome of our actions, and selfishness, or the doctrine of acting only for the self. They are inherently materialistic – meaning that they recognize no dimension to reality except the physical comforts, wealth and convenience we can achieve – because they are based on removal of giving a damn.

However, they're also completely destructive because they are limited in scope to *right now*. What do you want right now? How to look cool right now? Life is a process of many moments knitted together, and when we deny that future and past, we lose the ability to build. There is no need to be productive or constructive when you are living for one moment only, but if you live for many in sequence, you start wanting to have your life show its meaning in what you have done with it.

Fatalism and selfishness will be eternally popular because they're the same thing. Don't reach out into the world and challenge yourself; you're fine just the way you are! Don't strive for anything. Don't grow. Just be, and you're *equal* and we're all happy. If people aren't convinced, hide behind the idea that nothing ever changes and there's no point doing anything, except living for your own comfort and convenience (of course).

In our modern time, we've elevated fatalism to a positive value. Instead of admitting that we need to evolve as a species, we're looking inward and congratulating each other on how moral we are. Instead of striving so that we improve as individuals, and that we produce heroes and exceptional people, we focus on making sure we accept each other as equals. We're all one, we're the same, we're all OK, everyone wins!

This is the mindset of a solipsist who fears the world and doesn't want to challenge herself, so has created a social doctrine that demands no change to the status quo. When you think about it, equality and selfishness are the same idea, because with equality no one will strive and no one will tell you that you should strive, so you have ultimate freedom to consume, work, buy – anything but push yourself to achieve. And if you do, others will sabotage you with many pointless demands.

What is Nihilism?

If we could successfully encapsulate philosophies in a paragraph, we would have far fewer philosophical tests or debates. However, any sufficiently unique idea requires explanation not so much for its essence as symbols, but for its implications. If I say that my philosophy is to eat only the brains of cretins, I'm going to need to explain how to harvest those brains, what the justification is, and what implications it has for a social order that needs to breed captive morons for slaughter. And that's a super-simplified example.

The definition of nihilism expands. It's like a doorway, more than an endpoint. We can start with the simplest definition:

Nihilism is the belief that all values are baseless and that nothing can be known or communicated.[5]

What do values, knowing and communication have in common? Each relies on us representing our world or parts of it with symbols. A symbol uses a part of the whole to communicate the whole, and depends on its audience knowing enough about the topic to know what the symbol represents. Even our memories are stored in symbolic form such that we recall a summary or a conclusion, but not the whole of what is going on. Many of us can remember the end result of a conversation in a room; few can remember the steps of conversation, or all of the objects in the room.

Nihilism is a rejection of the "false world" of symbols, memories and the "knowing" of others. When we say all values are baseless, we mean they are a choice and there is no writing on the wall or Word of God or scientific "proof" which can justify them. The world does not tell us what to believe; the world just *is*. Nothing is inherent and we cannot prove that some value or truth is inherent. We can only elect to believe them.

A nihilist for example recognizes that even if shown proof of some truth, people may choose to disbelieve or may simply not understand. A person with no short term memory can see people walking through two doors, a blue door and a red door, and observe that everyone going through the blue door gets a hollow-point round to the forehead. But without that memory, even if told the blue door is death, they may have no idea of the context and walk through it anyway (thus curing their memory problem).

On a practical level, most human beings possess enough intelligence to be functional in a narrow range of tasks, but not to predict the outcome of some behavior they have not seen before. They therefore do not understand consequences of their actions beyond the immediate, and like basic algebra, are limited to measuring one variable at a time. Even worse, because they do not understand

---

[5] Alan Pratt, "Nihilism," *Internet Encyclopedia of Philosophy*, retrieved from http://www.iep.utm.edu/nihilism/.

any idea more complex than one they have conceived, they view such ideas as wrong, and because they cannot see where their own thinking is limited, compare all ideas to their own and reject those which are not of their own conception – which includes *all* ideas more complex than their own.

> *When people are incompetent in the strategies they adopt to achieve success and satisfaction, they suffer a dual burden: Not only do they reach erroneous conclusions and make unfortunate choices, but their incompetence robs them of the ability to realize it...The skills needed to produce logically sound arguments, for instance, are the same skills that are necessary to recognize when a logically sound argument has been made. Thus, if people lack the skills to produce correct answers, they are also cursed with an inability to know when their answers, or anyone else's, are right or wrong. They cannot recognize their responses as mistaken, or other people's responses as superior to their own.*[6]

We see immediately a split in worldviews:

- *There is no meaning.* Nothing means anything, or can mean anything. It's all pointless. When philosophers say that "A true nihilist would believe in nothing, have no loyalties, and no purpose other than, perhaps, an impulse to destroy" this is what they are speaking of. However, in our view this is a confusion of lack of inherent purpose with a perceived natural purpose to destroy. The lack of meaning does not mean that one cannot have preferences, even logical ones.

- *There is no inherent meaning.* Meaning, values, memory and symbols are artifacts of judging, perceiving minds. Without humanity, the world just *is*; a tree falling in a forest makes sound, but there being no one there to recognize the sound and call it

---

[6] Justin Kruger and David Dunning, "Unskilled and Unaware of it – How Difficulties in Recognizing One's Own Incompetence Lead to Inflated Self-Assessments," retrieved from http://www.wepapers.com/Papers/70939/Unskilled_and_Unaware_of_It_-_How_Difficulties_in_Recognizing_One's_Own_Incompetence_Lead_to_Inflated_Self-Assessments.

sound, the world remains unenlightened as to its soundness. However, lack of inherent meaning does not preclude humans from choosing meaning, or from noticing that they as humans will find some things more meaningful than others – specifically, as related to the task of *human survival.*

People who seek an inherent meaning in life, like writing on the wall appearing from a mystical world that is guaranteed to be 100% true 100% of the time, find nihilism depressing – they immediately see that they have no perfect argument to convince others they are right, and no perfect way of communicating it, so they give up on meaning entirely. Their view is that if meaning is not inherent to the same degree that, say, oxygen is, there's no way to discover it or share it. This is caused by the false objectivity of human consensus, where we assume that because everyone in a room thinks something is true or can understand it when we communicate it, it must be true.

Others however do not share this view. They reason that without a being that can prove itself inherent, such as a god who can work miracles and communicate with us in a scientifically verifiable format, there is no way to prove anything inherent. The universe does not have a human consciousness, and will not give us truths in a form we can recognize as being similar to our memories. Instead, per the scientific method (otherwise known as any systematic method of discovery) we must observe, formulate theories about how the world works, test them and share as much as we can what we have learned.

In many ways, this is parallel to our transition from childhood to adulthood. A child needs parents or other adults to provide absolute right answers that the child can trust and act upon; an adult is comfortable with greater degrees of ambiguity, and at some point says "this makes sense to me" or "this is what I want" and so pursues it. Children need inherent or quasi-inherent values; adults view values as, well, value choices. Not everyone has the same values but much like not everyone gives the same answer to a test question, some answers are better than others.

What is Passive Nihilism?

Nihilism as a philosophical doctrine is simple: the denial of inherent meaning. Nothing inherently, automatically and irrefutably "means" anything. Meaning is a projection of the human mind and does not exist outside of it, much like while we may use a symbol for "God" we cannot say God exists in the human form we project; we're using a variable or metaphor to describe God but that symbol is not equivalent to the thing itself.

When we look for inherent meaning, we are inevitably talking about morality of method. This type of morality assumes that the instance of any one thing is equivalent to its essence, like our word and conception of God being the same God who exists to other species on other planets. For a morality to be inherent, it must be a morality of outcomes (effects) and not their causes, or the effects they in turn create. The only moral object that is inherent is the action; its consequences unfold over time and so are not inherent in the same way that material change is.

For example, our civilization has become thoroughly neurotic about killing: murder is bad, except when we kill murderers, or wage war. If we wage war, we also need to be murdering murderers, or we are the aggressor who attacked first. However, if we murder a killer before he murders, or wage war against a civilization that by growing lots of cheap food will eventually produce an invasion force that will destroy us, we are committing immoral acts in terms of outcomes, but committing moral acts in terms of the effects of those outcomes.

Passive nihilism is the rejection of all inherent meaning. It tends to reduce life to what can be measured and observed, and to file everything else as unproven. As the first step on the path of stones that is nihilism, passive nihilism does nothing more than strip away the illusions imposed by civilization as a means of policing itself, unaware that those same means lead to its dissolution into individualism, or the citizens pursuing many chaotic directions and failing to unify behind the idea of civilization itself. Unlike active nihilism, passive nihilism does not then reconstruct meaning by assembling what is known into patterns and deriving a sense of cosmic and natural order from those. It merely rejects all; what separates it from fatalism is that passive nihilism also rejects individualism and the group conformist idea that humans can define reality. It thus sets the stage for active nihilism.

Through this reasoning, we see that inherent morality is like tying a hand behind our backs. Outcomes and methods exist in the moment, and may cause us personal fear, but what we must look at is the long-term consequences of our actions. Our human instinct is to demand inherent morality from fear for ourselves, but what this shows us is that what we want to consider "inherent" to the world is inherent to a different globe entirely – the human head.

What is Active Nihilism?

When people ask how you can be a nihilist and still be striving for something other than self-pleasure, remember this: nihilism means denial of inherent value. It does not mean denial of functionality, or loss of a desire for our actions to be constructive and produce aesthetic beauty in life. Nihilism simply states that there is no inherent morality, or in other words no morality of method, so we must be willing to do immoral things for moral ends.

Nature parallels this vision. In nature, predators consume their prey with vicious violence but that consumption creates smarter animals. The majority of intelligent creatures are the predators; the majority of stupid creatures are primarily prey. There is no morality of murder, or other outcome-based judgment, because such logic would stop the whole process of evolution. Instead, nature works by a basic principle of morality of consequence: if the ends (evolution) require vicious means (predation), so be it.

When Plato wrote his metaphor of the cave, he was talking primarily about instance/essence confusions. (While most scholars prefer to think he is speaking of a dualistic world where perfect archetypes exist, his point is actually the opposite – no such world exists, because essence is defined not by duplicating instances in a purer form, but by being the attributes in common between all instances.)

73

In the Platonic view, most people are looking at instances (outcomes) and believing they see a pure essence (meaning), when really what they see is specific to their participation in the event – and therefore, like morality, is easily gamed into a "I demand freedom so you cannot force me to change, even as I force you to change to avoid inconveniencing me wherever I go" mentality which Plato identifies as the root of decay of a civilization.

When we are children, the difference between instance and essence is clearer to us. We have recently learned words like "chair," and know that not all chairs are alike. We even draw the distinction "all chairs are like my chair" without assuming that all chairs spring from that one chair. But as time goes on, through a sleight of hand, we are convinced to build up an idealized, socially-driven version of more complex ideas that conflates to "all things like this are like the version I have most closely experienced." For example, in morality we conclude that our deaths would be an injustice, therefore all killing is wrong – but how easily we are lured into paradox when it comes to killing those we perceive as threats.

The principle of active nihilism is one of ultimate reality: we are real, in a physical world that is real, with real consequences for any given action. There are no inherent goals, so we must pick one. If we like life, that goal is survival. If we want to maximize survival, we pick a systematic method (the scientific method) for discovering truth, or mental constructs that correspond to constructs existing in the physical world. After all, the one inherent thing to life is physical reality outside of us; everything else is up for grabs or ambiguous.

Thus there are two essential ideas in active nihilism:

- *Adaptation not judgment.* We judge; the world does not. What the world does, like a machine, is function on some input and fail on others. As organisms who want to survive, our goal is adaptation. While life and physical reality are inherent, the choice to adapt is not; we can choose suicide. But only true idiots argue over "validity" when there's a lack of inherent value. Nothing is valid or invalid; there are only results. Did you get the results you desire? Did your desiring make sense given the reality around you? Does your notion of sense make sense, both in the *a priori* zone of pure logic and the *a posteriori* zone of knowing how similar decisions in the past have worked out? Judgments are human and as such are (a) representative of a small segment, or partial truth, or truth or reality and (b) inherently anthropocentric in context, and to humans they appear inherent.

- *Correspondence not absolutism.* Absolutism means that something is true (a) because it is internally logical and (b) as a result, it applies in a universal context – it is not situational, or specific, or time-dependent or context-dependent *at all*. Some logical ideas may exist *a priori* from the concept of logic itself, such as that one proposition must follow from another, but anything more complex is usually dependent upon factors from our world. Absolute thought exists in a universal context, in a perpetual present tense, to all people equally, without variation no matter what the balance of power (for moral actors) or context of the question is. If we said "donuts are good" is a universal truth, we would use donuts to end wars, feed cattle, balance machinery and soothe hemorrhoids. Sound insane? It's just an easy to recognize example of common insanity.

Active nihilism denies inherent value but does not deny the inherency of reality. It tells us there are no default or universal judgments, and all that we can expect is that reality is consistent such that specific actions achieve similar results every time they are tried. This is the basis of all learning, and without it, even the basics of our understanding (gravity, time) would not make any sense because we could not expect them to be consistent.

Historically, the most popular theory of truth was the Correspondence Theory. First proposed in a vague form by Plato and by Aristotle in his Metaphysics, this realist theory says truth is what propositions have by corresponding to a way the world is. The theory says that a proposition is true provided there exists a fact corresponding to it. In other words, for any proposition p,

p is true if and only if p corresponds to a fact.

The theory's answer to the question, "What is truth?" is that truth is a certain relationship – the relationship that holds between a proposition and its corresponding fact.[7]

From this consistency we hope to construct truths, but it is understood these are not universal; they apply only in our minds to such degree that our individual minds are ready at that moment to accept them. The most profound truth if told without context seems like arbitrary babble, or if told to an idiot, seems like pretentious drivel.

If active nihilism has a tenet, it is the denial of anthropocentric desires for "inherent" truth – really, consistent patterns to our consciousnesses that we would like to believe are inherent to the universe, but are an artifact of the object we are using to perceive, namely our brains: social preferences, feelings and emotions, the "official" declarations of public institutions or individuals, the promises of advertising – in preference for the adaptive model provided by the scientific method. "Deny no perception," says the fatalist; "Deny no reality," says the active nihilist.

Toward a non-Hollywood Nihilism

Nihilism will continue to confuse its audience because the actual concept is so much less emotionally satisfying than the false one. The kind of active fatalism that is required to deny anything but the self and the self's material comfort in the present moment carries with it a satisfying rage against all that we dislike in the world. Nihilism itself however sees the rage of rejection and the errors of calcification as one, and provides an antidote: remove the human definition of "inherent" that is essentially solipsistic, and replace it with a knowledge of events over time as a sequence of causes.

It is for this reason that nihilism, unlike fatalism, does not proscribe striving for ideals, even ones that might overlap with what is considered "moral." Nihilism denies that values are inherent, and by doing so, denies human solipsism; it does this as a means to having clarity about why we choose to be moral, which is a form of adaptive

---

[7] Bradley Dowden and Norman Swartz, "Truth," *Internet Encyclopedia of Philosophy*, retrieved from http://www.iep.utm.edu/truth/.

strategy similar to the scientific method where we observe the world and pick a response that is most likely to bring about positive results.

Nihilism may be our ultimate weapon against the consequence of human solipsism, which is backward rationalism. Because our selves are the formative archetype we know, we argue "from the self and toward the world," instead of the converse where we would observe the world to determine how to adapt to it. This means that when we find something we desire, we effect it, and then argue backwards from that effect toward a justification outside of the self.

"I'm just drinking this alcohol so no wayward kids get it" could well summarize human logic of this nature. We rationalize from what we have done to the reasons for doing it, using tokens that will manipulate our audience, usually of an emotionally universal or logically absolute (contextless) type. Nihilism denies this solipsism by denying these universals and absolutes, and by rejecting inherent values that are cornerstones for manipulation, forcing us instead to formulate forward logic: "I am doing this action for this effect toward this goal."

The rejection of the idea of inherent values negates justification because it means there are no universals toward which we can always ascribe our actions; instead, each action must be considered situationally not by a moral standard of outcomes, but by a moral standard of goals which will be measured by the outcomes they claim (before the action) to be attempting to achieve.

For this reason nihilism is less a philosophy in itself (or like fatalism, a substitute for a philosophy) but a philosophical framework. When we understand like as not the false inherency of our solipsism, and as being composed of many moments knitted together by cause and effect where immediate outcome of an action is not its sole effect, life makes sense again. In the odd mode of paradox that afflicts many of nature's greatest creations, in human life we must accept nothingness in order to find meaning in something.

July 20, 2010

EXPLORING NIHILISM

For a simple philosophy, and one that serves as a gateway and not a set of concrete goals, nihilism unleashes much confusion as people try to leave the mental ghetto in which civilization itself places them. This ghetto unites individualism, or the prioritization of self-interest before all other interests, with the tendency of human groups to pick what is mentally convenient and easy to understand over realistic responses to their situation.

Primitive men with their talismans and devil dolls, scientists with studies based on statistical reasoning, and the modern person armed with his dual combination of atheism and humanism are all wielding symbols against the uncertainty of reality. Like cleansing ceremonies in a new barn, the driving of the scapegoat over the cliff, or even the modern habit of neurotically moving into "good neighborhoods" in the hope of escaping crime, the modern mental ghetto of rationalism has us insist that the symbolic – a part standing for the whole – can replace knowledge of reality itself, which includes context and consequence far beyond what the average human can consider.

Nihilism also rebels against the idea of universal ideologies and values. Not everyone shares the same values; however, this does not mean those values are all equally legitimate. The only arbiter is reality itself. Those that produce good results are good values. Those that do not are illusion, or the person desires bad results, which in itself says much about them. Since nihilism is so anti-universal, it applies itself as a series of mental tools which then translate to particularized results in different areas.

Rationalism as Religion

Two worlds exist on earth, as they do in the theology of the Christian religion, where there's this imperfect world contrasted by a perfect Heaven-world where things are exactly as they seem (sounds boring to me). The two worlds on earth are reality as it exists, to the best degree that we can perceive it, and reality as a psychological construct *projected* onto the world.

Most people live in that latter world, and usually justify it with the former. Life is unclear, ambiguous, so they impose an Order upon it. Although analysis of the former should convince them of the illogic of absolutes, they prefer their world of simple certainties.

A form of nihilism which recognizes the primacy of the design logic inherent in nature, which we might call *naturalist* nihilism, removes the latter world and embraces the former including its ambiguities. The world created by humans considers only the human perspective; something instead is needed that includes the whole. To get to this world, we have to first strip back the illusions we have and then look at what exists in the objective.

Our perception of this will be "subjective" in the eyes of the Herd, but to varying degrees in much the same way that many opinions describe a real-world scenario, and some are more accurate than others. In the case of the best minds, enough of the objective will be understood, even if imperfectly, that it can be acted on for ongoing evolution and growth. This is natural in the finest sense of the word, meaning what is intuitive to those of high intelligence.

The latter world, which could be described as a socio-emotional construct, is comprised of our reactions to our world, which occur in the form of mental judgments. Death = bad, feces = disgusting, violence = bad. While death, violence and feces may have negative effects on our lives, we've confused the human perspective with the perspective of the whole.

Consider for example the mass murderer. Without ideology, or plan, he kills to feel the power of control over another (this same phenomenon can be observed in bosses, high school principals, and authority figures across America). If death is brought to the mass murderer, should we feel it is "bad"?

To obsess about his death would be to fixate ourselves on the isolated perspective of the human, and not to look at the whole, which is just fine without him and moving on, with someone of potentially better caliber taking his place. This concept shocks most people, because they are somewhat depressed and have low self-esteem, thus automatically assume that any competition or predation would eliminate them. They project themselves into the mass murderer and feel pity for him when they really feel fear for themselves.

That we defecate, disgusting as it may seem, forms part of what sustains us. From that defecation as much as consumption we derive life. Breathe in, breathe out: the CO_2 you exhale is a poison, in enough concentration, but it's a useful building block for plants. As is feces. As are corpses.

To recognize this nature of nihilism, we see feces and death as the "dark side" of the mouth, and through that recognize life beyond the human perspective. Humans fear things that disturb them personally and then assign to those things a universal status, like a monkey trying to convince the tribe that his enemy is its enemy. Escaping this is the essence of nihilism, or a reduction of all value except the inherent and holistic. "Disgusting" is not important; the function of the world and the human body is. Function, measured in real-world changes and results, is more important than sensation or moral judgments, feelings and emotions.

By naming that which cannot be named, we break through the line between what is publically recognized by humans, and that which is reality as whole. Anuses, death, violence, predation and the fact (not opinion) that some humans are more intelligent, stronger, etc. than others are all threats to the human-only mental reality.

It doesn't need to be a religious experience, but it usually is, to realize in any small or large part this awareness. It's like a meta-sorting: suddenly you are given a tool to literally divide your world into real and not-real, and to discard the not-real. You can then focus on the real, and rebuild.

What is it to "rebuild"? First, you will need to replace the mental constructs which were supported by the unreal world. You have to reinvent your own ethics, and your values (preferences for one type of outcome over another). You have to reinvent your own sense of personal destiny and mission. It's scary, like being alone for the first time on a strange street on the first cold night of winter.

But it's also a sense of self-ownership. The hand that swung you is gone, and you are now both hammer and anvil. There are no barriers to the world as it is, and you know how it can be operated and have preferences that you have derived, using only your brain, which you hope to fulfill. Everything you earn and create is yours and yours alone.

The major questions of life still remain, at least initially. Why are we here? Is death as real as it seems? Does anything matter? You are approaching these as a nihilist, however, and so the confusion caused by an illusion and your reactions to it are eliminated. For this reason, you can observe the natural world and develop some working hypotheses.

Since any vision of reality only works insofar as it doesn't run into contradiction, the human fantasy world requires finite, absolute answers to these questions for which there may be no immediate answers (or at least not answers we in human form are ready to perceive). Nihilism avoids contradiction by not creating symbolic answers to such questions. It preserves most of life as mystery, as it shall forever be, instead of creating symbols that assert human control over the unknown by taking a small fragment of it and turning it into a token which represents the whole. That is the method called rationalism, and it leads to an illusion of control at an opportunity cost of increasing instability when reality peeks through our carefully-constructed mental categories.

This allows nihilism to avoid the problem of the modern world, namely passivity. When you generate an absolute and objective substitute reality, the process of thought in life goes from "what must I do to achieve" to "what must I do to not offend the gods" (or analogues thereof, including in our modern time *the customer* and *public opinion*). This psychology is responsible for the passivity of the modern time, which cannot admit outright disagreement or difference between people, and thus tries to norm them with religion, politics and social factors.

This in turn creates the environment where to talk about a fact of life, such as an anus or the inevitability of death, is "offensive" and therefore taboo. Society retaliates against those who cross the line between social illusion and reality.

When one takes the narrow bridge of nihilism, a perilous crossing in which the long fall into endless despair funneling toward death is present on both sides, one reaches a point where acceptance of this new philosophy is possible, and values can be reconstructed. Where the previous social illusion depends on forcing its values on the world (through passive means), the nihilist path involves accepting the world and working with its methods.

In this nihilism is far healthier, as one accepts the world as whole and nothing is offensive, or taboo, or shocking. This doesn't mean that one blindly accepts destructive or stupid behaviors – in fact the contrary, because as a consequence of having an active and not passive philosophy one assumes responsibility for outcomes and not feelings – but it does mean that one is free from fearing things which would draw the social illusion into contradiction and thus shatter a worldview, and with it, a world.

November 3, 2004

Misanthropy

We live in an age where there is almost no philosophy; yes, academics joust over whether the verb "to be" has made us feel uncharitable toward the dispossessed, but there is no assertive discussion of philosophy as a means of assessing values systems, because to discuss such things would mean that someone in the audience finds his or her values are seen as illogical; then not only is tenure threatened, but future book sales are hovering near dubious. As a result of this aphilosophical thought structure, most of the terms we could use to describe certain aspects of a worldview are not only without definition, but have been loosely associated with such absolute, kneejerk behavior as to make no sense.

One good example is "nihilism." This originally described a frame of thought where nothing was seen to have any pre-existing value; it had both active and passive examples, with the latter ranging from stoicism to fatalism. In our current time, even the educated have trouble comprehending nihilism as something less ominous than "evil," as their minds work through absolutes, in which case even the verb "to be" is threatening: nihilism = no value, no value = ("therefore") no values; in conclusion, ladies and gentlemen, nihilism = really bad, like "evil" but more scientific.

This runs in contrast to the healthier values of the ancients, who believed that if you looked deeply enough into any system of thought, you could find where it approximated the same set of eternal truths and values, things which did not "exist" but were perceivable and thus, although "subjective," were consistent and therefore real even if invisible to most. The modern disease is to like a machine see categories as impassable divisions, and thus to miss this, in part because our society grew up believing in gods in other worlds who sorted every object, person and idea into exact, immutable categories like "good" and "evil." This is the false absolute that persists today; when we have enough data to associate an idea with an existing extreme, we assume that it must "equal" that extreme and thus discard all of its contextual thought. Rationalism has us impart the quality of categories to their contents, rather than the saner method of finding commonality between objects sufficient to declare a category.

Obviously, this is defective, as it has us imposing barriers where none exist, such as between "subjective" and "objective." We assume that subjective is one polar extreme of thought such that all subjective things are arbitrary, and not only do not need to correspond to reality, but are "choices" and not analysis, interpretation, or logic. This shield of the subjective helps us tolerate the neurotic and schizoid ideas of others, as we gaily say, "Well, that's subjective," and thus approve of no analysis being applied to *belief* which is seen as entirely separate from *thought*. Similarly, we take it for granted that anything "objective" – usually statistics, scientific categories or digital output – is not at all influenced by the arbitrary beliefs of its human handlers, and is thus an absolute truth which rules our world. It hasn't occurred to these people that all perceptions are subjective, even those filtered through scientific instruments, but that as all subjective knowledge is interpreted from a consistent world, if the subject is not insane *or in the grips of some insanity like absolutism*, the subjective data can very accurately describe the world.

In a time like this, it's thus nearly impossible to categorize one's own belief. If you say you believe in what is ancient, the braindead mob begins chanting that it wants something new, as what is past has failed. If you say you believe in something from the future, the braindead mob starts agitating for "proof" of an "objective" nature that what you say will work, which if you look past the smokescreen of their bad psychology is more likely a demand for inaction, because inaction offends no one. Inaction affirms that what exists now is just fine and that everyone in it is fine and no one will be seen to be in logical error, because after all, their arbitrary life choices – taking heroin, spending all their free time playing video games, having lifestyles based around recreational shopping – should be "subjective" and for that reason, *beyond all criticism*. In the light of this chaotic and broken mental state, it is important we analyze misanthropy.

Many great thinkers are said to be misanthropes, usually because they did not embrace *all* people around them as the greatest thing since sliced bread (which is actually a terrible thing: it massively reduces flavor if you keep it more than a day, which the shipping process by very nature imposes, so they need to add fake flavors to compensate). This enables us to write off their opinions as "subjective," with an airy wave of our hand and the all-knowing proclamation, "You know he was a *misanthrope*" or "Her misanthropy kept her from knowing the good in humanity." This dismissive outlook is designed to protect the meek among us, who might be offended by the knowledge that recreational heroin use is actually a somewhat illogical outlook (to avoid absolute categories, we say "for most," since for some people, dying of heroin addiction is the best solution). Misanthropy goes into the file with evil, terrorists, hackers, Nazis, pot smokers and Montana cabin-dwellers – people who have rejected society, and thus cannot be trusted.

Whenever one looks deeply into the definition of the word, there is always some loudmouthed segment of the crowd that can be found pointing a stubby finger at a book and saying, "No. You're wrong. It says right here that misanthropy is 'hating humanity,'" as if that settles the issue. They view the dictionary as an absolute, just as they'll view the words of a scientific proclamation as an absolute, without looking into the categorical structure of that scientific thought; declare that birds are closer to reptiles than mammals, and these types will call birds reptiles and scream at anyone who does not obey the same simplistic thought. It is profitable however to break "misanthropy" from this mold, and realize that instead of meaning "hating humanity" it implies a generalized hatred of how humans as a mass behave. Misanthropy is like any other form of elitism a preference for the best of people and a rejection of the idea of including and "validating" (= social inclusion) *all* people, because most people are insane and people in groups are even crazier. Misanthropes rarely deal with the set of "no people," meaning absolute zero, but they are selective, and this is a sin to the voting public.

It is offensive behavior because it bridges the subjective/objective line that has been established by popular consent for the purpose of protecting each individual from criticism. This is how you form a crowd – tell them that they can be individuals because the crowd protects the absolute form of the individual, and then in order to secure that individual "right" and "freedom," the crowd will turn on any who do not obey such a division. In crowd-logic, all choices are "subjective" and all data is "objective," because this makes personal choices immune to criticism and makes it easy to manipulate the crowd by bringing out some "objective" data with a broad interpretation hidden within that tells them what to think and do. Selectivity means that you refuse to socialize with some people, and in fact judge them as destructive, by their "lifestyle choices," and that you esteem others more highly for intangible things like character, intelligence, and emotional outlook. As with any belief that ranks some above others, this is offensive to the group-think entity of "individuals," who would prefer that absolute barriers exist toward criticism of any individual choice.

Misanthropy is thus, like nihilism, something that initially seems like a blanket condemnation of a category – humankind or values, respectively – but turns out to be a highly selective system of finding only the meaningful in those groups by denying their objective absolute status as law. Some would call this "elitism," but what is elitism except a form of meritocracy: choosing the best and holding them up as an example to the rest, so that the rest rises to an approximation of that level? We either aim high, or normalize the lowest common denominator, which then descends in level over the generations. The crowd is fine with that when you pick the best by wealth, or looks, but when you start picking them by character, they feel threatened. They should. For several thousand years now, our society has made the assumption that people of any character can be shaped by external rules and made to function as a social machine. Now that civilization is fully plunging into its self-created abyss, the few thinkers who haven't been killed by the crowd are looking more critically at that idea, and instead electing once again to esteem the internal values that, a long time ago, made our civilization reach for higher concepts. These higher concepts have been dragged into the mud by the fear of the crowd, and it is selective and cynical philosophies like misanthropy and nihilism that oppose this.

February 9, 2005

The Young Nihilist in Love

The concept of love and being in love is central to not only human life, but our hopes. We all want love in some form or another. Like the ancient Greeks, who used many words for love, we can divide the concept further: love by family, by friends, romantic love, appreciation by others, or even to be desired or desirable. But love presents a challenge in that our tendency is to *project*, or assign our hopes, desires and intent to another object, specifically, the beloved in whatever form that person takes.

What is scary about relationships is that they create a new world, an "our world." Suddenly, like a microcosm of civilization itself, two people must get along by agreeing on what is true and what should be done. These two questions – *what is true?* and *what should be done?* – form the basis of most philosophy because they are intensely related. If we discover the world exists in a certain form, or for a certain purpose or lack thereof, that shapes what we should do about it. Without that, we have only survival: food, water, shelter, defense and the acquisition of comforts. While survival only is comforting to us in its simplicity, it also reduces meaning, which is our connection with the world out there such that we wish to interact with it and change it. We find comfort in ourselves, but meaning in our interaction with the world and our achievement of actions which, by creating a balance to inevitable death, show us that our lives are important in some way more than our own desires.

Poor humanity! Confused, it bleats out the same message every time, which is (not coincidentally) that the world means nothing more than our desires – and it includes love in that scope. This creates empty humans who wander like zombies, hungering for meaning which they invent out of the set of things that already make them feel good, but this changes meaning from interaction with the world to concealment of the truth about that interaction. Humans live by lies. The empty form an ideal audience as they rush after desires, then find themselves empty, and then rush after meaning. Shuttling between the two wears them out and keeps them distracted, pliable and unlikely to interrupt the flow of commerce, power and social importance.

But, back to love. It is impossible to love an object without loving the conditions of that object. With the beloved, we know that our desired person must eat, defecate, and even engage in questionable behaviors as they learn to become whole people, a process like maturation but reaching farther into both the inner self and the world out there. Even more importantly, we cannot love an object without loving the ground of all objects, or existence itself (required to perceive those objects) and the world which makes those objects come into being. Love is not love of something; it is a belief in love, and in that the problem emerges along with the beauty, namely that with this belief in love, we begin to give ourselves license to see belief as more important than reality.

Most of our failures in love involve self-deception. The other was not all that excited about the relationship, but we projected our enthusiasm onto the other and charged ahead. Or the other was hopeful, but we were cynical and attributed that same motivation to the other. We can ignore the needs of an other because they are not impulses we feel; we can ignore warning signs because they do not fit into our vision of what should be. Sometime we mistake love for a sense of obligation, and take others for granted. These originate in our belief in love, as well as the good. At that point, whether in the individual or the union, love becomes taken over by the kind of manipulative hyperbolic promises made by the advertisements they show to kids on Saturday morning television.

Some nihilists disclaim love entirely as purely a biological impulse to reproduce, or a hedonic pressure toward sexual gratification. Clearly these are part of love: one does not logically commit to someone with whom a lifetime would be unbearable, sexual attraction impossible, or children a disaster. And yet love cannot be only biological because of its ties to human hope and our estimation of the world; we can only love a good place, and through that love, be able to love others. In a nihilist sense, love might not be a belief so much as a commitment to life itself, and this is a realistic decision if one finds life to be beautiful.

Marriage is the commitment to make a lifetime of a love, as one will most probably be creating new life forms merged of the parents. Love is what happens when one finds someone else one respects enough to wish literally union in the form of one's irreplaceable time and possibly spawn. If you look at the process of breeding, it's quite romantic: We work, so let Another be made of Us. My warmth and heartspirit goes out to you teenage lovers; may your idealism never die. It goes out to the older couples who've lived through everything and made it work, should they still have tenderness for each other. And most of all, it goes out to my generation, you intrepid Generation Xers, who think you know what you should have and are trying to copy the image from TV screen to life.

But one must acknowledge love's instabilities. First, the choices involved depend on the people involved and more importantly, their knowledge and experience (one doesn't need many lovers for life experience: one needs life experience outside of love to apply to love). You are every experience you've had, and every lover you've had. Over time, the process can become rote and you can cease to be able to tell the difference between lovers. Also, the concept of love depends on what one sees. Your beloved may be hiding a murder, or a betrayal; it's hard to think of ultimate union with something diseased. Finally, love itself may become a prison, when one tries too hard for love and not enough for the literal situation of two people coming together (no pun intended). When I see love held up as a *signum imperium* in this way, I shudder and think of Saturday morning advertising.

August 15, 2004

Forgiveness

Although the idea of the individual, judged by morality and beholden to others for the form of being human and not the degree of striving toward a goal of greatness, remains filthy and horrible underneath its coating of cupcake-frosting sentiment and submission to the winds of life, there is one area where a nihilist could look Jesus Christ in the eye and tell him his doctrine succeeds: that of forgiveness.

People come into this life like drunken men caught by an ocean current, bewildered at these new shores and saddened by the paucity of life to be found there. The past is either barbaric natural selection, or a series of good intentions that bulked our species up like fat men, bulging with emotion but devoid of passion for a real sense of right in the only sense that matters, which is carving from the pattern language of life a beauty which transcends the ugliness, as the universe has been doing since its inception, converting void to light.

Politics is either authoritarianism or anarchy, if you take each thought to its logical extreme (as the years, and iteration of failure and dramatic action, will take it). We are born bitter or we check out early, and become doers of the rote action, evaders of the doubt and death through preoccupation with things we do not care about in the inner parts of us that can think of more than one thing at once and construct from them beauty or emotion. The solutions given to us are bad, and our ancestors, afflicted by the same things that will soon imprint us, have treated us like possessions and left us to the wiles of a world motivated by fear and thus greed, control and snide witty remarks to conceal an inner hollowness.

At some point, those who still have red healthy blood become possessed by a desire to take the fight to the enemy and leave scars of mortal wounds across its jaws. But who is the enemy? In a metaphysical "Where's Waldo," we're left stranded in our angst to try to locate the source of all of this bad, and we always come up short or pick targets that occupy us but obscure what we really want to change. The enemy is no one, or it is everyone; it could be ideas, but even those "isms" we learn in college eventually decompose into simpler thoughts, or rather biological impulses misdirected by illusions so basic we cannot even construct dogmas of them, and there is no way to take an axe to the intangible.

We have reason to be bitter not only from the past but for the future. Since our fellow citizens are checked out of reality, and we need consensus to address a problem, we see them as our obstruction because they, selfishly, refuse to see reality because it is more convenient to remain in denial. We see them as pigs and whores and we would like, if we search our hearts, to murder them all so the few who have chosen to face reality can move forward to do something better with our time than the cycling exhibits of rote-task jobs, shopping malls, traffic-choked streets, news reports of random shootings and government offices where we always are one triplicate form short of what we need. Our reality is hell, unless we have made ourselves oblivious like most have chosen to do.

In the state of oblivion, it is impossible to recognize fault with the design of a system. The patterns we live by are invisible, as are the larger patterns around them, which are invisible because they are mathematical and informational, not tangible. Oblivion makes us see life as being always this frustrating, and the goal of oblivion means that we are busy stuffing our minds with garbage, and occasionally, bad and terrible things happen and we do our best to forget them immediately. One reason we may not see UFOs filling the night sky is that all civilizations face this threshold, and either surrender to oblivion and self-destruct, or reorganize themselves through great effort. Distant stars may harbor only ruins and bitter, devolved apes flinging broken circuit boards at each other.

This balance would make anyone uneasy. It might make them sick. Do we live for the now, and try to keep our minds distracted, or do we do what might make us feel whole, and struggle for clarity, knowing that others will be alarmed that we interrupt their oblivion and slash at us with their words, their money and their censure? What a feast of bitterness – what a tragedy of inattention – what a horror, through that inextricable process of nature that kills things that have lost the will to live, all without flashing a neon sign in their faces saying OBLIVION REACHED: DOOM AHEAD, PREPARE FOR GALACTICA FAILURE. It is no surprise so many smart people either outright kill themselves or live increasingly recklessly until drugs, alcohol, disease or pimped-out ghetto dwellers finish the job for them.

Most people take a middle path. They try to live as best they can, and to push those bad (but real) thoughts away behind the TV shows and CDs and shiny new gadgets, and try to live inside themselves as much as possible, while making some concession to the need for ideology. These people – 99% of those who aren't so incapacitated by congenital stupidity, poverty, self-abuse and/or power that they still notice things – will choke us with their sad paradox. They know a need, but in an effort to balance it with themselves, they have reversed the logic. Instead of doing what is right, they go through the motions of doing what is right to make themselves feel better about being alive, and to hold up a rhetorical sword to others: "I am on a mission! I have a goal! Where you, grey lumpenprole of the cascade of Rome's future failure, may endure only for your sofa and television, I have a *cause!*"

Those who find life frustrating, but cannot yet commit to doing something about it and possibly giving up the little they have, come to it with their supposedly unique personal philosophies to wage war on us in a desperate attempt to prove they are right and we are wrong (nevermind that they have misunderstood the relativity equation, and assumed that a drowning man can rise by pushing down others to drown faster: the water level remains the same!). They bloviate violently, they cajole us for not seeing their point of view, they act like petty philosophers and tyrants – in fact, their actions are indistinguishable from honest ideologism until we look deeply into them, and see the logic is reverse. They do not act toward a goal.

They act toward themselves, and use the goal like those little crabs who glue shells and sand in a clump around them for camouflage. They hide behind "activism" so they do not feel the cold hard fear for this time, for the past and for the future, and realize how tenuous their own grasp on wanting to exist in it can be. Haven't we all felt that touch of cold night, a velveteen breeze with the promise of dew, sneaking in that window we must have forgotten to close and stroking us with a scent that touches on the beautiful freedoms of childhood, and so in contrast to the present, pointing out what we're missing and converting a thing of beauty into the touch of death, fear, horror and failure? When we are blocked by anger and frustration, things of beauty become hateful, because they are not what we have, and they remind us of our two options: go into denial (anarchy) or force ourselves ahead through personal fascism (authoritarianism) even though it means our whole lives will be unrelenting work.

Forgiveness intrudes into this state of mind, and gives caesura, because like all states of transcendence ("grace" in the Christlexicon) it reminds us of the goal as a pattern in a pattern language of reality, placing the tangible aside so that we can see what complements our souls and completes us as people. This completion is not individualism, which means "placing of the individual before everything else," but a transcendence of both individualism and the Crowd around us. It is a clarity of mind through beauty, and one of the few times in life we can think clearly of more than one thing at once, because we have woven all into an upward current like the thermals of a fire, the sinuous waves of an ocean storm, or the image left in our mind by a tree full of leaves where we cannot see anyone but can see all as a ragged, beautiful shape.

We forgive those who abused us as children, or did stupid things to us during the day, not because we care for them, but because we want to free ourselves from them, and by freeing both parties from the resentment that keeps us earthbound, return focus to the goal. Some say it is better to light a candle than curse the darkness, where others say it is better to forgive the darkness, and light a candle so you can read, or cut some pushups, or ignite your own flatulence and send a blue flame into the night proclaiming "I am alive!" Forgiveness is giving up on the treacle of what has failed and moving toward that which is more ideal. It takes us from a negative logic of detesting something, to a space of emptiness, from which we can reconnect with creative logic and instead of acting out our fears of the negative, reach toward what may be beautiful. (Most people fear emptiness too much to let go of their hatred and impotence, because at least it's something tangible. It will be there tomorrow. It seems immortal. The more miserable it gets, the more immortal it seems, which is why people love to suffer – so long as they can bore us with the details.)

I encourage us to forgive on several levels:

- *Forgive the idiots around you.* It's not that they don't know what they do; it's that they're designed to not even consider knowing. They can do no differently. This is why in greater civilizations, they were told what to do and removed if they could not do it.

- *Forgive the past.* Let go of the old symbols, of the *Lord of the Rings* style visions. That which is truly eternal will be recreated if you act logically according to the pattern language of life. By holding on to images, you reverse your logic, and act so that the goal leverages you, instead of leveraging yourself toward the goal.

- *Forgive the future.* It looks horrible, doesn't it? It's an illusion. Nature's mathematics are designed with strict boundary functions that regulate systems so that a small amount of abuse makes them apocalyptic, but that gives them the ability to right themselves quickly. The idiots will plough ahead like lemmings and at a future moment, in free fall over the churning surf, will whip out Wiley E. Coyote styled signs saying "WTF FAIL," and then plunge into the abyss. Mourning them and cursing them are less productive than eating your own waste. Move forward toward the creative goal.

- *Forgive the bloviators.* They are your future allies, once they accept that trying to uphold themselves as the universe, with all else (in backward logic) a leverage toward the self. They bloviate because they need a cause so they do not feel doubt, and through this process of cognitive dissonance, where the individual invents an alternate reality to compensate for lack of importance or satisfaction in the one ultimate reality which may not be fully material but converges on materiality, they create "activism" of improbable things. The more improbable the better, because when one leverages activism to justify oneself, the goal is not to achieve a better state, but to have a cause for existing. So try to find those unicorns and sodomize God, because it'll keep you busy until you're too old to take yourself so seriously, and can look forward to coasting into an oblivious death.

Forgiveness is a form of nihilism that cuts us free from an obligation to consider this time sane, and the actions of insanity which adapt to its lack of sanity, important. Forgiveness slices it away from us so we can use our real powers to make changes to the design of reality, reflected in its pattern language, and allows us to use the principle of nihilism: believe in nothingness, and use that nothingness to remove the unimportant, which is that which does not have a necessary causal relationship to the interconnected design of the cosmos. Act not for practicality, but beauty, because what is practical is illusion, and when we forgive it, we give up on it in the one positive context of giving up – we move past the dying to the living.

If you take a reverent attitude toward forgiveness, and forgive this world and its people for their illusion, a stillness will settle over your soul. You will feel the past leave you like a headache at dawn, and leach out of you like an illness fading away. You will feel silence in your mind and soul, and what is not silent will be possessed with contemplation of a goal, which in a non-linear fashion involves combining all of the factors of life into a holographic rope fashioned from the pattern language of the universe. You will feel power as you see what you can do to move past the confusion and horror of recent history, the lies of others, and the bloviation of those stranded in not forgiving these lies.

This stillness will be followed by action, but – not yet. Wait for another moment. In this new stillness, you will for the first time experience the reverence for the universe and the grace that mystics speak of, where its beauty will return. Yin and yang, darkness and light, anarchy and clarity, chaos and order... they form something that is like a warm hand, cuddling you its child. Somewhere a voice like the hum of the earth is encouraging you to go onward, to create, to make beauty wherever whatever exists. Nihilism has removed both hatred and apathy. And as you think this, the cold air of the night – reminiscent of those rare moments of freedom in childhood when you forgot the rules, and played fearless in the darkness – intrudes on you in your lonely room with a hint of dewfall, and you feel a love for the universe that you can craft in seed and sword, for as long as you live.

April 27, 2008

Nihilism as Holy Grail

In one of the oldest, and most popular, stories in English-speaking countries, a handful of knights seek a mythical object called the Holy Grail. In the course of their adventures in seeking it, they overcome illusion and fear and become one with a natural order to the cosmos, being thus able to do what is required to transcend the supernatural protections of the grail and to "achieve" it.

To anyone who has read much literature, or is familiar with the structure of legend, it is clear the grail is a symbol and that the real acquisition is the knowledge and strength gained from pursuit of the grail. Whether the grail itself has mystical powers, the mythos of the journey is that of the knights gaining mystical powers, and by it, passing from one level of power to another. This power affects the organization of their consciousnesses, and therefore, grants to them a higher degree of effectiveness, much as martial arts training improves one's combat skills.

When we speak of nihilism, it is extraordinarily difficult to come up with a basic definition of it for the same way that explaining language to a cow is difficult – unless you already have an understanding of the basic archetype on which the definition is built, it's almost impossible to comprehend. It is like a thing from another world, in the stories of H.P. Lovecraft, that appears to us as terrible because to correctly perceive it requires more dimensions than those in which we are conscious. Nihilism is to most of us this thing from another dimension, as being accustomed to Judeo-Christian morality, we have no knowledge of why such a thing would be valuable.

Nihilism can be described as a rejection of knowledge, a rejection of belief and morality, or a rejection of decision-making. It is all of these, but rarely in the way we describe. It does not make sense to reject all knowledge, or one stops in the middle of this sentence (here) because one has rejected the memories of language. It makes little sense to reject all belief and morality as that destroys even our faith in logic, or our ethos of wanting to discover truth. And to reject decision-making, as a whole, is passivity, not nihilism. So how to define it?

One way to look at it would be that nihilism is a rejection of any belief system that is exclusively human, e.g. does not have a paired structure in nature. That means that unless we see reason to believe in the Gods, we do not believe; that unless we see reason to believe in equality, we do not believe; it is a form of skeptical, educated, and yet open-minded empiricism. It does not make absolute rejections, but pares down our knowledge to what is realistic, passing on the Judaic-style moral systems that create arbitrary systems for artificially equalizing the wills of different individuals.

More than empiricism, however, nihilism could be described as a gateway to realism, but a form of realism in which the intangible is recognized; most realism translates rapidly into materialism, or belief only in the physical world, which is not what nihilism means. For the uninitiated, materialism seems fine until one realizes that in the philosophical definition, having any values outside of material things – comfort, wealth, survival – obviates materialism.

Nihilist realism is a grasp of reality that preserves our knowledge of the abstract structure of the cosmos, and thus avoids the blockhead interpretation of realism as literal materialism. Much like knights going to find the grail, we often must experience it in our lives before we can understand why it has value; this brings us back to the question of morality. Judaic-style morality revolves around the individual, and preservation of that individual. Nihilist morality frees itself from this absolute to consider only realism.

From a realistic view, for example, an overpopulated planet needs to be cleansed. Therefore a nihilist does not worry about whether it is "murder" (and thus taboo) to kill people, but concentrates on killing the right ones so that humanity and its world get healthier. For example, to a nihilist, it's very obvious that seven billion people are too many, and that killing the dumbest of those on planet earth will be a positive step toward sanity. Some may waffle on about sterilizing versus killing, but to a nihilist it is not a question: one does what fixes a bad situation, rather than worrying about the individuals within it, as individuals are like water – a commodity of nature, and more will be created.

A nihilist does not adhere to Judeo-Christian views about morality in other ways. Most nihilists are not inclined to violence, but where it is the right tool to better a situation, they would have no moral prohibition against it. Nor against war. Nor against laziness, or drug use, or any other "wrong" behavior – with the only caveat being that, in a realistic sense, it must have purpose. To a nihilist, an action without will is an admission of fatalism, or a lack of ability to make decisions, and probably merits death if repeated consecutively.

Only reality is real. Relegating what is in human minds without a natural correspondent keeps us in touch with what is real, so we don't drift off into fanciful notions of God, Justice, Freedom, Money, or other things which are our symbolic systems for interpreting life, but not relevant to life itself except when used accurately in that capacity. When one becomes a nihilist, it is no longer a question of accepting absolute values, but which values to pick – based on reality, and an enduring realism that recognizes the holiness of life as a whole.

This ultimately is the paradox of nihilism: as a philosophy, it is a gateway to an understanding of cosmic order as it is, not the creation of an alternate cosmic order (God/morality) with which to compel others to act for the benefit of the individual. It is the only transcendence of the individual, and thus of death-fear, which is available to us, and its tenets have been found in all of the ancient cultures and religions of merit, but its most enduring appeal has been through common sense: reality is real; get over the fear of death and low self-esteem, and do what is great, not what is a phantasm of a lonely and fearful mind.

July 14, 2005

NIHILISM

Civilization is a disease which is almost invariably fatal. – Sir William Ralph Inge

The problem that humans face is simple: we cannot think. Or rather, we think too well, but therefore arrive at a state where we cannot tell the difference between our notions of what we want to believe is true and what is real. Nihilism is a type of discipline applied to our thinking that steers us away from our innate tendency toward illusion. It is not a complex concept, but because the path from our current beliefs is so circuitous and fraught with confusion, it is difficult to understand. All things must start somewhere however, and doing something – where otherwise doing nothing is a path to certain failure – will always be a worthwhile attempt.

What Nihilism is Not

Any form of organized thought is a belief. This offends those who would like to make convenient categories that absolve them of the need to actually understand the issues and take particular action instead of merely reciting slogans or endorsing universal solutions like "equality" or "work hard."

Most people approach the question of their future with a mix of futility and cunning. The fatalistic belief that nothing they do can have a positive effect is a subterfuge intended to allow them to do nothing and still feel smugly self-righteous about that choice. Their mission is to spread fatalism by encouraging others to give up on anything more exciting than a full day at a job, a six-pack of beer and something good on television. Their need is like that of a drug addict: their response to the eventuality of death is to declare that everything sucks and therefore to be happy with mediocrity. If all of these people died tomorrow, nothing of value would be lost.

Another form of fatalism is mainstream politics. By selecting a political belief like a product off a department store shelf, people have chosen an excuse for their own dysfunctional response to the future. Political alignments are ultimately proxies, or substitutes for action through symbolic acts, and allow people to vote once a year, repeat the same "wise" ideas in every conversation, and then have an excuse for why things turned out poorly or well as they scream at the television screen. Like the talismans and devil dolls of primitive cultures, these are merely superstitions, banishing fears with symbolic gestures. We tend to categorize such things under *cognitive dissonance*, which consists of balancing internal beliefs against real-world experience, and when the two come up short, changing our perception of what is real instead of altering our internal beliefs to reflect the new knowledge.

Let us now examine how dissonance may be reduced, using as an illustration the example of the habitual cigarette smoker who has learned that smoking is bad for his health. He may have acquired this information from a newspaper or magazine, from friends, or even from some physician. This knowledge is certainly dissonant with the cognition that he continues to smoke. If the hypothesis that there will be pressures to reduce this dissonance is correct, what would the person be expected to do?

I. *He might simply change his cognition about his behavior by changing his actions; that is, he might stop smoking. If he no longer smokes, then his cognition of what he does will be consonant with the knowledge that smoking is bad for his health.*

II. *He might change his "knowledge" about the effects of smoking. This sounds like a peculiar way to put it, but it expresses well what might happen. He might simply end up believing that smoking does not have any deleterious effects, or he might acquire so much "knowledge" pointing to the good effects it has that the harmful effects become negligible. If he can manage to change his knowledge in either of these ways, he*

100

*will have reduced, or even eliminated, the dissonance
between what he does and what he knows.*[8]

Still another deception is a belief in materialism alone. This system
of thought says that only material objects, comfort and convenience
are important, and everything else is illusion. It denies our need for
meaning and tends to produce empty, greedy individuals. But it cuts
to the essence of human decision-making which is fundamentally
entirely existential or focused on the quality of and meaning to
individual experience. Even our political and religious ideas we filter
through the needs and sensations of the self. Our choices reflect
what we think will make our lives more comfortable, wealthier and
more significant.

This puts to the forefront the questions of mortality and meaning.
We defend our lives as concept as if arguing to our social group that
we are important, and to convince ourselves that we are making
the best of an irreplaceable – whether there is an afterlife or not,
this life does not repeat – mortal life. Humans face a threatening
world in which the question of death features prominently. If what
comprises us as individuals is merely matter, to die is to disappear,
which makes life a brief span of time to develop a personality before
permanent extinction with no chance of seeing what comes of what
we do. That eliminates any positive attitude we can have toward life
itself. Similarly, "meaning" is understood to signify participation
in something larger than ourselves and most people view that as
requiring an inherent, or inbuilt and universal, order to provide
that context. This creates a belief in God or gods as a container for
questions of afterlife and an order beyond materiality to give our
lives meaning.

To many, among them Friedrich W. Nietzsche, "dualism" or the idea
that a perfect heaven existed in which the actual significance of life
would be decided in opposition to and differently from as it is in this
world, is a form of fatalism or failure to embrace the possibilities
of life out of fear of mortality. A nihilist might see materialism and

---

[8] Leon Festinger, *A Theory of Cognitive Dissonance*, Stanford University Press
(1957), pp. 5-6.

dualism as two sides of the same coin, where either life has zero potential for meaning or its potential for meaning is determined by forces we cannot discern from the rules, patterns and natural laws of this world. In both cases, the individual has surrendered the obligation and freedom to choose sources of meaning through understanding the world and how to make beauty (or another transcendental good) from it, and is looking for guidance like a lost sheep at the shopping mall. In this view, life represents a binary option between an empty and random existence with no purpose, and purposeful and immortal existence under a divine force that imposes an arbitrary order upon it.

Yet none of these are satisfying, because at the end of the day, they place us no closer to a coherent vision of human purpose and enjoyment of life. Fatalism absolves us of responsibility and nothing else; it instead is the oldest human mental fallacy, that of isolating a sub-set of reality and using it in a symbolic method to insulate us from the consequences of life as a whole. People who enjoy fatalism act entirely in narrow self-interest; in their minds, they have "proven" the futility of any action but the personally convenient and by doing so, have made their own selfish acts look like the noblest course of behavior. This enables them to both demand others consider them important and simultaneously contribute nothing beyond what they are forced to do, which makes them as parasitic as leeches, ringworm, Ebola/Marburg or attorneys. The question of human purpose includes questions of metaphysics, politics and personal behavior and shares among each of them the question of the root of meaning.

Political questions strike us in this time especially because to even the numbed observer it is clear that this society is embarked on what we call in business a "death-march": a fundamentally doomed approach whose flaws are not immediately visible that is nonetheless demanded by higher-ups because it visually resembles decisive action, and by doing so, allows them to justify and defend their jobs for the intervening period until the ultimate crash. Much as metaphysical questions tie in to purpose in life, politics and personal morality relate to the same underlying question of meaning. Do we require an inherent order for meaning and purpose? If so, what is it? This vital kernel of all philosophy to follow forms the basis of our personal moral decisions, our feeling about where civilization should direct itself and therefore all political questions, and relates to whether or not we find its origin in metaphysics, material or some third option.

The human habit of scapegoating, trusting talismans and making sacrifices to gods extends to our view of life itself: we like having a boss or authority above us that, right or wrong, can be blamed for our shortcomings. Much as humans target life itself with negativity while continuing to live, many are content to labor on doomed errands so long as they can blame whoever is in charge and thus absolve themselves of responsibility for their own happiness. Of course, no one is really "in charge" here, as we are just following mass trends and opinions, media and political constructs passed along for so many generations that it is now impossible to find someone who is definitively to blame, for whom we can have a comforting execution, then dust off our hands and proclaim the problem solved because we dethroned the bad guy.

Nihilism offers a third option because, unlike almost all beliefs, it is a conduit and not an endpoint. Most belief systems lay out a series of static objectives and claim if these are achieved, everything will be as peachy as it can be; the most dangerous are the Utopian ones, which promise an absolute near perfection that has little to do with reality. "Someday we'll eliminate all war" and "free markets make free souls" both fall into this category. Believing such homilies is akin to thinking that if you buy the right guitar, you'll be able to magically (metaphysically) or automatically (materialism) create the best music ever, et cetera *ad nauseam*. Nihilism does not claim a Utopian solution, and is in fact contra-Utopian: by the nature of its being a philosophical viewpoint, and not a mass trend around which you're expected to rally, it defines itself as a way of viewing the world including such political mass trends. There is no ultimate solution, no absolute Utopia, only a better mental tool for perceiving and analyzing whatever situations arise. Unlike political rallying points, it is a highest level abstraction, and one under which all other ideas form a hierarchy assessing their degrees of logicality.

Trend-whores and savvy political manipulators will try to group issues under any belief, including nihilism, thinking that a bullet point list makes it easy for the proles to agree on a course of action (so far, history suggests this is either outright lying or wishful thinking). It's unlikely that such a thing could occur. Nihilists embrace "extreme" viewpoints because they have seen past the cognitive dissonance, and thus have no problem looking at the world analytically. It's not extremity for extremity's sake, which is almost always a psychological device for creating an impossible goal and thus, by claiming to labor toward it, removing responsibility of actually doing something achievable. One reason to detest extreme rightist, leftist and green communities is that this is their *modus operandi*: suggest something insane, then accuse all who don't agree of selling out, and continuing to labor on with the attitude "only I know the truth, and the rest of you are pretenders, therefore, I'm better than you." Can we be honest and refer to this as defensive egomania?

Nihilism needs no justification. It follows the pattern of nature, which is evolution: successive replacement of previous forms of organization ("order," "design") with better ones. There is no moral imperative to do any given act, only a practical one, in that if a proposed design works better even in some small way, those design details can be incorporated into the status quo, thus forcing it to the next level of evolution. Of course, making any changes introduces new powers and new problems, so the process of evolution continues ad infinitum, unless (as in the case of French and Italians) an evolutionary "harbor" is reached, by which adaptation balances adequately enough to an unchanging environment. If one is, for example, the remnants of a fallen empire, there is not much to do except to live well and not worry too much about greatness receding slowly into memory so far removed it is mythic legend and not a part of current reality. Nihilism is a means of exploring the truths you cannot say in social situations, which conflicts with the tendency of most people to engage in illusion and have others validate it for them. With that truthful approach in mind, we then see the actual question before us which is to rise through realism or sink through social illusion, and if we love life, that question compels us to act for the former and against the latter.

Background

I was arguing once with a fellow who, when I proposed a high-level abstraction, said, "But isn't abstraction a Judeo-Christian thing, and therefore, bad?" He fell into the same trap that many at our universities have, in which they assume that language misleads us, therefore we must deconstruct and "go beyond" language, essentially creating incoherence instead of improving language *qualitatively* so that it works. Instead, *we* mislead language. Look at it this way: some sentences are true, and some are not. Some abstractions make sense, and others do not. How do we tell? How well does each stack up to reality, and by that we mean the process through which reality is created and not its persistent objects, should be our yardstick. An abstraction of some fanciful world where a benevolent unicorn in the sky will sort good from bad, right from wrong, and lead us to a place called Heaven is an abstraction that has little to do with the world in which we live. It is a solipsistic abstraction: it applies to the desires of the individual human, and does not take into account the world in which all humans live. (Nihilists are brave enough to recognize the obvious: individual humans have different strengths and intelligences, and thus, not everyone can perceive or understand such an abstraction, and those who cannot will invent abstractions of a solipsistic nature to compensate – see "cognitive dissonance" above.).

> *Narrowly speaking, the correspondence theory of truth is the view that truth is correspondence to, or with, a fact—a view that was advocated by Russell and Moore early in the 20th century. But the label is usually applied much more broadly to any view explicitly embracing the idea that truth consists in a relation to reality, i.e., that truth is a relational property involving a characteristic relation (to be specified) to some portion of reality (to be specified).*[9]

If you take a highly abstract view at the real-world problems of creating a conscious creature, you will see rapidly that the major threat to such a being would be the possibilities of its own mind. Our

---

[9] Marian David, "The Correspondence Theory of Truth," *Stanford Encyclopedia of Philosophy*, retrieved from http://plato.stanford.edu/entries/truth-correspondence/.

strengths are our weakness. Because such a creature can imagine, and can predict, and can create in its mind a partial replica of the world to use in guessing what the potential outcome of any action might be – "sun and rain always come in spring, and things don't grow in winter, so I'll plant in spring, assuming that this pattern is consistent" – it is also susceptible to conceiving an inaccurate notion of how the world works, and/or becoming emotionally unstable and thus creating a solipsistic version of reality in the mind and claiming it as the one true reality. "When I bless the gods, winter ends and the spring comes" is such an example; a more insidious one is "If I do not harm others, no harm will come to me" (tell that to a village being attacked by a band of raiding looters or pillaging Vandals).

Still more developed is the root of cognitive dissonance: I will think on how things should be and content myself with that, since I cannot or do not believe I can effect change in reality. Each of these errors is formed from the fundamental mistake of assuming that what exists in the individual human mind is higher than reality as a whole, or can be used to compensate for tendencies in the whole. We die; it sucks; let's invent "heaven" and perpetual life. Would not it be more ethical, more honest and above all else, more realistic, to simply admit we have no idea what follows death – if anything? (Add to this the complexity of a world we know through the progression of time, yet which might encompass additional or fewer dimensions in some other view, and you have a formula for endless unprovable conjecture taken as fact because well, we'd all like to believe we don't die; to this I rejoin that if we're all immortal, this means that the morons who afflict us daily are as well, which might make us reconsider the wisdom of "life eternal.")

Humans, being highly abstract creatures, are prone to creating abstractions which make sense only in their minds. These are "dead end" or "ultra-discrete" abstractions, in that their only error is a failure of realization that the individual human is part of a larger world, which goes on with or without them. If a tree falls in a forest and no one is around to witness it, does it make a sound? Of course, but the forest won't call it a "sound," and no one will note it or talk about it. We can play definition games all day, and claim that either a sound only exists in the human mind, or that the idea of "sound" is innate and external to us, but this is a case of redefining the word, not the phenomenon it describes. We might as well call a leaping predatory animal a butterfly, and then be shocked and surprised (awed?) when groups of people fail to respond to our urgent warning. Similarly, we can call death "life eternal" if it makes us feel better, but that causes zero change to the phenomenon itself, which remains unknown to us.

Thinking creatures have a great strength, which is their imaginative and analytical facility, but it is their greatest weakness: they can create "artificial" thoughts which do not relate to the world around them, and thus mislead themselves based on what they'd like to believe, not what they can know from an inspection of their world. There's much talk about the scientific method – experiment based on conjecture, observe, conjecture, repeat – but isn't it the same process we use in less formal incarnation to discover our world, from our time as babies nibbling on different objects to test their solidity, to our last moments on earth? In this sense, debugging a computer program or exploring a new continent or taking LSD is the same task as a scientific experiment. We observe the world, make theories about how it works, and then test those theories. Of course, the ones about death cannot be tested, and this opens a giant loophole for us to make a foundational theory about God or "life eternal," and in order to support it, to invent many other illusions so that it seems like a realistic, complete system of thought.

This human problem – distinguishing the internal world from the external – is not unique to humans, but as they are the only creatures with "higher" logical functions on earth, they are our only example. It is magnified as a problem when the question of civilization arises, because for the first time, groups must be instructed in organizing principles they cannot directly experience, e.g. "you grow grain, he'll make bread, and that other guy will distribute it to the people at large." Where individuals err in assuming their internal worlds are more real than external reality, civilizations err by making popular assumptions into law because people act according to them; whole civilizations have perished by upholding the rules that, in theory, will lead them to external life, but by denying reality allow crops to wither, invaders to intrude, decay of internal discipline to make people ineffective.

Mother: Why did you throw crabapples at cars?

Son: Johnny did it first.

Mother: If Johnny jumped off a bridge, would you do so too?

Son: What if my entire class did, and ended up "successful" like the people you always tell me to be like?

Not everyone must be deluded, but when enough are, the future of the civilization becomes a death-march. If you want a working definition of nihilism from a political-philosophical perspective, it is an affirmation of the structure and process of reality, in dramatic contrast to the appearances of objects and the seemingly-real perceptions that turn out to be phantasma of our internal minds, and have nothing to do with external reality. Nihilism is facing facts: whether or not we get eternal life, we have to keep the crops going and invaders outside and internal discipline high, or we will collapse as a functional entity. "Structure" in this context would be understand of our world as it operates, including that people need grain to eat and need to act on realistic principles, or invaders, disease, and internal listlessness will condemn us all.

Currently, our society is a linear construction of opposites that do not exist in nature – they are purely perceptual within human minds: good/evil, profit/loss, popular/unpopular. The best product is not always a necessary product (iPod), nor the best product (SUVs), nor even a good idea (cigarettes), but, well, it's popular and all that money goes back to its creator, so it is Good according to our lexicon. Similarly, we pick our leaders according to those favored by most people, and therefore, our leaders become those who make the biggest promises and find a way to duck the follow-through; since most people relying on such delusions are not rocket scientists, they quickly forget and go about their lives merrily assuming that because promises were made and the election was won, they'll come true and everything will be A+ from now on. Some might argue that in nature there is profit and loss, but a quick study reveals that be false: in nature there is success or failure that creates prevalence of effective genes in a statistical sense, and it has nothing to do with the popularity of those traits among the animals themselves. Similarly, some will argue that there's good (heterosexual intercourse) and evil (anal intercourse) in nature, but when one sees the function of anal intercourse in nature (among apes, appeasing intruders) it is clear that no such judgment "exists," except in our minds. In our minds... well, that's not a logical test, according to any methods scientific or otherwise. It's wishful thinking, in the common parlance.

What is most disturbing about this view, which invariably becomes popular in the later stages of civilization, is that it imposes a singular standard and form-factor upon each person and his or her desires, ambitions, needs – as well as what that person requires to stay alive and live well, a quantity often quite separate from what they think they desire (people, like lab rats, will often pick pleasurable sensations over long-term benefits, thus drink instead of investing their cash in future returns, u.s.w). In such a mode of thought, we are all form-stamped by a bureaucratic, mechanical or social machine, according to what is popular, and therein we see the origin of this thought process: it selects what most people want to believe, over what is real.

Through this mechanism, civilizations move into a senility formed of acting according to internal assumptions, and thus eventually come into conflict with cold hard reality, whether it's invading Vandals, crop failure, or internal lack of cohesion. While that end in itself may be far off, the intermediate problem is that living in such societies is, at the lowest and highest levels of our perception, disturbing. Not only is there illusion taken as reality, but it is an illusion created out of what ideas are popular and therefore (because most people are not wise) contra-wisdom and contra-realistic, which is terrifying on both existential and pragmatic levels. In later civilization, we all serve the whims of popularity and the illusions of the crowd, awaiting that future day when society collapsed into Brazil-styled *Blade Runner* anarchy-kleptocracy and we are forced to acknowledge our reliance on illusion.

What Nihilism Might Be

Solvents separate matter into its component parts. Nihilism could be viewed as a mental solvent which divides illusion from a realistic perception of individual and world as a continuous, joined, inter-reliant process. When one sees the world only in terms of appearance, and has no knowledge of structure, illusions and good idea look similar: death and "life eternal" are simply opposite extremes, not logical results of radically different processes.

To someone dwelling in illusion, a fern is a green thing that appears in forests and sometimes, lawn gardens; to someone concerned with design and structure, a fern is a plant of a certain shape, genetic background, and place in an ecosystem whereby it appears when the right conditions – sunlight, soil, water, surrounding plants and animals – exist, and serves a certain role in its processing of sunlight to water and oxygen, strengthening the ground with root mass, and providing homes and food to other plants and animals. While to someone dwelling in illusion human societies may be measured in terms of how little they harm the retarded and infirm and insane, to someone grounded in reality, the only measure of a society is its long-term survival – whether they murder the retarded, or keep them in gilded cages, is completely irrelevant to that final determination (although resources expended on the non-productive is part of what determines success or failure). We can live in our own mental worlds, perhaps, but the world outside of us keeps going, and our interaction with it is the only determination of success or failure; the rest is entirely cognitive dissonance.

(A great and practical example for young people especially is the difference between music quality and hype/presentation. Many artists will be presented to you as "new," "unique" or even "brutal," but this has no bearing on the underlying quality of the music. Similarly, neither does production; if the music is well-composed, using harmony and melody and rhythm and structure well, it should be excellent music if played on a single acoustic guitar, a Casio keyboard, or as presented by the band on their label-financed heavy-production debut.

Stuff that "sounds good" is often insubstantial, but has excellent production and an enigmatic image, but over time it fails to reward in the way that art does, by creating a poetry of life that enlightens and compels. It may not even hold up to musical scrutiny, when it is pointed out that behind the flutes and sirens and wailing guitars and screaming divas, the song is essentially a variation on a well-known and tedious ballad form or blues form. Hype and production are excellent ways to get people to buy a zero-value product, that is, a repetition of past successes, while getting them to convince themselves that they have found something new and enlightening.

If you are a nihilist, you look past whether it "sounds good" or feels right or you like the image or it makes you feel like you're part of some kind of revolution in behavior, and analyze the music: if it does not stand out from the usual patterns enough to be expressing something not new or unique but particular to its ideas, and demonstrative of those ideas, it's hype and not reality. It's "art" and not art. We can play word games here, too, but if you value your time and are not brick-stupid, you'll see why it's important to find the real art.)

Another way to view nihilism is transcendence of what we call, in the modern West, the "ego." Egomania occurs through cognitive dissonance when, reality not being to our liking, we invent our own; at this point, we can either invent it and recognize it as unreal but symbolically evocative, something we call fantasy, or we can invent it and claim it as either a higher reality than the real world, or a reality that supplants existence. Egomania (our vernacular for egotistical *solipsism*) is the assertion that our internal worlds are more real than the external world, which is paradoxical as the latter includes the former (we are necessarily accurately represented in the external world, but there is no assurance that it is accurately represented in our internal world).

When we think egomaniacally, as most people in the West do, we see the world as limited to our own perceptions and desires, and ignore the *continuity* between self and external world; we also think according to the form of ourselves, meaning that we see all decisions, ethical and otherwise, as limited to individuals. This cuts us off from a holistic morality by which we might for example see our environment as an extension of ourselves, both as a parent and a process upon which we are dependent; it cuts us off from considering unpopular decisions that nonetheless are right, when we consider the direction of our civilization. Our modern conception of morality is one that regulates the rights, survival and treatment of individuals, but it has no capacity for a holistic morality which sees individuals, environment and civilization as interdependent entities and thus makes decisions at the level of what is best for that convergent nexus.

This brings us to the crux of a philosophical dilemma in the West. The separation of mind and body creates a duality in which we see thoughts and external reality as discrete, isolated entities. One is either an idealist or a realist in this view, and never the twain shall meet. From a nihilist perspective, idealism explains realism, in that reality is not simply physical appearance but a structure and process; a "design," even if we decide there is no Designer (and for our daily lives: does it matter?). This conversion is accomplished by taking idealism, or "the philosophical doctrine that reality somehow mind-correlative or mind-coordinated-that the real objects constituting the 'external world' are not independent of cognizing minds, but exist only as in some correlative to mental operations" (*Cambridge Encyclopedia of Philosophy*, Second Edition), to its extreme, which is to assume that the external world and thoughts operate by a single mechanism; in that context, the world operates as an idea, and what is important in the world is not physicality or appearance but idea – design, concept, structure and process. Matching that supposition is an extension of realism, or a belief in the preeminence of external reality, which hyperextends to a study of how reality operates, and from that, a focus on its abstract properties. To analyze reality is to see that it operates like thought; to analyze thought is to see that the world operates much as thoughts do, and therefore, that putting thoughts into flesh is the supreme form of thinking.

Nihilism is a joining of these two extremes through a focus on the practical study of reality and a rejection of preconceptions brought on by anthropocentric viewing of the world, which is necessarily confined to the physicality of individuals and objects as they appear to humans. It is not an attempt to create an obligation, or an ideal, in and of itself, but a reduction of things to their simplest, most real elements so that higher ideals can be created, much as the creation of new civilizations produces a collective focus on the forging of something better than previous civilizations.

F. W. Nietzsche wrote of the necessity of "going under" the higher concepts and moral binaries of modernity, and one interpretation of this is that one cannot create "higher" ideals when our concept of higher/lower is linear and predefined; one must remove all value and undergo a "reevaluation of all values," focusing only on those which survive the test of a his "philosophical hammer," much like knocking on a wall to find hollow areas. Nihilism is a going under in the form of removal of all value, and construction of values based on reality instead of potentially internalized abstraction. In a nihilist worldview, nothingness is as important as somethingness, as only nothingness can like a midnight predator carry away the somethingness that has outlived its usefulness, is illusory, irrelevant or fanatical. Nihilism is a mental discipline which clarifies outlook by disciplining the mind to understand the structure of reality, and exclude anything which regardless of appearance is not true to that understanding.

In this, it is possible that nihilists witness civilization as it actually is: an eternal process of birth, growth, and then an aging brought about by self-obsession, leading rapidly to a distancing from reality, thus irrelevance and death. To remove all preconceptions of value is to have to re-invent value that is relevant to things as they are both right now and eternally, in that throughout history the basic rules of civilization have never changed; either there is a system of organization that makes sense, or there is illusion and ruin. Civilizations start out young and healthy, unified by whatever ideals made their members come together in the first place with the intent of building something new; when succeeding generations take this for granted, they drift into illusory ideals, at which point no "higher ideals" can overcome the illusion, because one cannot get "higher" than the notion of individual self-interest enforced by group fear. One must instead go lower, to the state before civilization reformed, to re-design its ideals.

What Nihilism Does For You

If you live in a time when illusion is seen as reality, and reality is an unknown continent, nihilism can on a personal level save you time by removing illusion and leaving only what is honestly relevant to your life and existential happiness. A simple version of this is undergone by many in corporate America who, finding it relatively easy to succeed, then because they have filled that need, find themselves with a new need to spend less time in the office and more on those things that are eternally human to desire: family, friends, local community and increase of wisdom and balance in the self. The illusion is that money is more important than anything else; the actuality is that if you have enough, and you have the ability to do the things in life which are more important in the long term (imagine seeing your life from your deathbed) than money, it is not only sufficient but superior to a hollow existence where life is secondary to jobs and payment.

Further, nihilism drives away fears through illusion. If one believes public rhetoric, it will seem necessary to cower under the bed as if hiding from a host of fears: public ridicule, global warming, racism, nuclear war, fascism, drug users, hackers, Satanists. These vast apocalyptic fears operate for the most part as distraction, keeping our minds off the emptiness of modern life and the inevitability of our society facing consequences of its reckless action. What is important is not the collection of fears, but real threats and most importantly, *how to fix them*. Much like people who hide behind cynicism, most moderns fixate on "raising awareness" of problems, and rarely do anything to address them practically. This creates a culture of fear where in the name of amorphous fears, or balkanized infighting between political and ethnic groups, we miss the point: we can fix our civilization, but we'll have to do it at a more basic level than politics, economics and social popularity afford.

Nihilism helps many lead better lives. When they cut out the meaningless garbage that infiltrates from television and neurotic people, they can see their actual needs are simple and easily satisfied. From this, they can see how the larger unaddressed problems – the tedium of modern society, the pollution of nurturing environment, the degeneration of culture and heritage, our loss of wisdom as a civilization – can be important not only for the fragile individual but for future generations; nihilism leads people to holistic moral thinking.

(If you want it in boring, everyday terms, nihilism is a bullshit eliminator. If someone tells you something, look at it with eyes abstracted from everyday life and what people think and what is profitable; look toward what is real, and then find what ideals maintain that status. You like being alive, right? – If not, consider suicide. If you like living, you believe in life, and you'll do what furthers life in the same way Darwinism furthers life, which is by improving it *qualitatively*. Garbage is not life. Illusion in religious form, political form and social form is one part of this; another is overhyped garage bands, or oversold commercial rock, or trendy books that tell you nothing of importance. It is better to sit in silence and contemplate the universe than to fill your head with garbage. Do you need to watch the mundane movies and pointless TV shows, and entertaining commercial messages? Do you need a sports car? Will owning one more DVD, video game, or CD of not-that-great-after-all rock music help you? When you pull aside the curtains, the truth is there, naked like the contents of your lunch on the end of a fork – apologies to William S. Burroughs.)

The Doctrine of Parallelism

When you accept that there is a structure behind reality that acts in the method of thoughts, and when you observe natural surroundings and see how consistent this is, you are then ready to think in parallel. Put simply, parallel thinking is the ultimate refutation of the linearity and binary morality of modern society. If we are to construct right and wrong, they are specific to the situation at hand. Some will condemn this as "situational morality," but holistic morality is a form of thought that is best applied in specifics; after all, a different rule applies to the wolf than the dove, and different standards apply to the behavior of plumbers, computer programmers, and political leaders. Some will see this as relativism, but under analysis, it becomes clear that relativism is one standard of morality applied with forgiveness for disadvantages to certain situations or experiences of individuals; the morality of thinking in parallel says that there is no one standard except reality itself, and that many different types of things acting in parallel create this.

One area where this can be seen is homosexuality. For most heterosexuals, having homosexual behavior occur in neighborhoods or other areas where children are present is not positive; they would rather raise their children according to heterosexual role models and behavioral examples. However, homosexuality occurs, and the best data available suggests that in most cases it is inborn; obviously, some are induced into homosexuality much as many heterosexuals are brought into forms of deviant sexual behavior, through sexual abuse or conditioning in youth (hence the desire for normal, heterosexual role models; most heterosexuals also do not want promiscuity, anal sex, coprophagia, BDSM, etc. occurring around their children even if solely in a heterosexual context). So what to do with homosexuals, for whom being raised in a heterosexual society can be oppressive, and heterosexuals, for whom having homosexual behavior around can be equally oppressive and deleterious? We think in parallel: some communities will choose to be heterosexual, and others homosexual, and when they meet on neutral ground, it is likely that neither will assert its morality as a dominant, inviolate rigid code. Morality after all is not something we can prove exists, but something we derive from natural structure in order to establish a civilization of the type we desire. Some civilizations will endorse promiscuity and coprophagia, but in doing so, they miss out on some opportunities granted to civilizations with a more disciplined moral code. The converse is also true. There is no one law for the ox and the raven; to do so is to commit tyranny.

Another area where this can be applied is that of recreational chemicals, a term which is our modern shorthand for perception-altering drugs. Some communities will deny alcohol and cigarettes; some will embrace LSD and marijuana and mushrooms and perhaps even go further. It is likely that the two will never find common ground except where the question of drug use does not arise. When we see experiments in drug legalization, like British Columbia or Amsterdam or Christiania in Denmark, we see an artificial gold rush toward hedonism caused by the fact that, worldwide, there are few relatively safe places to go take drugs. Were it such that in every continent there were some area where the rules on such things were relaxed, it is likely that those who seek drugs could go there and pursue them at a fraction the cost of illicit use. This would not only curb crime, but keep drug use out of normal (heterosexual and homosexual) neighborhoods where such things are not desired as unintentional role models for children, and the cost of drug use – including, let's be honest, increased laziness and pizza consumption – is considered funds misspent that could otherwise be directed toward bettering other aspects of the community. There is no one rule. We cannot "prove" that drugs are good, or bad, but we can see how in some places they would be helpful and in others, destructive. Do the Hindu communities where marijuana is a sacrament have greater crime and pizza consumption?

The area most controversial where this could be applied is the taking of human life, and the enslavement of others. Some communities, such as a community formed by those who live according to the doctrines of black metal music, would not have any prohibition on honor killings, death in combat, or even brutal removal of ingrates. In their worldview, honest combat produces a survivor ("winner") and one judged less able, the dead ("loser"). Most societies find this concept reprehensible, and would never permit it, so it makes sense to have communities where combat to the death, duels and other honor violence, are seen as a way of selecting the more capable citizens. Further, in many communities, it would be seen fit to work by the old Texas standard, "Judge, he needed killing," whereby bullies, cattle thieves, morons and other undesirables could be removed with tacit consent of community. While many communities would prefer intricate and expensive legal systems, in some areas, if a person was known as a child molester or cheat or thief, it would be cheaper and easier to look the other way while a local hotblood challenged that person to a fight and attempted to murder him. Cormac McCarthy describes such places in his book *Blood Meridian*, as they are also described in Burroughs' *Naked Lunch*: lands where there is no law except strength, and as a result, where all citizens are ready for combat and by process of evolution, over generations become more apt at it. Are all peoples warrior peoples? Clearly not. Would all communities tolerate this? No. But much as we need plumbers and computer scientists, we need warriors, and if some greater threat manifests itself, it is probable that the people of these warlike communities would be esteemed as valuable combatants.

"It's too nice in here," he moans. "It's not hell at all. In this country prisoners get a bed, toilet and shower. It's completely ridiculous. I asked the police to throw me in a real dungeon and also encouraged them to use real violence!"[10]

Another controversial area where localization – the best thought from the leftist side of things has emphasized this theory under that term – becomes preeminent is that of race. Even mentioning race, or that there are physical differences between races, is currently taboo in the West and will get you fired, removed from office, drummed out of volunteer capacities, blacklisted in industry and crucified in the media. History tells us that human races evolved under different climates and different pressures, and therefore have different abilities. We cannot "prove," objectively, that any one collection of abilities is superior to another. Communities are united by common belief, and some communities will opt for this to be a unification of culture, language and heritage.

Some communities will opt to be cosmopolitan, mixed-race communities like New York City. Others will choose to be ethnocentric and to defend their ethnic-cultural heritage as necessary to their future; this preserves their uniqueness, and is the only realistic basis for true diversity. Without this bond, you have Disneyland-style fake communities which give nods to heritage but are basically products of modern time. Let there always be Finns, Zulus, Germans, Basques, Cherokee, Aztec, Norwegian, and even Irish – this is diversity; this is multiculture; this is all of the good things that exposure to different cultures can provide. This is the only mature attitude toward race, instead of trying to produce, as

---

[10] Article on Black Metal, *NME*, September 5, 1998.

the Americans have, one global standard of liberal mixed-ethnic democracy that essentially destroys culture and replaces it with malls and television. The race taboo is propelled by those without a clear cultural heritage who want to revenge themselves upon those who do, much as in high school those with low self-esteem tried to antagonize both nerds and class leaders.

Still another area where localization saves us from our current civilization's misery is that of intelligence. A nihilist has no use for social pretense that says we are all equal; some are fit to be leaders by virtue of their natural intelligence, and no amount of education or government programs can make someone else be able for that position. Some prefer to correlate this with race, but a nihilist has no use for this, either: even within what George Santayana calls the "favored races" there are many completely stupid people, especially those with the worst kind of stupidity, which is a combination of cowardice and bad leadership skills. Few people mind a dumb person who is humble and follows orders well, but dumb people who agitate for change that benefits dumb people quickly destroy any civilization. Some localities may opt to admit anyone without regard to intelligence or character, but others will wish to only accept those of a commensurate mental level to the best of their populations, and will therefore exclude morons, blockheads, fools and ingrates. This conflicts with the idea of universal rights, and shows us why the concept is illusory: if morons have the "universal right" to move anywhere, what about people who want the right and freedom to live apart from morons? Modern society tells us that the way to do this is to earn enough money to live in an exclusive neighborhood, but even then, one must interact with morons daily for goods and services, in addition to dealing with those morons who inherited money or earned it through stupid means. Social Darwinism, or the idea that those who are the best and smartest earn the most money, has two holes: first, not all intelligent people opt to chase the money wagon and second, most morons are greedy, and many of them succeed through luck or persistence. A nihilist naturally laughs at the idea of correlating money to intelligence, and would prefer to live in a community where morons are excluded.

There are numerous issues that divide communities which can be resolved through this model. Anti-abortion devotees might need their own community, as there's no way to make a law that both pro- and anti-abortion people will find fair. The constant combat between different groups, whether divided by sex or race or preference of values, exhausts our current civilization because so much of its time and energy is spent on internal conflict. The major reason that we choose this insane method is that it enables us to believe we are united by the form factor of being human, and therefore, that there is no need for belief beyond that. It enables us to ignore nature. However, as Carl Jung observed, by nature humans are of several different personality combinations, and those serve a role in the larger social construct (for example, a Meyers-Briggs "INTJ" personality will be a philosopher). There is no single archetype of human, but different types which match different roles in nature, much as there are different ecosystems for which there are specific combinations of host species. Our environment creates a pattern, and we evolve in a form that matches its unique contours; in the same way, humans have adapted to a self-created environment, civilization.

Paul Woodruff, in his book *Reverence*, pointed out that in modern times we have lost the ability to revere nature and our world. Part of our loss of reverence is this insistence on one-size-fits-all rules for civilization; we are so unstable as individuals that we want a solid, clear-cut, and absolute rule, but nature does not fit this pattern and so we override. One step to regaining reverence is to stop judging objects, actions and people by a linear binary (yes/no) rule and to start thinking in parallel. In some places, there should always be debauchery, and in others, there should always be quiet conservative living. Communities will shed people from newer generations who do not find that type of locality valuable, and those will in turn have to find their own living elsewhere, and define their own path. In this, we escape the illusion that a perfect social construct can be engineered for us all, and that by forcing us through it, something Utopian will emerge. Such illusions convince us to be passive, and to think solely in terms of governmental solutions applied by rote force, which limits our perspective on the manifold options available in almost every situation.

Nihilism in Politics

MORROW: How do you define politics?

ACHEBE: Anything to do with the organization of people in society. That is the definition. Whenever you have a handful of people trying to live harmoniously, you need some organization, some political arrangement that tells you what you can do and shouldn't do, tells you what enhances harmony and what brings about disruption.[11]

We define politics as the process of convincing large numbers of people to do something. No belief system can escape politics, unless it deals with the individual outside of civilization, at which point writing it down is hypocrisy.

For this reason, although nihilism is a mental discipline and not a political platform, there are some areas in which nihilism will influence modern politics. The first and most obvious is that, unlike most who are either bought off or blind to the inadequacies of the status quo, nihilists will recognize that it is a death-march: an illogical path that will ultimately lead to failure, but because saying so is taboo and unprofitable, we all go along with it even though we march to our doom. Look into the future. Our earth will be more, and not less, polluted, because no matter what we do there will be more people than ever using technology and producing waste. A consequence of our population growth will be a lack of natural spaces to enjoy, because every single continent on earth will be divided up into salable land and covered in fences and concrete to the degree that unbroken wilderness will not exist. Nations will no longer convey a cultural identity or heritage, so we will all be citizens of the world and have what is offered in default of culture, namely Wal-Mart, Coca-Cola and re-runs of *Friends*. Bred for jobs and obedience, we will lose the best of our people because they are no longer relevant in a world that prizes money and docility over

---

[11] Bradley Morrow, "Chinua Achebe, An Interview," *Conjunctions*, Issue 17, Fall 1991, retrieved from http://www.conjunctions.com/archives/c17-ca.htm.

leadership, wisdom, and independent thinking. Endless commercial messages will adorn our cities and, because there is no culture, most will spend time watching television or engaging in equally debasing virtual entertainment. Since leadership will be useless, most people will have such flexible spines that they will be utter whores, and conversation will be worthless and friendship a meaningless term. Won't be much to live for, so instead, we'll survive, and hope "someday" it will get better.

The cause of all of this disaster will have been a fundamental inability to deal with reality. Our society, wealthy and powered by cheap fossil fuels, grew at an exponential rate with an inverse relationship to the quality of intelligence, leadership ability and holistic moral outlook of its population. We've bred a horde of fools and bred out the quality intelligences, replacing them with "geniuses" like Jay Gould and Bill Clinton. Since consumption is the only logic we understand, we have consumed much of our planet, and focus on symbolic factors like global warming in order to avoid looking at the enormity of the problem. Our governments get better with their computers, cameras and social security numbers in order to ensure that dissidents are more quickly quashed, and they've found better methods than locking them up; instead, they proclaim them as taboo-breakers, and let the rest of the citizens boycott them as dangerous to future business. All of this comes too much attention paid to the popularity of ideas, and a denial that what is popular rarely corresponds to an intelligent response to reality. We've had leftist governments, and rightist governments, and neither have dealt with this underlying problem.

Nihilism is not a bullet-pointed list, but there are some clearly definable ideas that nihilists will embrace while others do not. Extreme ecology makes sense if you wish to preserve your planet's life, which directly contributes to maintenance of its climate and land as well as to your peace of mind knowing that you are not a destroyer of beautiful things. Localization makes sense if you wish to spare us all from having to find one rule for diametrically opposed ideologues. Preservation of national identity, and granting local communities the right to exclude or murder morons and perverts and other unwanted detritus of the human gene pool, also makes sense.

Giving the individual greater existential autonomy than a society of products to buy and jobs at which to serve is more realistic than assuming we can all be crammed into the same mold and out will come perfect, uniform citizens. Realizing that using commerce as a motivator does not address the subtle and long-term issues of our society liberates us from having to constantly manipulate each other through money. Finally, recognition that popularity of an idea has no bearing on its fitness for our collective survival frees us from the tyranny of the crowd, and lets us have leaders again, who instead of finding out what is popular and espousing it, find out what is practical and pursue it. Nihilism ends the society of illusions by shattering the power of the Crowd. Societies age and die when popularity becomes more important than pragmatism, and nihilism offers us a way to "go under" this process by removing value and discovering it anew. In this sense, nihilism is immediately political, although it is unlikely that an organized nihilist political presence will be seen.

How to Apply Nihilism

The underlying control level which supports politics is public attitude. If the public is "educated" to expect a concept as positive, and another as negative, it is a trivial matter to associate political issues with one of the two and thus to manipulate them. This creates a *metapolitical* battleground where ideas and their valuation determine the future means of gaining intellectual currency for ideas; this translates into political power like a form of celebrity for the idea. While nihilism applies to political viewpoints, as shown above, it is primarily efficacious as a change in attitudes and values to those within society, and can be used from that level to later alter political fortunes.

More importantly for those who see to what degree our civilization has become stagnant, nihilism is a guiding force for analyzing the task of creating a future civilization, whether a breakaway colony or a restarting of life in the ruins. Such an outlook is not favorable to a need for instant gratification; unlike conventional politics, which prescribes highly polarized immediate actions which do not change the underlying structure, nihilist thinking proposes enduring changes made slowly through individual rejection of garbage values.

To apply nihilism, start by viewing the world as a nihilist: reject that which has no value in the context of the whole, or the structure of reality, and replace it with things of solid demonstrable value, as found in biology, physics and philosophy. Do what is necessary to have a quality life, but go no further down the path of luxury and materialism, because it is meaningless. Use nihilist principles wherever you are given a choice; if even a tenth of our population refused to buy junk food, that form of mediocre nutrition would not endure. Contrast nihilist principles to the "normal" illusory view that most of the population prefers, using short and friendly but insightful statements to point out where null value can be replaced by something of meaning. When people bring up "problems," give a few words that show where nihilism reduces the illusion to garbage, and suggest a better course of action. Abstain from all of the idiotic things that people do, and apply yourself toward constructive tasks. Those who cannot both reject garbage and create better are unworthy of any accolades; they are passive and deserve whatever slavery this world will throw at them.

What is Nihilism?

Having discussed the modes of thought through which an individual passes in being a nihilist, it is now appropriate to use the dreaded "to be" construction to describe *nihilism*: nihilism is an affirmation of reality so that ideals based on the structure of reality can be applied to thought and action. Like Zen Buddhism, it is a form of mental clearing and sharpening of focus more than a set of beliefs in and of itself; this is why nihilism is a belief in nothing, being both a belief in nothing (no inherent belief outside of reality) and a belief in nothingness (applying nothingness to useless thoughts, in an eternal cycle that like our own thinking, balances a consumptive emptiness against a progressive growth and proliferation of idea). It is a freedom, in a way that "freedom" cannot be applied in a modern society, from the views that others (specifically, the Crowd) apply out of fear, and a desire to use this freedom to create a new and more honest human who can view life as it is and still produce from it heroic ideals. When Nietzsche spoke of the "super-human," this was his concept: that those who could accept the literality of life and fate and yet still do what is required to create a braver, more intelligent, more visionary human, would rise above the rabble and become a new standard of humanity. While our current definition of "humanity" applies more to pity and blind compassion for individuals, the super-human would think on the level of the structure of reality as a whole, both thinking in parallel and holistically, doing what is right not to preserve individual life but to nurture overall design.

Behold human beings living in an underground den, which has a mouth open towards the light and reaching all along the den; here they have been from their childhood, and have their legs and necks chained so that they cannot move, and can only see before them, being prevented by the chains from turning round their heads. Above and behind them a fire is blazing at a distance, and between the fire and the prisoners there is a raised way; and you will see, if you look, a low wall built along the way, like the screen which marionette players have in front of them, over which they show the puppets.

I see.

And do you see, I said, men passing along the wall carrying all sorts of vessels, and statues and figures of animals made of wood and stone and various materials, which appear over the wall? Some of them are talking, others silent.

You have shown me a strange image, and they are strange prisoners.

Like ourselves, I replied; and they see only their own shadows, or the shadows of one another, which the fire throws on the opposite wall of the cave?

True, he said; how could they see anything but the shadows if they were never allowed to move their heads?[12]

The best thinkers in all doctrines have reached this state of mind. While they may not call it nihilism, and many rail against the form of "nihilism" that is essentially fatalism, or a decision to declare all thoughts and actions impossible and thus to relapse into mental entropy, all have accomplished this clarity of mind and transcendent state of seeing structure and not appearance. Plato, in his metaphor of the cave, describes humanity as imprisoned in a cave of its own perceptual dependence on visible form, and portrays philosophers-kings – his version of Nietzsche's "super-humans" – as those who leave the cave and, while blinded by the light of real day for the first time, find a way to ascertain the true nature of reality and then to return to the cave, to explain it to those who have seen theretofore only shadows. This state of mind is heroic in that one sees what is important to an overall process, and is willing to assert that higher degree of organization whatever the cost, thus combining a realism (perception of physical world "as is") with an idealism (measuring the world in contrasts between degrees of organization in thought) into a heroic vision, in which life itself is a means to an end, and that end is a greater organization or order to existence as a whole. Nihilism is a gateway to this worldview.

The belief, whether known in language to its bearer or not, that the individual should predominate over all other concerns is Crowdism. We name it according to the crowd because crowds are the fastest to defend individual autonomy; if any of its members are singled out, and doubt thrown upon their activities or intentions, the crowd is fragmented and loses its power. What makes crowds strong is an inability of any to criticize their members, or to suggest any kind of goal that unites people, because what makes for the best crowds is a lack of goal. Without a higher vision or ideal, crowds rapidly degenerate into raiding parties, although of a passive nature. They argue for greater "freedom." They want more wealth. Anything they see they feel should be divided up among the crowd.

---

[12] Plato, *The Republic*, trans. Benjamin Jowett, Chapter VIII.

Crowdism strikes anyone who values individual comfort and wealth more than doing what is right. People of a higher mindset leave situations in a higher state of order than when they were found. This requires that people form an abstraction describing how organization works, and create in themselves the moral will to do right, and thus embark on a path that is not accessible to everyone: the smarter and more clear-sighted one is, the greater likelihood exists that one is realizing things that an audience of average people have not yet comprehended. For this reason, Crowdists hate people who leave situations in a higher state of order than when they were found.[13]

The Crowd serves death because through their great fear of it, its members create rules which do little more than restrict the best among us, who they fear because they cannot understand them. What defines a crowd is its lack of direction, and its need to be led, and if it is to be led, a preference for one among it who will throw out a popular idea and thus congeal its unformed will into some lowest common denominator which is actionable. Reality does not play by this game, because to adopt a constant lowest common denominator is to descend in both ideals and evolution, because that which applies evolutionary pressure is a striving for larger goals. The humans who were content without fire remained little more than apes; those who needed fire were driven into the northern climates, away from the easily nourishing jungle, and eventually thrust themselves forward toward other goals which supported the need for fire: organized civilization, language, learning, and the concept of ideals versus materialism, or a simple assurance of comfort. Evolution forced them to consider "reasons why" and therefore, to develop themselves in such a way that those who could understand reasons why could compel themselves to do what was otherwise inconvenient and uncomfortable. From this is the root of all heroism that produces the best of what society offers: philosophy, art, architecture and morality.

The Crowd creates a reality to serve its fears, and by imposing it, crushes realism, because to point out that the emperor wears no

---

[13] Brett Stevens, "Crowdism."

clothes is to offend and disturb the crowd. Why might a nihilist insist on accuracy in taboo topics such as eugenics, race and environmental needs to reduce population? – because the Crowd will go to its death before it will ever do such a thing. To notice reality is to point out that Crowd reality is a complete lie, an illusion, and a sick farce designed to supplant the flagging egos of those with low self-esteem and relatively low intelligence (attributes necessary to be a member of a crowd, and not an independent thinker or leader). Those who create civilizations are succeeded by those who could not do the same, and by virtue of this opulence, societies soon breed crowds that through their greater numbers demand to control reality. One either illustrates the lie of their artificial reality, and directs society in another direction, or drowns in the weight of lowest common denominator demands; all societies perish this way.

Before the invader at the gates can conquer, or the disease can enfilade the population, or internal strife can tear apart a nation, there must be a failure of organization and even more a failure of will toward something higher than that which is convenient and materially comfortable, commercially viable, popular, etc. Dying societies inevitably create a Satan or Osama bin Laden to which they assign blame for their failing, but the actual cause is within; this is why while a nihilist may recognize the truth about race or eugenics, it is impossible to logically blame minority groups, extremist religions or the retarded for the downfall of a society. Blame is not useful, but diagnosis is, and an accurate diagnosis suggests that ordinary capable people become misinformed and accept mediocre ideas, at the behest of the Crowd, and thus condemn themselves to doom. The Crowd will always exist, but in healthy societies, it is kept in check by the wisdom of others.

Much as there is a "super-man" possible in our future, in our past and present there are Undermen, who are those with no higher goals than philosophical materialism: a denial of all value outside the physical world and its comforts. Those who take this lazy attitude to the form of a political agenda are Crowdists, and they can be found in Left and Right alike, supported by those who are emboldened by pity, or the feeling of superiority one gets for helping someone of lesser ability or fortune.

Nihilism addresses such illusions and negates them, using nothingness as a weapon to clear the earth so that somethingness can again take root. A nihilist has no use for pity or the kind of low self-esteem that needs the response of others in order to feel good about itself. Like Zen monks, or European knights, a nihilist acts according to what is right by the order of the universe, and does so independently of consequences, including personal morality. To be thus independent from social conditioning, which is not as much a process of evil governments/corporations ("Satan") as by the neurotic concerns of peers ("the enemy within"), is to crush the worthless and destructive opinions of the crowd, so expect retribution wherever one of them has power. Yet to have this state of mind is not to blame them, or those who wield pity, as they are misinformed rather than malevolent, and with better leadership – achieved, in part by acting independently and thus putting the lie to their false "reality" – they will act in a better state of mind. It goes without saying that such people are incapable of becoming super-humans but, while thus obsolete for our optimal future, will be the parents and grandparents of those who, if bred according to rigorous evolutionary standards, will become superhuman.

To distill this to a simple equation: one can either accept negativity (death, defecation, loss, sorrow) in life, or one can use cognitive dissonance to create a pleasant-sounding reality which denies it while asserting only the positive comforts of life, but to do so is to miss out on the challenge of life. To accept good and bad together as a means toward the continuation of life, and as a necessary part of the evolution that shaped us from mice into apes into humans, is a fully mature attitude and one that only a small portion of the population can understand. *Most of you reading this will not understand nihilism and physically cannot*; breed well and hope your children are smarter.

Nihilism vs. Fatalism

Much has been written about nihilism, most because for any great good in life, one needs an opposite, and that is the belief in nothing: that nothing is worth striving for, that nothing can have any meaning, that the individual and the world together are nothing.

I refer to that mental outlook – specifically, the bit about nothing being worth striving for – as fatalism because, quite honestly, if one believes that little, not even in the pleasures of being alive, the basest of joys, then death is a gift and a deliverance. If your fate is so terrible, embrace it, and die well. Perhaps you can bestir yourself long enough to strap an explosive device onto your person and, running into some commercial orgy such as a mall during Christmas shopping, detonate yourself, clearing others of a subtler fatalism from amongst us.

Nihilism is the removal of all value to things except reality itself. Human perceptions are not inherent, but we pretend they are so; reality alone is real and usually conflicts with most people's perceptions. If it did not, everyone would be a genius or top-level talent. When people wail about Satan, or the war against terrorism, or the great quest for equality, you can look those straight in the eye and say, "These have no value except what we impose upon them." By the same token, when people tell you how important it is to see the latest movie, go to that exclusive party, or own a fancy car, you can similarly dismiss the concerns. Nihilism is a removal of all except the inherent.

It is a gateway philosophy, meaning that it is the initial realization on a course of learning. In contrast to the "devotional" or "exoteric" philosophies such as mass culture Christianity, where all who come and recite an oath are considered to have received wisdom, the philosophies of life that are not a charade embrace esoteric views. Esotericism – the contrary of the above – says that wisdom comes to those who seek it, and in varying degrees and by degree of ability and moral character towards the inclination to seek wisdom, in a Calvinistic twist; there is no magic threshold to cross after which one can write the holy sign on one's forehead and be considered knowledgeable. Infinite learning and infinite potential pitfalls await instead. When one embraces nihilism, one has undertaken the first step of this initiation, by removing all value externally imposed, including by other humans. Herein begins discovery.

Most philosophies of our time either enshrine some absolute, universal wisdom as the One True Path to righteousness and power, or de facto do the same with the individual, stating "reality is anything you want it to be." These aren't philosophies as much as extreme social sentiments addressing the question echoing through eternity, "What is real/true/meaningful?" Nihilism offers a way out of this paradox, by affirming life itself as the answer to the question of life: what is meaningful? renders to "life is meaningful," and leaves us to realize that life is an ongoing process that cannot be quantized into some devotional answer, or even a finite technological answer such as "money." To have a good life is to have beauty, truth, and meaning.

But how to define a good life? If we look for absolutes, such as the best comfortable living, or the most power, or the most money or popularity, we find externally-defined things that do not reflect much of satisfaction, except of material want. It makes more sense to look to the ancients and to say that a good life is fulfillment of destiny, or of taking one's place in the inherent order and structure of reality. Nihilism removes the sense of a good life as something that can be created outside of the individual, but also acknowledges the frailty of the individual: none of us will always see "truth" in the sense of what is accurate given the external world around us.

To say this is not to endorse a shallow "objectivism," such as that of Ayn Rand, for whom materialism became a philosophical object in the tradition in which she was raised, that of Russian Judaism, which despite its dualistic faith-character sees nothing of supernatural or ideal value above material comfort: power, wealth, stature in community. These philosophies of "objectivism" become a parody of themselves, as they have replaced meaning in life with the means to life, bypassing the question of life in actuality, although they grasp the utility of capital over wishful thinking economics. The objectivism of nihilism is closer to that of science or the ancient religious traditions of the Vedas: we are all enclosed in the same space, which operates according to consistent rules, and it acts predictably upon all of us, whether we perceive it or not.

Another way to say this is that when two people play catch, the ball is thrown and follows an objective course, regardless of whether the catcher has her hands in the right place to receive it. If the thrower misjudges her throw, the ball will land afar from the catcher, but the catcher can also compensate, having seen the ball move, and thus catch it. The motion through external reality is "objective," while the thoughts and perceptions of thrower and catcher are "subjective," and the two do not always come together; the game of catch is a fun way to calibrate one's internal sense of reality to external reality, which operates much as a machine does, predictably according to its structure and the mechanisms therein.

Marcus Aurelius gives us part of the puzzle:

> Surely it is an excellent plan, when you are seated before delicacies and choice foods, to impress upon your imagination that this is the dead body of a fish, that the dead body of a bird or pig; and again, that the Falernian wine is grape juice and that robe of purple a lamb's fleece dipped in shellfish's blood; and in matters of sex intercourse, that it is attrition of an entrail and a convulsive expulsion of mere mucus. Surely these are excellent imaginations, going to the heart of actual facts and penetrating them so as to see the kind of things they really are. You should adopt this practice all through your life, and where things make an impression which is very plausible, uncover their nakedness, see into their cheapness, strip off the profession on which they vaunt themselves.[14]

To dwell in the physicality of life is to be obsessed with the signs of meaning, and not meaning itself. In a game of catch, what is not important is the quality of the ball or the sensation of seeing it whiz by, but the ability to match hand with ball and thus connect the motion of thrower to receiver. A nihilist, initiated in the value of no-value, thus recognizes that while neither objective nor subjective is supreme, bringing them together is a value in the inherent, as it makes the individual stronger as interacting with "ultimate reality," or the physical and very real world that we all share and the implications of its pattern structure for the metaphysical. Similarly,

---

[14] Marcus Aurelius, *Meditations*, VI, 13

to get too far into symbolism is to create a "dual" world, in which symbol is more important than meaning to life itself; either dwelling solely in the physical, or solely in the symbolic, is an error of reason (these roughly correspond to mass culture interpretations of Judaism and Christianity, respectively).

However, this type of thinking is beyond all but a few, hence the hordes of people who criticize this site for being nihilistic and yet daring to believe in anything more than fatalism. The most educated of this type are the Russell-Wittgenstein devotees, who are victims of essentially the most advanced phishing scam in philosophical history; told that language is frail and thus error, they are asked to invest their belief fully in subjectivism, and through that to achieve objective proof of the truthfulness of non-truth. Zen philosophy offers a more benevolent take on this insight, one that is wise enough not to express itself in language, but to rely on raw experience – and sometimes, a Zen master's slap – to reinforce that reality, itself, indeed, is *real*.

Nihilism is a gateway to appreciating the inherent by denying falsely inherent universal "truths." Being thinking machines isolated in ourselves, we are contra-intuitively isolated from the reality of life, and our most common error is to be the catcher expecting the ball in the wrong location or the thrower, blinded by the sun, throwing to the wrong place. It is not a linearization or a moralization to state that the expectation of the ball is at the wrong place in both cases; literally, the humans involved have been deceived into believing their own perceptions higher than external reality, which is the force responsible for space, and time, and indeed all other natural tendencies which make the game of catch possible. This is the ground of the inherent.

Life itself is indefinable, except when we constrain the parameters of definition to be very narrow. Existence might be a better term, but eventually even existence is predicated upon natural law and "reality" coming to being in the first place, at a level lower even than physicality: that natural laws exist such that matter is even conceivable, or that regularity or logic even existing, predicates the being of matter. What Aurelius endorses above is an acceptance of the nature of existence, but a realization that meaning does not exist except in our minds: it is an abstraction based upon the inherent, which includes life itself.

Another way to phrase this is to say that we find life good when we perceive that life has meaning, which is a factor of life being lived well, or being "good," in the first place. It's a giant loop if one approaches it linearly, but from natural terms, it makes sense. Our environment grants us existence, and either adapt to it or drift off into our own little fantasy worlds, and where we are able to adapt to it, we derive pleasure from having matched our own desires with its tendencies – much like catching the ball thrown by another perceiving being and conveyed according to natural forces through space and time to our hands. This is the nature of the inherent, and there is nothing higher or lower than it.

To get to this stage, however, one must first undergo the cleansing rite of nihilism, by which all "meaning" as told to us by others or "seeming" to us by physicality, is removed. Sex is not what gives meaning to life; the relationship between the two is what does, as pleasure is transient and cannot by itself hold off pain (indeed, as any thinking pothead can tell you, even the absolute bliss of being gloriously stoned loses its luster over time, as the *agenda never changes*). To counterbalance that, however, the symbolism or love or purity or chastity is equally not what is real; it is a shared perception of the inherent, and not the inherent itself. Only the actual matters, and each of us can see it to varying degrees depending on our ability.

Additional definitions of the inherent can be found in transcending the "mind/body dualism" of life; most embrace either mind, and the abstractions we consider real such as "good" and "evil," or body, and the material comforts of life as highest value. However, it is more sensible to avoid a mechanistic approach to analysis of life, and recognize that the value of the inherent is value to whole and self-as-part-of-whole; we cannot separate ourselves from the whole, nor view it as something independent of us. It created us and equipped us with all that we know, and even in nihilism one recognizes a refutation of fatalism: we are its agents, and what we do changes the course of the future, in varying degrees according to our abilities.

Thus we come to the thorniest realization of nihilism: we are not all "equal," either in some cosmological sense or in ability. Some are smarter, some stronger, some of better character, and to realize this is to cast aside the great social illusion that blocks nihilism. The crowd of people who cannot perceive the inherent, or because of their own undifferentiated state in it deny it, would like us to think in terms of equality, such that we could partake in a devotional "truth" where repeating a few simple words would raise us – equally – to the level of holy knowledge. Nature is real, and in nature, many are born and a few survive; this is a failsafe method of producing better versions of the organism each generation, which means that for those who will live in the future, life will be better than in the past.

Nihilism opens the gate, and it is unwise to attempt to summarize it in a tidy essay that one can read on the Internet during lunch, doubtless before returning to a stimulating task such as sending faxes, fixing cars, making speeches or cleaning toilets. Philosophy for those concerned with accuracy is an esoteric task, and reveals itself slowly, through experience, and any attempt to shortcut that is devotional egalitarianism and thus illusion. But for those for whom the normal "meaning" of life is ashen and formless, an invitation to a gateway is issued in this essay; believe in nothing, so that you may find the *somethings* which have actual meaning.

December 15, 2004

Transcendence

Reverence is the capacity for awe in the face of the transcendent. - Paul Woodruff

When one is philosophically mature enough to look past good and bad and see them as component parts of reality which work in opposition to create a larger good, or "meta-good" as we might be tempted to call it, good and bad lose moral value in and of themselves. They become a means, where the end is the continuation of reality. Much as humans respond to nature in parallel structures, the destructive and the creative are balanced forces that maintain equilibrium of a sort; without forest fires, forests choke; without predators, species overpopulate and deplete food sources and become extinct; without war and predators, humans become fat, lazy and useless (whoops, no idea how that last one got in there). In this context, we leave behind binary, linear morality and see the world as a nihilist: a vast functional machine which permits us the experience of consciousness.

In popular lore, there is frequent mention of "mind over matter," but this is usually interpreted to mean using the mind to convince the flesh to do things it would not ordinarily do, like run marathons and lift cars from runover children. The concept of transcendence is an evolution of this which harmonizes with the nihilist emphasis on structure over appearance as well as the idealist concept that thoughts define reality more than physicality. Transcendence occurs when, acknowledging all that is destructive and uncomfortable in the world, we take a greater delight in the idea of what we are accomplishing, not as much what it means in the anthropocentric valuation, but an appreciation of its design in the greater working of our universe. While we are a small part of that whole, transcendence has us find a place in it and to appreciate its design and significance in that context, even to the degree of "forgiving" the world for our suffering and eventual death, and thus lightening our burden by recognizing that physicality and demise are secondary in importance to achievement of idea, whether that is a moral concept, a symphony, a painting, or even a life lived normally according to moral principles in which there were intangible rewards like learning, time spent with family, and personal betterment achieved by facing fears and surmounting them, gaining new abilities.

It might be said that the ultimate process of idealism, in which reality is "mind-correlative" or composed of thoughts or thought-like phenomena, is transcendence, or the achievement of valuation of idea over all physical comfort or discomfort. It is not asceticism, per se, in that it is not gained through denial of physical existence, but on the contrary, asserts the importance of organizing physical existence according to idealized design. It converges with heroism in that the idealist in this context acts regardless of personal consequences, because if the world is idea, the only way to truly express that idea is by putting it into action in the world. This form of belief unifies the previously divided mind and body, and raises the human from the level of a reactionary animal to a planner and a creator who is also undivided from his or her natural role. Historically, two of the most important philosophers in European canon, Arthur Schopenhauer and Friedrich Nietzsche, are united in this belief: Nietzsche sought a "pragmatic idealism" while Schopenhauer was a "cosmic idealist," yet both appreciated the role of heroism in creating higher degrees of order. While Nietzsche derived his greatest inspiration from the ancient Greeks, Schopenhauer found great meaning in an ancient Indian text known as the Bhagavad-Gita, which introduces its view of philosophy through the viewpoint of a warrior concerned over the death and destruction he is about to unleash on his fellow humans. Through that question, the text explores the idea of placing idea over physical consequences by explaining that all reality is continuous will originating in a mystical source, and thus that while lives come and go the eternal order of reality remains, and creating a more organized harmony with that force is the goal of any heroic individual. As if proving parallelism through history, the ancient Greeks lauded similar concepts in their worship of heroic death and tragedy, in which triumph is found through assertion of higher ideal even when death and ruin inevitably follow. Praising what is right in a holistic sense over what is advantageous to the individual is the primary trait of all heroic, idealistic and nihilist philosophies.

In such modes of thought, the human being unifies imaginative and analytical facilities, using a method not dissimilar to science to interpret the world, and a method not far from art in projecting a next evolutionary stage, driven by such non-linear thought processes as informed emotion and calculated creativity. In the great transcendental thinkers of the West, most notably Ralph Waldo Emerson and Johannes Eckhart, the desire to merge these two seemingly disparate mental operations was the foundation of a spirituality based, as is Buddhism and ancient Christianity, on a quietude of the soul and a mystical state of mind in which one was "in" Nirvana or Heaven, a state of clarity both regarding life as suffering and a purpose and vision of what can give life meaning. All

Romantic philosophies and art have this basis as well, and are equally mystical, as such states of mind cannot be achieved through linear description. Nihilism can be seen as a spiritual device for achieving this quietude of soul by abrading the meaningless and insignificant facts of physicality in order to clearly see the Idea, much as a philosopher leaving Plato's cave would stand in reverent silence at the first glimpse of the sun. It is thus despite its primal origins as a "going under" through removal of meaning, a reevaluation of meaning and value, and a dramatic opposition to philosophical materialism, or the doctrine that the physical world and individual comfort are of overriding importance and thus outrank thought and idea.

Materialism is the essence of every destructive action taken by humanity, even though most who practice it would have no knowledge of it by that name. Most people, being well-meaning but misinformed and physically unable to undergo the cognitive process of holistic vision, drift toward materialistic ideas and strive toward what gives them personal physical comfort and wealth. In the modern time, materialism manifests itself in three primary fronts unified by their reliance on "preference utilitarianism," or what most people want to believe is true and beneficial for them:

I. Democracy
II. Social popularity
III. Consumerism

Consumerism is the choice of the most popular product regardless of actual utility; social popularity (or *oversocialization*) the organization of society according to who is most popular (usually he who promises alcohol, sex, and money); democracy is leadership not by what is right but what is popular. Materialism encourages the individual to think only of their own preference, and to limit thought at that which directly impacts individual comfort, and thus is blind to thinking for the whole of humankind and environment. When one thinks on that level, self-interest replaces finding the right answer according to the structure of the external world, and humans become solipsistic. Further, because materialism is an opposite to idealism, it causes the Crowd to gather and tear down whatever idealists dare rise among them. Only such a misinformed and dysfunctional thought process explains humanity's ongoing attempted genocide of its environment, its contentment to labor in horrifically boring jobs, its seeming satisfaction with petty interpersonal strife and a lack of reverence toward humans and other life forms alike, and its reliance on a world of illusion whose empty values render individual souls empty, causing neurosis and anomie at all levels of existence.

(Many humans are so divided between mind and body that they prefer ideas of a solipsistic nature to physicality, much like some drug addicts prefer intoxication to reality. Nihilism allows us to see reality as the one and only expression of both life and thought, and therefore, to see the true stakes in our dilemma, especially regarding our environment, whose destruction – a process not of complete obliteration but of disrupting its complex internal machinations, which require more land and sea and air than humanity – will not only be the greatest tragedy of our species, but an unforgivable offense.).

Nihilism is the soft earth at the start of a wooded path toward seeing life in a more developed way. Before this path, life seems to be suffering and boredom punctuated by horror (paraphrased from H.P. Lovecraft), without meaning or direction, even when one creates an absolute God and corresponding Heaven where things are otherwise. This state of depressed mind must be like that of the inhabitants of Plato's cave, who find themselves bored at an endless procession of shadows yet unaware of another way. A nihilist is anointed with knowledge, and must return to the world at large to speak of the sun which filters through the woods toward the end of the path. There is hope; there is meaning; there is reason and purpose to life. Whether one is a Christian, a Jew, a Buddhist, a Hindu, or a Muslim, this truth can spoken in a familiar language, as it has been discovered by the best thinkers of all religions and cultures. It is universal not only to humanity, but to all thinking beings. From nothingness comes everything, and when the two are seen as continuous, we are finally aware of the infinity of life and the great continuous gift that consciousness must be.

THE WORLD AS WILL AND REPRESENTATIONS

Philosophy is a convoluted world. Writers try to find some central theme to their writings, and through that unify a system of belief, but since reality doesn't fit under any heading in an outline except "reality," these end up being contorted organizations. Despite thousands of people working in this field over the past centuries, not much of a definitive nature has been produced. One of the great classics, and one that best formulates the "transcendental idealist" position on philosophy, is the work of Arthur Schopenhauer.

Schopenhauer wrote his classic *The World as Will and Representation* to express two basic ideas as indicated by the title. The first is the one grasped by almost everyone out there; that the universe, like individuals, is not purely rational but is more like a personality, in that it is like individual animals motivated by an attachment to life, or "will to live." The second idea is more important in a broader context, and relates to the first; much as Plato saw "objects" and "shadows of objects" in his metaphor of the cave, Schopenhauer separates the world into its essential force (Will) and its forms, which are a human Representation based on sense-data of the world as is.

Unlike many who followed Plato, Schopenhauer avoided the trap of dualism, in which one would say that there is a pure world and it is mirrored in our physical reality. Will is a force that animates the world, and there is something like a representation generated from it, which we can't know as a "thing in itself" because we are included in it and its scope is too broad for us to comprehend in a linear thinking system. The representation in Schopenhauer's works was a revolutionary concept: he said that humans never know the world as it is, but only know a representation of it, formed of their interpretation of sense-data and memory.

These were a shock to a philosophical world which had so far operated in the populist Christian tradition of an Absolute, believing

140

there was a dual world (or an abstraction that constituted a pure and singular form) which was the blueprint from which the world of appearance is made. This is one viewpoint on the classic division of philosophy: what is the world, and what is the human, and how can the latter best approximate the former? The question "Why do we suffer?" even has its origins in this, as to the world, the suffering of humans is inconsequential, but to a human, individual suffering can take up most of his or her awareness.

Although all of these ideas had vast political and social effects, what this article targets as its topic is something else: the addition of another Representation to Schopenhauer's list. This is not an addition to his actual cosmology, but a political notation. It is that in a modern time, when we have no uniform religious tradition and are accustomed to devotional belief as our means of finding truth, we view government and media and organized religion as sources of truth or at the very least, information about reality. This comprises an additional representation that a modern must address.

This representation is not unique to a modern time; we are always influenced by others, and there have always been doctrinal headlocks by various sources. However, in the age of technology, which asserts concepts as "scientific" and "proof" in an absolute sense, it takes on enough political and social importance that it's worthwhile to comment on Schopenhauer's philosophy and point out this additional cause of confusion. In the most rigorous academic sense, it would not be included in Schopenhauer's description of reality, as that is analytic of process and not situation. But for moderns, for the purpose of this article, it bears commenting.

Nihilism by its very nature negates this social representation. Most people confuse nihilism with fatalism, which is the belief that one can't know any truth or do anything about it, even if one could find out. However, nihilism is purely this: a negation of value in any sense removed from the actual, real world. It is not a negation of reality, but the values which are associated with a value-representation of reality, and while it removes that which exists, it does so to enable the individual to analyze reality and from it derive values on the terms of the individual in the context of a task, not an absolute.

Fatalism says there is no ability to interpret, value, perceive or think; nihilism says that such thinking must occur outside of what humans have already projected onto their world.

Of course, reinterpreting this through Schopenhauer, we can see the reason for nihilism existing within the individual: the individual knows the world through his representation, and therefore, can act only on that data according to his degree of will. There is no absolute to which the individual can appeal, but there are grounds for "truth" or at least *accuracy* in statements about the nature of reality if the individual interprets it according to its structure. In turn, this interpretation is only allowed by nihilism, which by removing values outside of the inherent de-emphasizes perception of *what* something is, and turns the mind to focus on its importance in the context of a task or goal.

There are two ways to interpret Plato's cave. The first is that there's a pure world, and physical objects are shadows of it; this presupposes that we know physical objects as they are, instead of as data from our five senses. The second interpretation is that there's a physical world, and it casts shadows on the cave wall that are what we know; these are the sense-data perceptions of physical objects, and this view presupposes that we can know our own representations fully. However, it is more logical that we can master thought than that we can achieve perception of things beyond our knowing, and for this reason, nihilism is the only sensible gateway.

It is a rejection of the artificial world imposed upon reality by the additional representation mentioned here: the social and economic reality that is trumpeted in our ears and eyes daily by any number of technological devices. It is repeated in newspapers, on television, on radio and on the Internet; government leaders and news/entertainment people give basically the same view, disguised as oppositional theories. All of these debate things that are not immediately important for the long-term triumph of replacing the reality we perceive, a representation of our world in our own minds, with another representation, that of a collective reality based on social values.

One thing that can oppose this mindset is nihilism, but it does not exist as a philosophical system as much as a method of liberating concentration to be able to apply other methods and intellectual systems. The basic idea of nihilism is accepting ultimate reality – the physical world that surrounds us and, whatever it is made of, is consistent in effect upon us all – and discarding all inference-information from others; it rejects both the absolute and the subjective, and replaces them with human adaptation to the external world in varying degrees of accuracy. Although this is more complex than what most embrace, it clears the part of the mind that values to consider life anew without being unduly manipulated.

Undoing the best efforts of philosophers, there is no central concept or theme to life, except life itself. It is its own goal. Schopenhauer gave us some basic tools that can help us understand our relationship to the world, but there is no complete, single answer – only a series of starting points. The individual can use these starting points successively as the changing basis of a goalset, with each realization leading to something new. But that path begins with something like nihilism, or the mind is awash in the absolute representation of the herd.

January 9, 2005

EXPERIENCE

To live and think in this time is to see humanity as a vast screw-up; to think a little further is to realize that there is more than enough good to go around in the world, but that it is disorganized, based upon a few wrong turns not in history but in our collective beliefs as a modern, global society (by "good" it is meant all the good things in life, and not some absolute moral abstraction, a neat category into which we can divide things as having one source or another according to an ironclad, absolute law that applies equally to us all). In other words, while we can point to any number of symptoms and *carriers* of our bad ideas, which are essentially vectors for justifying erroneous thought, it is that erroneous thought itself that is the root of our problem.

(This essay is written for those developed enough in their thinking to realize that, no matter how much we might *think* we live in separate, absolute worlds, we live in the same world and the same laws of nature apply to us all, and there is no escaping them; in this realization we see two absolutes, the first being the mistake of thinking there is one categorical way of life that can apply equally to each of us, and the second being the mistake that we each exist in an untouchable category of our own, separated from reality. About the only equality in life is the status of these errors. For this reason, "erroneous thought" can be translated as "unrealistic thought," "illusion," "lies," "delusion" or any synonym of your choice.).

At our first pass, it seems likely that our thought went wrong with some tangible entity; money, or the Church, or corporations, or "patriarchy," or the gods of the sandal-wearers from the Middle East. This answer is unsatisfying in that first, the beginnings of the decline predate these things, and second, waging war against these things on a test basis – in smaller communities or ourselves – hasn't stopped the pervasive nature of problems on that level. Thus we are left unfulfilled, and go on to our next level of thought, at which point our conclusions resemble the sappy lines from get well cards and bad short stories. If we only knew that love is all we need – if we only took time to care about the downtrodden, to realize their humanity is equal to ours and their suffering is real – if we only cared more, if we only took more walks on the beach at dawn, if everyone just got stoned and started thinking about how fascinating life is... the cynic in us asks, "So how did it work for you?" and the answer, universally, is that it worked for a few things, but the practical problems of how to conduct life remained, after all the new age-y, starry-eyed bullshit was over.

So: at this point, most give up and fall into what is called "nihilism" but makes more sense when referred to as "fatalism," namely the belief that nothing means anything, that nothing can be done, that no value can be found, that nothing can reverse the decline. "Fatalism" is thus a fancy word for giving up on giving a damn, and settling down to a life of self-pity and what medical professionals call "symptomatic treatment," or giving the patient care to release suffering from symptoms, having assumed that the cause of the disease cannot be stopped; the extreme of this is "palliative care," in which scenario the disease is fatal and the only thing that can be done is to dope up the patient and wait for death's swift kick to the rickety door of the soul. In our time, this is the most common philosophy, this palliative fatalism, and it explains in part why "conservatives" have fundamentalist, positivist religion and "liberals" have marijuana and wine – lots of wine – and everyone else has money, and/or cheap and effective street drugs.

Another aspect of it is pity, or the feeling that if you have the ability to give someone less fortunate something, it makes you feel good, in no small part for having the status of being higher than them and having the ability to give a gift. You're not doing it for them; you're doing it for yourself, and because of this, what you're doing is rarely what they actually need, but some form of condescension. Hand the poor bibles and temporary food relief, but don't cart them off to work or, if they're mentally deranged, to a desolate and lonely patch of freezing ground for a quick and relatively painless death. To others who suffer, give little encouragements of the theme "you're alright," even though what they might need to hear is that they have to make changes or they'll keep suffering. This feel-good condescension is the antithesis of "tough love," which is a reality-embracing wake-up call to all who are suffering needlessly, and doesn't gently suggest change but spells out clearly that they either change or die. Another aspect of "tough love" is taking lame horses, mutant livestock, and fatally diseased animals out behind the barn and applying a .30-06 to the skull. When you have no pity, you kill that which is having no hope, but unlike palliative medication, you actually end the pain and give space to new life by removing that which has failed.

And what exists beyond this fatalism? Surely the author of this piece believes that something might...? Otherwise, it would be pointless to even communicate, whether exhorting or preaching or cajoling, and it would be most sensible instead to find some way to swindle you into buying some *product* so the author could apply palliative medicine more effectively to himself. Does some aspect of that thought depress you – those who lead the blind, becoming blind, such that they might profit? Maybe you recognize it as a common occurrence and in fact, the motivation behind most advice you'll get that isn't outright pity, making the giver feel smarter for having a solution the pitied have not yet seen. You were warned this is a fatalistic time, but it was some paragraphs ago, so you're forgiven for forgetting it – on a standardized test, your options would be clearer. But what everyone says about standardized tests is that they're not close enough to reality, and test you more on your ability to fool a test than on knowledge of reality, or knowledge of how to summarize knowledge. Communication in this time makes even bridging this subject difficult, much less communicating how to surpass it.

We'll start with the basics. There may not be an answer for you; you may literally be condemned, by character or ability, to live thrashing about in ignorance with no hope. Sorry – have some marijuana, or have you tasted the Mogen David 20/20? Well. However, if you've made it this far in reading this document, and still haven't started skimming for swear words or sexual references, it's likely you can process the information at hand (if this were a postmodern piece of writing, the author would try to communicate exclusively through sexual references and swear words but, alas, I'm not that clever, and far too pragmatic for it). Philosophers like to talk about sensitive but warlike souls (Mr. Nietzsche? Your car is ready—) who by combining these attributes have a selective aspect to their aggression; indeed, such a description merits the Indo-European people in healthier days, in that unlike the more passive populations to the east, and the unrelentingly aggressive populations to the south, they became selective; contemplative; philosophical. In shorthand, this means that you must not declare the cause lost or won, but return with a critical eye to the task we explored in the past four paragraphs; however, you must also do it with a determination to not find a solution but *make* a solution, and do it with both warlike discipline and the playful joy that characterizes most healthy primate behaviors.

By way of backward analysis, if we debug our own thoughts to this stage, we have a powerful clue about where "we" as a species went wrong: we were not active enough, and were too passive, and therefore when selecting future roles as "active" and "passive," we could not see a middle path between the two; we either opt to be 100% warlike ("conservative") or 100% passive ("liberal") and in both cases, fail to find working solutions because life does not operate in absolute categorical terms, but requires any ideal of an absolute categorical nature be applied in the language of life itself, which is far more flexible. As the English say in musky oyster bars and discotheques, "Quite." It's important to take a brief detour here, which is represented by the appearance of a Buddhist monk in saffron robes – saffron cloth was originally used to bury the dead, and was selected for that reason as the icon of Buddhism, which like most modern religions is a death religion: it spends so much effort explaining away personal death that soon conversation on death dominates all discourse, and the result is that no matter how many delightful things Buddhism or Christianity have, in practice they remain obsessed with death, and thus stop short from making positive changes; theirs, too, is a palliative medicine.

If we had a Buddhist monk here, one of those tidy and dispassionately friendly little guys who seem to exist without unnecessary memory or inefficient action, he or she would probably politely point out that the West, like the East millennia before it, has become obsessed with the *ego*, or conception of self as individual. Good point; back to your rice and pickled vegetables, now, while those who think toward sculpting a future discuss the real issue. The ego is with us – or rather, the socialized self-image is with us, too much, in that what we have for our egos is displaced into the absolute and generic perception of other people: the assumption that there is some standard by which all people will view us, and that this represents more of "us" than our inner attributes, such as our character and our spirit and our preferences and values.

What is important is not the person, but the person as demonstrated, or shown off in public. It is no longer an individual, but a series of boundaries, as agreed upon by every person in the observing audience, like a character in a movie. It doesn't matter that she loves animals and will, if she gets out of this absurdly symbolic drama, run off gratefully to veterinary school and spend the rest of her life tending to them; what matters is that she has chosen the Dark Path, because her character is summed up in a certain way, say a preference for power over emotion, and thus she – like every good chess piece of symbolic intent in art – gets quickly shuffled offstage and goes to the fate that, as you saw earlier in the movie, she merits by her actions. This is not religious; it is not political; it is not social; – it is all three, unified by something more basic than a symbolic division of thought into discipline can symbolize.

Yet it seems that this self-image/ego problem is with us, in that the major cause of our world's decline is people doing not what is right by all things, but what enriches them most in the short term, whether through money, or power, or social status. Is this directly a cause of self-image/ego, or is there something that underlies both errors? The lack of collective goals points toward a deficiency which existed before the egomania of the current era, so our philosophical inquiries should probably target whatever created the void into which me-first-ism fell. This task is complicated by the nature of selfishness, which although it works through the individual, produces a revengeful crowd; the individual dislikes anything that threatens its boundaries, and thus will work with others to tear down those who have higher goals that individual enrichment and comfort. Although this seems a paradoxical proposition, history bears witness to the downfall of the West as a form of mass revolt by the less distinguished against the part of their population that traditionally bore the responsibility of leadership. If this is not envy in action, it would be hard to place a finger on what it is. Those who could not be leaders, wanting what leaders had, destroyed the principle of leadership through crowd rebellion, and thus created a void in which their egomania was unopposed.

For this to happen, however, there has to be some failure in leadership that allows such an unbalance, where the majority of the population are so clueless that they are undisciplined and destructive. It may be this failure was as simple as the leadership minority becoming so small it was overwhelmed. Yet – using what we have observed from day to day life, balancing probability against probability, this seems unlikely. Experience dictates that such an overthrowing could not have happened without some fragmentation, or lack of consensus, among the leadership population *first*, followed by its increasing irrelevance and thus weakness. We could claim that what afflicted the leaders was what later deranged the bulk of the population, namely, a nutty desire for personal power and wealth. This, at least, is common when a society has no great task before it, such as growth, or warfare, or struggle with a natural threat. It makes sense to keep going, however, because our analysis has not found a common thread basic enough to reveal this widespread falling apart. We have found plenty of clues.

Such a common thread would have to be so universal it functioned as a bedrock not of government, or society, or culture, but of perception itself, which is influenced by the attitudes around it and can thus re-program humans to see the world in a different way; the smarter ones might find their way out of a logical trap, but the most subtle and prevailing logical traps are the ones that take *lifetimes* of experience to decode. These are the errors that cut to the core of our existential outlook, meaning how we value life itself, and what we find as meaningful goals within it to pursue. They shape what we expect out of life, and what for which we strive, and by those, what we're willing to endure. This is a form of managing both joy and fear, and thus motivating the individual to work in concert with civilization and nature to live the best life possible. And, to cut to the chase, that leads us to the question of experience, through the question of what happens when fear eclipses joy, and out of fear we enshrine our doubts as holy, and deny our joy – remembering, of course, that great success in civilization is a form of joy, as is heroism. To give of oneself, and to make something better than what existed before – can there be a greater joy, a greater triumph?

Experience is what happens when we make contact with the world, gaining knowledge which shapes our internal "map" of the world, or the impression of it and its operations we store in our heads. When we think of an action, we plot it according to what we know will occur according to the world as we have observed it. A thrown ball will travel in a balance between its momentum and gravity, and at some point will fall to earth as gravity overwhelms what is left of its momentum. We understand our world by this mapping of it we have in our head: its geography, its natural laws, its cycles. While we have some knowledge of it via intuition, as our brains are shaped by years of genetic adaptation to the world and are as products of its mechanics prone to operate in a similar method to its laws, our basic method for adapting the world in our heads to the outside world is experience. Some refer to this process as part of the "inner war": gaining awareness of the world, and the discipline to act on it as is right for what is healthy (the "outer war" is applying this discipline in physical reality). Experience can bring great joy, and also great doubt, and from doubt comes a kind of fear that is different from fear of physical pain or loss; from doubt comes the fear that our lives are not worth the price of death.

This doubt could be characterized as "existential" doubt, meaning that we no longer live secure lives in our inner world when we have it; we wonder if our lives are misspent, if we could be doing something better, if the self and the self-image are not rewarded enough. After all, no matter how much we spin the process of death as a transition to another world, we never know *for sure* if it will be the case, so we focus on how we live and what those lives mean. And there we enter a new dimension of questioning, because to have something that is self-evident, such as survival, "mean" something introduces another layer of assessment. Thus we question our own lives and choices, and think about making different ones for the sake of having more "meaning" in our lives, even if we don't phrase the question that way. Existential doubt afflicts us more passionately when we are trying to overcome doubt, and make the most meaningful decisions. At this point, we hover in a grey area where much error or much greatness could be decided.

Doubt denies experience, as when one doubts, one would rather grasp something predetermined and uphold it as an absolute. Each time we venture out of our inner worlds and look to the larger world outside, we face possible rebuke, in the form of our preconceptions of what might happen not turning out how we'd expect. The most extreme case of this is death, where something fails so badly we are physically destroyed. Much as in religion, if one devotes all of one's time to explaining death away, death becomes a god, when one devotes all of life to explaining reality away, anti-reality (our inner worlds, sealed off from any kind of feedback loop with reality which could point out where illusion exists) becomes our new god, and it insidiously does not have allegiance to any named philosophy or entity within society. Instead, it is pervasive, and no matter what ideal we take on, because we have this preconceived method of parsing the world around us into internal tokens, we literally have blinded ourselves to the significance of our world, and have relapsed into internal symbolism. We are prisoners in our own minds, and we cannot escape until we address the construction of our prison, which is under our control, unlike the larger social and political apparatus around us.

The walls that confine us are made of our own fear of experience. It is easier to trust in an absolute truth than to experience the world; indeed, most people need to, as their own facilities and time resources do not allow for a study of philosophy. However, our entire society has at this point been infected by such a delusion. We would like to believe in predetermined outcomes, such that if we simply follow a sign or a path, we can arrive at the successes we see others as having. We fear taking the risk ourselves, however, and when we see no one else undertaking that difficult passage, we assume it is unnecessary. In doing so, however, we cut ourselves out of the equation of life, and see only the starting point and the product. Witness the average equation:

$$x \; (\text{ random mathematical stuff here }) = y$$

We look merely at Y, seeing X as our current circumstance (or, our selves and self-images), and skip the middle part of the equation. We don't want to take the risk, the chance, and the chance of failure, that comes with the unpredictable middle part. We'd like a nice clean path: press button A (not button B!) and you will be rewarded with success. There may be some ups and downs, but basically, you'll be OK, and death will be something that comes in the way distant future – you will not risk death in combat, or in struggle, or even in play. Keep it safe. Don't rock the boat. (This delusion can also occur in a spiritualist sense, where one finds oneself saying, "I didn't win the game, or get the girl, and I'm still starving and miserable, but at least, *I did what was right!*" It is for this reason that some philosophers, namely Nietzsche and Schopenhauer, rail against the idea of absolute Christian morality, all while upholding the values of that morality as sacred. They're saying that if the method of reaching a goal corrupts our minds, we will never have truly reached that goal; this is the "inner war" common to every Indo-European religion and personal mythology.).

From this fear of the middle comes passivity; from passivity comes absolutism, and from that come baffling and unreal worlds patterned after our inner minds that cause us to relapse into our personal versions of reality, ignoring the obvious by ignoring the whole. When we look at reality, we see a single "thing" because all of its elements are connected; sky to earth, earth to water, water to fire – individual acting on world, and individual adapting to (being shaped by) world. Our fear of reality has made us prisoners in our own heads. This enables us to deny experience, and look only at a certain type of outcome, known as the final state – and to keep things safe, we measure this in material terms. We want our world to be exactly like our inner world, and we exclude everything else, as it is threatening. Whether we do this with money, with morality, or with politics is irrelevant, as the outcome (in the whole, not in the tangible part left over) is the same.

Experience also marks us. Like it or not, for every act we undergo, we strap wiring into our brain. We are our acts and experiences. Our minds are entirely physical, and the way we retain our programming is by building components of the brain, akin to those little squiggles on circuit boards, for each experience we undergo. This includes our decisions within it, which explains how learning occurs: based on past decisions, we have the ability to take on more refined tasks for present decisions, and thus all learning is cumulative. If you do not make the decisions required to get to a certain point, you cannot make decisions after that point. This is why traditional morality emphasizes selectivity in experience. If you have wiring in your brain for every sexual partner you've had, they are literally a part of you; if you screw around too much, you soon have only generic wiring, and don't even notice with whom you're sleeping. Focus on outcomes, not on experience, is revealed there. Similarly obsession with money and power denies the rite of passage one undergoes to get such things, a travail which in a healthy society would involve proving one's character and inner strength as well as the mechanical ability needed to reach an outcome.

We fear the risk of that undertaking, so we focus on the mechanical ability, and since that is accessible to everyone, we cheer ourselves for upholding "equality." This is philosophical error, and while it seems to function now, really we're living off the fat of what our ancestors achieved, and the piper awaits payment in the distant but closer-now future. Uh oh. Does it mean that our inner worlds will someday be compromised? Wait and see – the answer is one you can create for yourself. Other aspects of experience that terrify us include natural selection, or the idea that we might be insufficient to a task and just like the slow mouse under wings of eagles, be slaughtered and thus end our lives. Death-fear comes to rule us, doesn't it? Natural experience occurs both outside and inside our brains. If we opt for the easier, less obvious choice in all cases, when the time comes for us to face a significant choice, we are unfit for the task; we have selected ourselves out.

A potent metaphor for this realization comes from computer science. There are no random numbers in computers; how do you think up something without precedent? Instead, computers create "random" numbers by sampling arbitrary data, either atmospheric noise or user input or time data. Similarly, humans cannot think of a random number, as they are basing their choice on what they know, even if they decide to invert the choice – "I'd guess a seven, but I want something that is not obvious, so I'll pick something crazy, like a 13." An astute reader might note that novelty – that which is new and exciting in form, but perhaps of the same content as previous art – is created the same way. Pick what is rational, and then invert the idea, and thus come up with something "new" and "unique" and exciting (you may see this process referred to as ironism, iconoclasm or contrarianism). We are our experience. Make rotten decisions, and you program yourself to be rotten; make good decisions, and soon you will encounter new levels on which to prove yourself, and slowly better yourself.

When we speak of experience, most people confuse that term with sensuality, or the idea that the substance of life can provide a form of feedback that is interesting for its own sake. But really, how fascinating is it? Is that there much difference between orgasms, forms of intoxication, and sensation? Or do our senses point us toward something which is of much greater importance, namely the structure of life – that an orgasm is most significant when shared with someone truly adored, that intoxication is meaningful when it leads us to realizations or lubricates a social situation, and that sensations when assembled by the brain give us a picture of the external world? Experience ultimately teaches us how intangible the tangible is, in a form of paradox only something as brilliant as our universe (substitute "God" if you wish – it really *makes no difference*) could concoct. What matters is not the sensation, but what it signifies. This gets us closer to wishing for outcomes as seen as error above, but not on the same level. Where outcomes are absolutes without experience, ideals – "what it signifies" – are products of experience, and are re-calculated each time we undergo an experience. There are no absolutes, sensation included, only an ongoing process of evolution of *idea*.

You can hold onto nothing. Your body will decay, those you know will die, and eventually even your civilization's romantic ruins will collapse into dust, and the planet Earth be swallowed by the sun. What might outlast it is a higher grade of human, one not as developed in external character as self-image or technology would afford, but fully developed in internal character, in values and heroic attitudes and greater subtlety of thought and self-discipline. This sort of creature would be organized enough to escape the pitfalls in which we now exist, and to use technology for something thoughtful, like establishing new worlds and continuing the evolution of the species. Is this Nietzsche's superman? Is this the state of being a god and not a mortal? Is this Nirvana? Possibly, all three: it is a state toward which we evolve, where we are not distracted by substance or outcomes, but focus on experience as a way of programming ourselves to a higher state.

Nature operates via a simple principle: create a proliferation of designs, and select the best from among them by knocking out the least stable, and then build on that design base for the next generation. Even when starting with a simple design, this process rapidly creates a sturdy and enduring design in its place, and advances the state of knowledge radically. We as humans do not escape this process, physically or mentally. When we choose to degenerate out of fear, as in the current era, we devolve to the point of having no vision other than our own immediate gratification, and thus create doom for ourselves (such as childishly fighting over resources by expanding our factions until we have consumed all resources, then becoming dependent on a machine-society, and thus fighting internally until we destroy that and, having nowhere to go, collapse with it). And what is the origin of this devolution? A fear of experience, and of experience shaping us, leading to us relying on absolutes – God told me to, The customers like it, We have orders from above – passively, instead of asserting what is right for the whole and acting on it, regardless of consequences. All of our downfall – mass revolt leading to dumbing down, industry that eats our planet, democracy and morality and bad breeding including racial mixture – comes from this core realization. This core realization comes from doubt as to the meaning of our existences.

The West – and now the world – has for too long been grasped by this existential doubt. Although we have done well so far, our success has been mixed, in that for all of our genius, and all of our inventions and successes, we are still plagued by this internal failure, and our illusions of reality have caused us to push ourselves onto a path to sure collapse. It would be nice, surely, to find something internal to this system of thought that we could eliminate, and thus move forward with only the good parts, but the plain truth of it seems to be that our basic philosophy restrains us. We could have all that we have, and more, if we were able to organize our energies toward positive ends, and not condemn ourselves with neurosis. Yet that neurosis comes with our basic worldview, and explains why for every good thing we've done, we've also brought doom upon ourselves in the subtlest of fashions, that of a long-term imminent collapse. With this slow death lurking in the wings, naturally neurosis worsens, and the hysterical paranoia that results divides us further and only hastens the collapse.

Since there are no obvious enemies, nor any allies without the enemy within, the only solution is to dissect the illusion and to begin cultivation of a healthy philosophy that can unite us in the future. Not everyone has to understand this; in any society, there is a small minority of leaders who understand things, and many others who form the support infrastructure for the ideas of those few. This minority needs to come together on a belief system, as currently it is so divided that its members no longer care about doing what is right, so long as the ideas and symbols that represent their faction achieve a relative victory (even if that means smoking marijuana and drinking wine in the ruins, having out-survived the others by a small margin). When we look toward this future philosophy, it makes little sense to rearrange the tokens we now use, but good sense to attack its origins, in which is ensconced our attitude toward existence.

The symptoms of our error, at the lowest level, are an obsession with self-image, including a selfish self-interest which denies the obvious reality in favor of what benefits us immediately, and a passivity which has us herdlike following symbols and images while remaining blind to the truth. The most primitive diagnosis suggests that, simply, we are disconnected from reality, and that this passivity and self-image obsession is the result of us having no direct interaction with the world as whole, thus having no idea what are the consequences of our actions. Like most errors, this begins with a few, and then as the rest struggle to compete, spreads to the society as a whole; most people today do not act in pure blindness, but out of a need to keep earning a living and surviving in a world that has gone blind. If someone stood up and clearly pointed out the error, and enough leaders agreed that it was so, these people would be liberated from the system of competing against others for the privilege of error. For this reason, finding consensus in a diagnosis would liberate us from illusion and allow for a commonality of philosophy which would disintegrate the illusion from within as individuals no longer found themselves compelled to act on illusion in order to survive.

We can reverse this process. Passivity would have us looking for a single leader, a symbol, or other absolute truth riding out of the mist, to which we could cling and say, save us – save us from ourselves. But no one is coming to break down our prison, to shatter the demons that haunt our dreams, and to lift us up into a pure world where none of this potential for error exists; we have to do it for ourselves, and escape our prison by discovering what it is and then replacing it with something else.

Don't bother with deconstruction. It's an excuse for wasting time. Once you have diagnosed the nature of the prison, simply replace it. This author suggests two things: (1) realism and (2) heroic idealism. The first is a recognition that our physical reality is all we need, and that mystical concerns come after here-and-now action. The second is an awareness that, much as in evolution, we are fighting for a better design, not greater comfort of substance or even individual survival. The survival of the whole, including our planet and its ecosystems, is the highest goal, and there is no sacrifice too great toward this end. Even if we die, even as we pass away into grey ash and dust, the process of experience is marching on, and if we believe in the good things in life we have had so far, we realize this process of experience *is* life – an intangible thing – and that to value life is to uphold it, and even die for it.

Dedicated to Antti Boman

April 12, 2005

GLEEFUL

Cue typical American public radio broadcast:

Once this pleasant, sunny courtyard rang with the cries of children at play. That was the week before disaster struck, and began a process that we know only too well.

(Audio: birds singing, children playing)

As the first tendrils of disaster touched this happy community, residents rallied together, and declared their intention to fight disaster with the bonds of a community – love, sharing, forgiveness and a helping hand.

(Audio: "I know this is gonna be hard, but I'm here for the long haul," a gruff voice of a local longshoreman, or maybe a painter. Someone who is not a radio-employed intellectual from New York, please. We have empathy for the other half living.)

But as the disaster deepened, those strong voices dropped out one by one. First the busy bus depot flooded in warm blood. Then people began to abandon these homes they worked for over long years of struggle. Finally, the children disappeared.

(Audio: sad music, preferably a minor key modulating to a lower key still in the minor, with a two-note pattern of bright incidentals for contrast.)

Now this once-happy community is all but abandoned. Buildings rust next to burnt out cars. The government promises aid, but it comes slowly. We all know the rest. And even though we give, we cannot stave off this aftermath of disaster.

We can see radio programs as a pattern, much like patterns exist from which we cut clothing, design furniture, or write computer code. The pattern of this radio program is repeated not only on government-funded public radio, but also on privately-owned big media channels, and even more alarming, on the indie stations. Monkey see, monkey do, and this successful product format can be emulated to share in the success.

Looking behind the visual and political cues, and the putative content of the program, we see the emotional content of this pattern. It both memorializes tragedy, and seems to affirm its inevitability, while offering token methods of resistance. This in turn creates a psychological pattern: the sense of living with constant small tragedy and being impotent to change it, and finding solace not in fighting that impotence, but in accepting it and sharing emotions with others.

This pattern can be found other places. The best spot to locate it is a drug and alcohol rehabilitation center. People stand up, say they've screwed up their lives and cannot manage their own lives, and so they need someone to tell them what to do. God, the law, morality and economics all get mentioned as part of the same process (revelatory). What is the psychological pattern? Submission to negativity through acceptance of the negative but endurable.

> *"I get raped nightly," said one slave to another. "But there's always food afterwards, and it's not as bad as the guys in the field have." The other shrugged. "Share that food with someone too ugly to be raped, whyncha?"*

When we look at the logic of submission, we see a convergence of human psychological factors. The "Stockholm Syndrome," where captives bond with captors, is part of the same psychological pattern that has beaten wives clinging to their abusers, or anally violated children defending their parents. Yes, the situation is bad; however, we can't face what we have to do to fix it; therefore, we endure and find some way to make our sadness into proudness. Although our lives are meaningless, and we fail daily, we are the greatest martyrs of all time.

This psychological pattern is a subset of all cognitive dissonance patterns. In these, reality is painful, so people invent justifications and use them to supplant measurement of reality. We could use the old cliché of an ostrich hiding its head in the sand, but only if there's a television down there, dramatizing the sadness. It is an inversion of art: instead of singing the beautiful, we find praises for the ugly and disguise it as beauty, because we *have lost belief* in beauty.

As good nihilists, we note that this loss of belief in beauty is vested more in belief than beauty. We have made beauty contingent upon so many moral justifications that it is socially taboo to note beauty without somehow tying it to the plight of the disadvantaged (morality for dummies: when we fear for ourselves, we want to find someone in a worse position than ourselves and demand they be protected, like a human shield; this unites individuals into crowds determined to destroy anyone who might not need the protection of the crowd, like a populist Mafia). What a beautiful vista – we can build public housing here.

Through this process, what was once adaptation becomes a perverse addiction to failure and ugliness, so long as we find some hip new way of presenting them on the radio or television. You can see it in the irony of the hipster, who if his band sucks, will tell you all about how using a tuba to blast jazz riffs over indie rock guitar makes them unique and different and worthy of your attention. The question of "Is it good?" has been replaced by the question of "Do we do ugly, boring and failing *well*?" It's like a yard sale of used colostomy bags.

Cognitive dissonance, by the nature of denying reality, puts us into dangerous territory. It is spread easily through social expressions because if our good buddy Joe30AF0B18 comes up to us and tells us that his job failed, he has AIDS and his children are mentally retarded, we want to say something nice to him to make him feel better. So we tell him that Jesus loves him, or he's unique, or that we've never heard such a moving story and he should call public radio. In doing so, we take some of the need to justify misery into ourselves.

What is enduringly positive about nihilism is that we cut ourselves free from this nightmare of justification and socialized praise of death, and instead, look toward the actual design of reality. People with no goal in life want to turn nihilism into fatalism, so they have an excuse to sit on their fat asses pleasing themselves but yet can justify it with competing moral logic. "All is lost," they wail. "Oh well, might as well tuck into this pizza that just arrived... and there's *Madden* on the PS3, soooo..."

Nihilism can be more coherently expressed as the scientific method with a desire to remove the scientist. We look at reality, its repeated patterns, and note them in a mathematical sense. We then remove the bias of the scientist not by erasing it, but by putting it into context, as in "you are a person within a world" and not "the world is the expression of yourself." We look at structure because it is consistent and in a sense is more real than tangible, physical factors. We can make a chair out of feces, wood or egg whites, but the only way we can recognize it is by its form serving a function made obvious by the needs of those who would sit, so even if it is without any conventional "this is a chair" cues we can recognize it.

As good nihilists, we look askance at this world of weepy public service announcements because it is not real. We see that reality exists in parallel everywhere at once, and so inevitably there is tragedy somewhere. What does it matter to us? We cannot change it, and might not be advised to do so, especially if the tragedy was a community built on a floodplain or supported by a degenerate industry. We can do what we must do, and the only ultimate measurement of that is what we create in the physical world. Our thoughts die with us, as do our emotions. We lose out when those emotions are repeated mass media indoctrinations.

What is real is the knowledge that, as one old empire (the global economy and moral world government) begins to find out that its design is inferior, a new empire rises for those who want to grab it. If 99% of the people on earth are incompetent morons and/or are delusional and weepy, that means those of us who cut ourselves free from the old and dying emotional pattern are able to create and enjoy ourselves – and succeed while doing it, meaning that we inherit the future.

The people who uphold the dying empire, even by criticizing it and creating endless radio shows that fit this maudlin pattern, show themselves to be not only obsolete but unable to see beyond appearance. They cling to the feelings they can derive from the pattern of praising dysfunction by mourning its consequences but not looking deeply into its structure, and in so doing, approve of their doom. Laughing at them lessens any guilt you might catch from them like a pesky cold in a crowded office.

Most people you meet in life who claim to be outsiders to the dying regime are physically outside of it, but mentally and morally inside of it. This includes the "nihilists" who want an excuse to do nothing and sound smart for having figured out the futility of it all. This also includes the smart, shapely, young, attractive, compassionate and blonde radio hosts who want to get all weepy over whatever vestigial limb of the human amoeba just got its ass handed to it by nature, economics or logic. These people are caught up in the emotional pattern that is opposite to nihilism.

They, like most people who are addicted to these negative emotions, are hoping to share their misery with us and neutralize us, and drag us down with them. Misery loves company, as the cliché says, but even more, miserable people are threatened by anyone who emotionally or physically might escape their debacle. They don't want to save themselves because it's easier to weep than take action. But they do not want to see anyone who might not have their disease, because that competition will best them, and they hate that.

Honest nihilism liberates us from that dying cycle. Nihilism eradicates morality as it is practiced, and gives us space to re-invent a civilization that is not based on pacifying the masses with morality, but on working together to build something beautiful. Our goal is not to praise the darkness, declare all is lost, and go home to our pizza sofa video game klatches. Our goal is to transcend this mess, and then put our ideas into action so they persist in physical reality.

The first step we must take is rejection of the weepy mentality. We do not need depression for there is no reason to be depressed. Yes, humanity is destroying its world, but that is already written in stone and cannot be changed until our numbers are reduced. Yes, most people are stupid, but they will be unable to resist that reduction. Let the dying face the fate it has chosen, especially since it considers itself so clever; we don't need its addictive, negative emotions dressed up as some hip radio program.

Look toward the future with a smile. Underneath that smile, make sure there's a grin of determination and playfulness. What collapses around you has been fated to die for centuries if not longer, because its design is adapted to human emotional neediness and not reality. As it falls away, spaces open for us to create something new and better.

March 5, 2008

REALISM

When the idea of inherent truth is rejected, the question arises that replaces that idea is the search for something that is always true as if inherent, and the answer can be found only in reality itself.

As human thought and projection fades away, what remains is only the world around us, the cosmos beyond, the consistent principles of their function that we can derive. This is reality. This definition baffles most because it includes both the tangible and the intangible, refusing to banish mysteries in the way of materialism or turn them into fairy-tales as the dualists do. The only inherent thing is reality including the "invisible world" of ascertained past and anticipated future, and all else is human projection, although sometimes we can reliably assess reality and offer brief insights that, if the other party is thinking along the same lines, can stir communication but are not communication in themselves. This outlook replaces "truth" and "validity" with a question of what exists and what it means.

All of the great unknowns of life remain untouched by this, which is unsatisfying to the human mind which likes a firm answer one way or another but not an ambiguity. Human minds spark at any notion which is level, even, square-cornered and aligned in neat rows. We adore order of the sort that fits our numbering system and extremely basic topography. Nature however works in curves, in nuances, and in a complex form of many layers, such that our human logic is like that of a toddler. Most of our human errors arise from the collision of our own perceptual assumptions of this nature and the greater complexity of reality. The more we try to impose ourselves on the world, and scapegoat and demonize those who recognize reality, the more reality pushes back.

It is like a man trying to cram one more brick into a loose-piled wall, finding that the harder he slams it into the hole, the more it displaces other bricks. Life is like chess, or a Rubik's cube, not a linear order. And yet the human mind only feels safe with the linear order, because in it, the individual human understands his place, and sees it as not an object within the world, but as an object *above* the world, with the perspective of a god and perhaps the immortality of one. The human mind likes to project an order of objects arrayed as convenient for the individual, like an overlord looking over his fields or a general reviewing his troops. This tendency creates false expectations from reality, and sends us in search of "truth" instead which constitutes both a human perception and the group enforcement of that perception as a substitute for reality.

The existence of an object, the presence of a natural law, and the passage of time are all ineffably true; assessments about these, which take the form of a symbolic or token subset of the whole, exist only in human minds and vary with the capabilities, aggressiveness toward completeness, and honesty – a function of moral character – of the individual human. For this reason, there are no universal truths, only those groups have decided to enforce on themselves. When groups agree on truths, they reflect not the combined strengths of the group, but where it could not formulate clear disagreement, which leads to it embracing the ambiguous, unclear and nebulous instead of fact that corresponds to reality. Like in a bad committee meeting, that which cannot be resolved is passed along through compromise, and humans tend to use these unclear tokens – formed of categorical delineations that are at best inexact, at worst like the "miscellaneous" drawer in a kitchen a repository for that which cannot be easily sorted – as if they were hard, verifiable objects. Categories are mental objects and as with all mental objects, can replace their referents in our minds.

For this reason, the nihilist finds himself at odds with civilization because groups such as societies tend toward lies made convenient by these ambiguous categories, and also estranged from most individuals who self-deceive through the mental process of rationalism. Rationalism works by rationalizing backward from what exists (desires, possessions, impulses) toward what is needed; in its perceptual for, it consists of looking for data to support a conclusion and selectively filtering out that data through the exclusion of other details. This makes humanity the start of perception, replacing reality. The man who has a hammer and uses it as a universal tool, despite the awkwardness of its imprecise utility, exemplifies this condition. The realist nature of nihilism generally rejects all authority, taboos and sacred cows that are in denial of discernible reality, and looks toward realist explanations for the unknown instead of merely declaring a symbol and treating it as truths.

Anti-realism takes the form of the perceiver (the human) and not the perceived (the world) in a process called solipsism where humans assume that their own experience is universal, and the objects in their minds are in fact more real than objects in reality. Realists reverse this formula but often find themselves unclear on how to start down this path, especially within later civilization where everything they are told and tested on since their early days turns out to be a lie. Since most humans tend toward solipsism, and realism breaks away in another direction, it requires re-learning all that is known starting with the principle of reality-first instead of human-first reason.

THE FIRST LECTURE

Randy Pausch shot to great fame with his "last lecture,"[15] in which he teaches all the things he learned from life shortly before he departs it. In this writing, I take the opposite approach, and instead present the "first lecture," or things I have learned from coming to consciousness in life.

By coming to consciousness I mean that I was born, my intelligence matured, and then I had to decode the world I live in, since no word means what it seems it should and hidden motivations lurk around many corners. So after years of consciousness, I was finally able to discover a true self-consciousness, and when I had overcome that, a world-consciousness.

Along the way, many steps could have been eliminated and many delays saved had there been in place some social order to pass along to me the learning of past generations. But in a society dominated by conflict, with no clear cultural path, instead you are thrown to the wolves if you ask others for assessments of value.

So here it is – the first lecture – what you need to know now that you have woken up, found yourself alive, and are casting about for a grasp on reality and how to handle it.

First Lesson: Life is a Quest for Adaptation.

The quickest way to find happiness in life is to find out what's real. You are not a God, or a machine; you are an animal trying to survive in this place. So you need to realize that your first task is to adapt to reality. Once you recognize that, you are able to throw out all the irrelevant material and focus on that task.

---

[15] Jeffrey Zaslow and Randy Pausch, *The Last Lecture*, Hyperion Books (2008).

Life has not changed in this regard since the first human, and it never will. Humans are products of the demands of their environment and intelligence, coupled with the tensions introduced by being self-aware and compelled toward individual survival. An intelligence race of lizards, artificial intelligences or brilliant jellyfish would have the same psychology and struggles. History shows us that patterns – formed of situations, actions and consequences – repeat over and over again for the 6,000 years of recorded human existence. We can learn from the past because the same rules apply to us now.

Next it's important to know what "adapt" means. It does not mean be spineless (which many describe as "pragmatism"). It means take care of business. You may level the trees and start a farm, but you're going to have to plant seed at the right time, or no food will occur. In society, you may find yourself leaving a bad job for a better one, moving to get away from idiots, or taking action against people who are doing something illogical.

You will need to do all of the above. You know what to do by picking what you can change, and what you cannot. You cannot change the seasons; you can change what you plant, who you associate with, what you buy and how you spend your time. These seem like paltry weapons, but they are not. As you improve your circumstances, you also give yourself a voice of reason and others will emulate you because they too want to succeed.

When you have learned this lesson, you will also learn a corollary. There are two types of people you will meet in life: those who adapt to reality, and those who want reality to adapt to them. Those who adapt to reality consider their situation, make goals, and proceed systematically. Those who do not feel entitled to certain things they can demand from society, but those are never enough, and as their lives become more disorganized they become bitter.

Second Lesson: Life is a Struggle to the Top.

No matter what fond notions people pitch to you of equality, and of being fine just the way you are, life is a struggle for adaptation. Those who rise are hated by those who are too delusional (meaning: they want reality to adapt to them) to rise. Not everyone can rise and not everyone will. At some level, this rising is binary: have you reached a situation where you have what you need materially, are content and like what you're doing?

You will find that people who are not content have made themselves discontented by their own hands. The challenges of life were not fun enough or too hard, so they spent excessive time pursuing their vices – distractions, intoxication, fornication, self-deception. As a result, they never get anywhere, and have to find something on which to blame their failure. They hate government, they hate nature, they hate society and, if you are content, they hate you.

Read this carefully: they *hate* you.

If you have more than them materially, are more content within, are smarter or better looking, they will try to smash you. The dumb ones do it with violence; the slightly smarter ones do it by forming social groups with which they can mock others. They feel empowered when they say "But all of us don't see it that way!" as if this is proof. Remember, they're expecting reality to adapt to them.

Time will of course prove them wrong, and they will end up looking over a life that wasn't what they wanted and will have to face at some level that this error occurred because they did not organize themselves, adapt to reality and create what they really wanted. In some cases, self-deception prevented them from seeing what they wanted. Still others were fooled by going along with social groups based on delusion.

But in the meantime, we are all ranked by our actions. Someone disorganized but given to pursuit of excessive pleasures stands below someone who took care of business first, and then was able to have time for pleasures. We are ranked by wealth, but this becomes unimportant if you have enough to live on and like what you do for a career. We are also ranked socially, and as celebrities by the media, but it's unclear if this makes people happy.

As you ascend – in wealth, in personal organization and discipline, in abilities, in social status – you will find that anyone who did not do what you did resents you and will try to pull you down. Mostly, they do this through passive sabotage: "You can't really like that new job, you're working all the time!" and will try to lure you away with their own excessive appetites.

Underneath their friendly demeanor however is a singular goal. They resent what they cannot have, cannot face the fact that they don't have it because of their own disorganization, and they want to destroy those who have anything so they feel better about having nothing. This motivation underscores almost all human conflict.

Third Lesson: Happiness Originates Outside the Self.

Probably the most controversial part of this lecture is the idea that happiness originates outside of the self. People who are disorganized will tell you that happiness occurs when you have the right toys, intoxicants and social status; organized people will tell you that happiness consists in finding a place in life. Place consists of career, family, friends, abstract goals and community.

Career is easy: find something you like to do that is valuable to others, and you will get good at it and be rewarded.

Family is handled in a later lesson. Friends are those who want you to succeed because they are sure they will succeed as well. They are comrades and equals in the oldest sense, which means they are of the same quality of mind, body and character as you are. Friends never sabotage you. They are not there to help you do what you cannot do otherwise, but they as equals may trade back and forth information about how to live, in a playful struggle that makes you both better.

Abstract goals: this is the category for your music, writings, or technologies you develop that are not necessarily tangible. These are areas in which you compete against yourself to make something great, and you do not expect reward in your lifetime. These are gifts to all of humanity so it may learn from your experience and the wisdom you derived.

Community: You may be sick of many of the people around you. A community is made of individuals, but it is larger than any one individual. It includes the people with whom you collaborate to keep society both functioning and functional in its outlook, and the people you enjoy, and the slice of civilization that is local to you comprise your community. Community-building activities include reinforcing infrastructure, adding knowledge, helping those who are going somewhere to get there faster.

If you try to live only for yourself, you will find your goal reduced to pleasures and comforts. When these are achieved, you have nowhere to go. You become stagnant. Even more, you're isolated within yourself because others don't care and there's no lasting importance to what you're doing. If you get over your fear of being proven wrong, looking stupid or being unpopular, and act to make constructive changes in your world, you create a feedback loop between the reward of seeing your work pay off and your own self-esteem. You are no longer just an atom. You have a role, a place, and you do things that make other people you respect enjoy life more.

Fourth Lesson: Ignore Other People and Their Ideas.

Maybe I should use scare quotes and say: Ignore other people and their "ideas." Real thinkers find a need, and create a theory, test it and then publish. Hollow modern people try to find reasons to justify their actions or rationalize their failures. While real thinkers work forward in time, hollow people work backward by trying to explain why they did something in reasons entirely different from their original motivation.

Hollow modern people, who come from that group which is irresponsible and can't get itself organized so scapegoats you for its failings, have "ideas" which are this type of justification. They're not thinking forward to a goal, but defensively, as if trying to make the bad decisions they've already made valid with some fancy "logic." Often, they'll try to use "ideas" to make you feel bad about yourself, or feel you should give in to the will of others.

These people are controllers just as much as a bunch of dudes in fancy uniforms with machine guns and an iconic, enigmatic yet threatening symbol. They are bullies. Their job is to belittle you, sabotage your confidence, and make you feel as if you owe them something or should pay attention to their ideas instead of your own.

If you doubt me, compare their ideas to the vast store of information that has withstood the centuries. You'll see quickly these hollow ideas fall short. People who dislike life tend to be deconstructionists, and to embrace an altruistic philosophy to hide their destructive intent and make themselves look and sound good. The chaos resulting from deconstruction makes such unstable individuals feel that they are hidden in a crowd.

As you go through life, people are going to ask you what you're up to, and some of them will then attack with their own "ideas" to destabilize you. You might think you should carefully consider these ideas so you've got a balance of perspectives. Why do that, when all the classics of philosophy, literature, politics and economics are open to you? Instead of staying in the social reality sphere, crack a book and learn from the true masters.

Fifth Lesson: Self-Discipline and Genetics Trump all Else.

The ultimate taboo in our society is pointing out that genetics, not wishing it so, make us what we are. However, to really succeed you need more than genetics, and more than "hard work" – which is rarely hard, but people reference it because they like the idea that putting in 70 hours a week at the office makes a moron rise above a born genius. You need self-discipline. This means being organized, systematic, diligent and alert.

Reams of paper and years of human-hours have been devoted to debunking the obvious truth, which is that intelligence is congenital. You are born with a varying degree of it, and while you can refine this ability with education and diligence, you never get more than you were given. It's like artistic ability. Someone born with a gift for music can choose to take up an instrument or not, and won't succeed unless they work hard, but they'll then be ahead of those without the gift.

Wherever you are in the spectrum of abilities, you will need self-discipline and organization. From my experience, these are the primary skills that determine how effective you are. Knowing where your tools and vital information are, being prepared for the calendar ahead, being able to work on projects ahead of time because you can estimate when they should be complete – these skills are vital. Without them, even a genius is just chaos.

Sixth Lesson: Participate in the Life Cycle.

Many people do not believe they have the capacity for a happy life. They believe, on the contrary, that they are doomed. This is a pleasant psychological fiction even though it points to an unpleasant outcome; it is pleasant because it lets them off the hook. "I didn't fail at what I tried because I was disorganized, drunk, fat, sloppy, and not paying attention, I failed because I was *doomed by fate!*"

Like most human psychology of justification, this translates to a simple dogma: it's not my fault. I was wronged. I am innocent, and other people are responsible for my failings. You will find this kind of justification in every part of society where failure or misery has occurred. A good memory trick: think of an alcoholic who wants to keep drinking. What philosophy lets him not feel bad about his life, yet stay drunk? "I was wronged. Someone else did it."

These people who blame life, others, government, abstractions, symbols and feelings for their own failures will try to convince you to join them in failure. They don't say it that way, of course... they tell you that they're more enlightened, progressive, hip, wise, cool, or just friendly. Their goal is to destroy all of your natural inclinations, including your knowledge that life is finite and there are different stages to life.

Now, when most adults use the phrase "different stages to life," it is specific to them but not to younger people. Let me put it more clearly: your enemy is not death, but decrepitude. Starting in your teens, vital systems begin the process of slowing down with age. This means that with each year of life there are decreasing options available to you. So you need to plan ahead.

Even more than that, you need to go back to the First Lesson – the goal of life is to adapt to living. That includes you. So if you believe in yourself, and believe in life, you're going to want to do all the stages of life. A feast of delights of curiosity when young; a stabilizing as a young adult; a spouse and family, then extended family; finally, solitude and peaceful contemplation when old.

The hip and progressive will tell you this is nonsense and you can stay an eternal child. This is their way of sweetening what they're actually saying: come join us who cannot plan ahead in life, and don't believe in our own lives, and you failing like us will help reinforce our illusion that we're not failures. Misery loves company.

They will tell you horrible things about responsibility. How having a family is work, how you don't get to have fun, how taking a career seriously is stupid. They would rather you do something trivial, like play in another hipster rock band, than really stretch yourself in a symphony or by writing a novel. They would rather you join them in food service careers and doofus indie bands for life instead of reaching higher.

But when you look at their lives, they still always complain about work because they're always working, even if it's a hip food service gig instead of a functional career. They still have obligations. And when the youth crusade is over, and they wake up in their 40s, they have nothing to their name. No real accomplishments – teenage bands aside. No family. No career. Nothing but more hanging out with the boys, putting back a few cold ones. What kind of life is that?

Seventh Lesson: Live Clean and Honestly and You Will Not Dwell in Filth.

I will admit to hypocrisy here. I have known and loved many bong hits, and many beers. In fact, I'll tell you right now that the best high on earth is four cups of water, two cups of strong coffee, a bong hit of high-potency *cannabis indica sinsemilla* with 15% *Three Castles* tobacco, and a shot glass of whisky. But that high has little to teach past the first experience, and eventually, becomes a means of avoiding life itself.

All substances feel good, like a burst of energy from another world, but there's an insidious dark side to that: if it feels good, life without it seems empty and unfulfilling, which means that the great high causes you to end up hating life because life is both less intense than the high, and in the way of getting high. Unless, of course, you can get high again. And while you're getting high, other opportunities – mainly time – go by, and you miss out.

If you want to live well, live (mostly) clean, keep yourself and your place clean, and maintain what you own. You will not end up hating life. Your cool hip progressive friends think it's ironic and interesting to live on the edge of a ghetto in filth and experiment with heroin; this is more of their process of realizing they're going to fail life, and so inventing reasons to hate life and justify failing at it.

Dwelling in filth seems like a form of rebellion until you think it through. Foolish people will try to convince you that the problem is government, authority, or order, and the only real life consists of "fighting back" by living in squalor and pursuing stupid, empty activities. But you aren't fighting anything except your own possible happiness. You're making excuses.

Eighth Lesson: Idle Talk is Less than Even Microscopic Action.

As you go through life, you will run into many people who talk a good game. They talk a lot, and they talk as if they were important, which makes them feel important – and that's the goal, as you'll see if you stick around. They don't actually do anything effective, if anything at all. They talk. And keep talking. That lets them pretend they're important and have big ideas (see the Fourth Lesson) while making you feel less important.

Think about it this way: if their ideas were that important, they'd write them down in a book and spend all their time trying to form a political movement around them. But they are, instead, starting as if they had a political movement – it's "let's play pretend" from preschool again – and then spouting ideas so that you can see how important they are. Watch: in ten years, they'll be on to something else that makes them feel good about themselves.

The universal human disease is negativity. Low self-confidence, fear of the future and mortality, bitterness, fear of lack of control, resentment, fear of unimportance, depression, fear of one's own lack of self-control. You can make those go away for a short time by making idle talk that makes you seem like the new Martin Luther King or Lenin, new Hitler or new Buddha. People love to play pretend, but what is their goal?

The answer is a tautology: their goal is making themselves appear to have a goal so that they look wiser, sharper, braver and more altruistic than you. That means this is just more posturing and an attempt to take from you what you have created, on the credit of being assumed to be witty because they have ideas that sound like a goal! Ignore such people.

Ninth Lesson: Natural Selection is With Us Every Day.

The Darwin Awards are popular now to keep track of people who drive their sports cars into tree chippers and the like. But the real natural selection is more insidiously normal. Do you beat your kids? Do you treat your wife badly? Do you live sloppily and eat badly? All these things determine how well you survive, and how well your kids survive.

Why are kids important? You're not going to last forever. In fact, starting in your teens, there's a death curve by which each year there are fewer people your age. You can never beat it; at some point, approximately 120 years after your birth, the death curve will be complete. What lives on? Your good deeds, your ideas, maybe, but your family definitely, if you do it halfway right.

Reproducing is not the end of the process. It's the beginning. If you raise self-confident, cheerful, brave and honorable kids, but also remember to tell them the things in this first lecture, they will also have good kids and you will live on. If you rape your kids, beat them, neglect them, undermine their confidence, or forget to instruct them in the ways of life... might as well just pitch 'em in the tree chipper.

Tenth Lesson: Most People are Oblivious to Reality.

Almost every human being agrees that most other people are morons, idiots or crazy. It's more direct to say that all of us are limited in abilities, and without someone to teach us knowledge gained from experience, we cast about in chaotic and unproductive activity. When we do that for awhile, we throw in the towel and start compensating, or doing things we think make us happy because we've written off the world.

Most people are caught in the feedback loop of chaotic activity, bad results, "small rewards" like excessive pleasures, and then their own lack of self-esteem at having a chaotic, pointless life. They are not all morons; they are not all insane; however, all but a small group are acting like insane morons because they haven't had someone to show them the facts, haven't read the right books, and have thrown in the towel.

With this in mind, you can stop trying to compete with them or make them like you for doing your own version of what they're doing. They are all hungry and thirsty for a clue. The only way you can give them this clue is by living intelligently, and never looking back. That includes ignoring what 99% of your species is doing, writing off their "ideas," blowing off their worries and demands, and doing what you know is right.

They value comfort and oblivion over facts about adaptation to reality because they don't believe they can adapt. Even before they've tried, they consider the game lost, and themselves doomed, because it's easier to blame someone else than to do a little bit of hard work getting yourself organized, educated and directed at constructive activity. They would rather dis-engage and start making excuses.

As you go through life, you will be surrounded by these people. They will be doing stupid, pointless, unproductive, careless, clueless, useless and otherwise distracting activity, and will look at you blankly like you're the idiot. They're just trying to bring you down to their level. Misery loves company. If you point out that they're doing something stupid, they will turn and attack viciously because they cannot think beyond themselves, so are oblivious to consequences to others, so interpret any notice of these consequences as an unprovoked attack.

Eleventh Lesson: Beware False Altruism.

Philosophers like to argue that altruism does or does not exist. They say that we know no motivation except for ourselves. I say that real altruism is an outgrowth of self-interest, in that if we like being alive, we want the world to keep improving so we help improve the infrastructure of our community. That's a type of altruism. But there's another, false type.

Competitive altruism is when individuals vie for social status by doing nice things for those who can't do such things for themselves. Competitive altruism exclusively targets individuals or groups, but not improvement of social process, and is a race to find the most helpless victims possible to help, because the worse off they are the more like a hero you look for helping them.

We have a better word for competitive altruism: marketing. The goal isn't to help anyone. It's to be seen helping others. It's a way of promoting yourself. People compete with altruism to try to appear like the biggest Jesus Christ of them all, the nicest person, the guy you want to know because he's that cool. But if he was really that cool, he wouldn't need the publicity, right?

Since most people cannot understand cause -> effect reasoning (every effect has one cause; every cause has multiple potential effects), they do not understand that competitive altruism has a goal of marketing the altruist to others. It isn't like spending time on a neighborhood barn-raising; it's like having the news cameras ready when you give the crippled impoverished burned cursed-by-God orphans free toys and the accidentally mention your furniture business. The promotion of the furniture business was the end; the altruism, just a means, like giving free candy to kids at the store entrance.

Other people will try to use competitive altruism to appear higher in social status to you. They know they can fool a mass of the dummies we described in the Tenth Lesson. Confused, depressed, disorganized people have no way to feel better about life except through little gifts: another bong hit, some TV, maybe some porn, buying themselves junk, and so on. They love to see altruism and cry over it because it makes them feel (briefly) alive.

There is only one known defense against competitive altruism: emphasize how you have no dependency on it. "I don't need to show others I'm a good fellow, so any charity I do is private," will not fool the masses, but it gives you a good counterattack: "Why do you need to show us this?" Then casually remind the few working brains in the audience that the altruism is just marketing, and the altruist, just promoting himself or her product.

Twelfth Lesson: Live for Positive Goals.

Nihilists refer to most people as *pungis* because they resemble an ancient device of war, the pungi stake. These nasty devices are sharpened bamboo spines smeared in feces and hidden on the likely path of your adversary. If he isn't careful, he will get cut by them or impaled by them and die of a nasty infection. Either way, he's off the path for some time.

Your average person functions in the same way. They hate their job, which they're "forced" to do, and their hate their life, which is obviously someone else's fault. They want to destroy anyone with more than what they have. They also want to make themselves appear important, when they haven't done anything important. While crushing them will eventually be necessary for humanity to further evolve, in the meantime you need a positive goal.

The definition of positive goal is tricky. I can say constructive, creative, or affirmative, but really what I am saying is that you need to have something you're reaching for, instead of defining yourself by what you're against. The *pungis* I mention above know what they're against, and what they blame, but they have no idea what they'd like to see instead. You can beat them by starting first on what you'd like to see.

If you think about it logically, if you act toward what you want, it will be like the species of more successful birds that drives others out of a valley simply by having too many members for others to have any room. You want to populate the world with things that work better, ideas that are smarter, symphonies that are more intense, anything that's a goal you're reaching for instead of something you're running from.

In this you find the true meaning of life, which is that in order to love yourself, you must love your world, and want to engage with it and make things happen that you find beautiful. Many are functional – better flushing toilets, tastier grapes – but the big things in life are subtler. You want to find those things that are worth doing and push toward them aggressively, letting no way force you off the path.

From this mental process, you can see what it is to be a hero. A hero is someone who figures out what they believe, from that constructs a vision of what is right, and does it – regardless of the cost. Modern people confuse hero with "victim," like when they call people who die in plane hijackings heroes. Being a hero isn't to be a casualty. It's a state of mind and putting your life on the line for what you believe in.

At that level, you have "sacralized" life, or through a process of reverence made a religion out of living. Instead of being fixated on the negative, you have seen that destruction and creation together create life, and that in life, you have a chance to make what is beautiful – and that this alone is more important than all else. Reach toward the beautiful and never say die.

Summary

You were born into a rotten time. Just like we start young and age then die, civilizations get old and as they get old, they get obese and calcified. This comes in the form of people, thanks to specialization of labor and herd morality, cutting themselves off from an understanding of cause and effect. Instead, they stick humans in the middle between cause and effect, basically assuming each thing we do is a personal choice directed at them.

This paranoid, defensive, reactionary outlook inevitably leads to liberal politics. The person does not want anyone to tell them what to do; like a hermit crab, they want to retreat into themselves. They trust their own personality, and other personalities they can control, but to their blind eyes nature is random and pointless and they hate it, especially that "personal mortality" part.

In the name of that fear they run away from reality and make a real mess of things. They tell each other delusional ideas, and force others to agree with them, making all of humanity a big circular logic argument for human solipsism. Social status and exchange of witty comments based on public entertainment replaces any kind of knowledge of reality. Much as the individual goes into his or her self, humanity has receded into itself.

You can end the retreat in yourself. Don't deny your mortality and end up throwing reality out with it; embrace both. You know you die, so make life count. This will help you discover how life is beautiful and important, and escape the negativity and depression that underlies modern society. Instead of trying to palliatively treat pain and suffering, ignore them so you can surge forward to the beautiful and powerful.

Because you have occurred in this time, you are surrounded since day one by toxic lies. People don't even mean to tell them to you; they were half-truths that sounded more right than the really crazy stuff, but they're designed for adults to use to justify their participation in a broken society. To young people, they are baffling paradoxes and a justification of illusion as more important than reality itself.

Despite all of this, there is no need to despair. Actually, you should be cheering: all of this chaos is slowly filtering out the clueless and the deceptive by forcing smart people to separate themselves from the herd. If you educate yourself, starting with this document, you will be able to view life again through cause/effect logic and so free yourself from the crowd "thinking," and so be able to rebirth society after the decay.

July 2, 2009

NIGHTMUSIC

Listen to the night, the next time you're up when others are asleep. Everyone has gone to a grateful slumber after whatever they believed would fill their days. Cars go by as others rush to amusement, but the traffic is slower than in daytime, and therefore it is fitful, spurts of lost souls racing over the concrete desert in search of – something: who cares. It is now you alone with the night, with the emptiness, with the lack of certainty, and with that, your future death.

When you are young, of course, it is less present on your consciousness. I'll die, some distant day, you think. Or maybe beneath the level of consciousness that puts things into words you don't believe it will happen to you. That's what goes on with old people, you think, and I'm not *old* – I have no signs of aging. Perhaps this is why young people like John Keats, afflicted with the certainty of fatal tuberculosis, or those who go bald or grey prematurely, have a wisdom that others do not: they've already seen the death curve and know their time is marked and running out. Slowly, however.

This is not to believe in the fear of death, but to remember to tell death off via the only means you have of understanding it: recognizing its certainty, and since there is no way of stopping it, finding something to make life worthwhile. To recognize death is to praise life. To feel the emptiness of the night and its lawlessness stir your soul is to accept what you want in the daytime, or that you might have the same things in the face of night: after all, *you* are the captain of this ship you call your life, and being a good nihilist, you recognize that your life won't mean anything to anyone but you. If you get famous, they remember a name, but they will not know your consciousness. They may remember your art or deeds, but how much of that is you? No: you pass on to dust, as does all knowledge of you. The consciousness that is you literally disappears, or ceases to be.

184

These morbid meditations will free you, however, in the only sense of the word "free" that is meaningful. You will not gain some absolute freedom, or immortality, as in pop culture spiritualist fairy tales, but you will "free" yourself from the mental hell that comes with illusion and denial. Want to beat death? There is only one way: accept death by realizing how much death is needed for life to have meaning. Eternal life... what would you do? You would follow pleasures, or maybe learned pursuits, but either way, your life would have no shape, no form. It would be a series of days. There would be no sweetness in a young love affair, or a family, since that could happen at any time. You'd have innumerable affairs, do uncountable things, and at some point, would face your boredom and find some excuse to die. *I didn't notice it was loaded, honest!*

It's the temporal nature of life, in part, that makes it sweet. Your time is unique. The choices you make in spending it are delicious. There is a world of conquest in saying "I will do this, but not that." When you make such divisions, you are lord of your own world, in a way that places everything else secondary to you. There is no certainty, but you make a decision anyway; you are telling the world that for your own purposes, you are better informed than they are. And you will not make every decision correctly, but that makes the winning ones far more treasured than a random win, as in a lottery, could ever be. Everything that you have in a metaphysical sense will be things you have built for yourself. Can one imagine a greater poetry than this? The infinite void spans dimensions we cannot even visualize, and yet, somewhere in the midst of it, there is a center of warmth and light that is one's own personality, one's will, one's choices and joys.

We fail to understand the universe because we approach it from a linear, rational aspect.

X +/- Y = some tangible result.

What if the universe operated *emotionally* instead? Its goal is not to churn raw materials into product, and to call it "progress" and congratulate itself on being enlightened – its goal is experience, and the feelings that motivate a desire for the same. It has a need to discover things in particularized detail, and eschews universal results where the precepts equal the conclusions; it is more like a general set of equations used to begin problem solving, than a hard over-arching answer like dogma. Why else would life exist? Surely not from some chemical necessity. More likely, there is a consciousness to (but not outside of and controlling) the universe, a unifying principle in the cosmos, and it loves the poetry. It delighted in the sensual contrast of the big bang, between a void so profound it extended to a lack of matter, and then the sudden impulse, the orgasm of exploding data becoming for the first time (this iteration) *somethingness*. There was that moment of shock where nothingness realized its lack of something, and that very realization created a somethingness, since to know that something can exist is to have made something out of that very thought.

When we look at this poetic universe, we understand the beginnings of Germanic idealism as philosophy. Life is this giant gift that kisses us with its shock of discovery, like a love affair in the teenage years a balance between good and terrible, the goods being so amazing that we cannot describe them, and the lows so profound that our souls shudder and tear at the thought. The contrast is like freefalling in infinite space, or even the lack of space; much as on a painting the brightness of colors is defined by the difference between all colors in contrast, instead of an absolute, in our lives experience is defined not by some absolute ("good," "best value," "evil") but by the stream of experience and the differences between its parts. Meaning "is" not; meaning occurs in our minds as a response to what we have known, and we must know something before its opposite has sense. Without pain, pleasure would be a mediocre sensation.

Our world works like our thoughts. Our thoughts are a product of the world. Without our world, our thoughts would have no context or meaning. Without our thoughts, our world would go unnoticed and thus all of our days would have the same impact upon us, leading to a mundane sort of boredom which, if we look at it critically, would be as much of a hell as a heaven where nothing could go wrong and therefore we would exist in a state of perfect tedium in stasis, forever and ever, amen. These permanent beingnesses would bore us to tears, and thankfully, they do not exist – it is instead our poetic one and only life that grasps us, and gives us meaning between the dark and the light, such that we have a situation forced upon us in which we either make meaning or drown from the lack of it. Even if an afterlife exists, we can never come back here, much like we can never return to the same moment in time, with its context making the experience meaningful in a unique way. Can you feel its beauty?

Now, it makes no sense to wax spacy about all of this. Idealism is well and good, but it has two components. The first is that both reality and thought have a common ancestor or thread, and the corollary to that says that if we wish our thoughts to become known, we have to carve them out in what we know as physical reality. Your thoughts are profound? Make them so: the world is thought, but thought is of the world, so you must create it by action. "Action" does not necessarily imply the typical idiocy advocated by the Internet people – not just people using the Internet, but people who thrive on the virtuality of the experience, "the Internet people" in the parlance of this age – of the form of demonstrations, or terrorist acts, or pointless attempts to call attention to ourselves with a narrow guise of ideology as camouflage. Action can mean planting a garden, or starting a war, or writing a book, or cutting a CD, but it only applies when this virus or creation is successful and perpetuates itself. Another bedroom CD-R of music "that matters to me, even if no one else wants it" – who cares? If you really felt that way, you would have hummed it to yourself; instead, your excuses are all too visible as the product of a lack of confidence and a fear of rejection. If you make music, thrust it into the world, such that the world changes from its touch. That alone is action.

Our deeds are thoughts, insofar as for the world to think, the ideas must leave the individual and be communicated through space and time and other beings in order to become manifest, to become incarnate, to become corporeal. And what greater way to increase the poetry of existence? To die with a pure thought of realistic poetry on one's lips, even if dying in defeat, is to be achieve a metaphysical victory beyond the bounds of those who never tried; it is greater to die having achieved victory over our fear of striving for victory, and knowing that one's idea and contribution is spreading like wildfire across the dry surface of earth. The idea is greater than the life, as the life is a product of the idea – that concept should perhaps be allowed to ferment in the partial form whereby herewith it is expressed. Life is poetry, and poetry is ideas in contrast with nothingness, a perpetual restatement of the process that brought us somethingness in the first place. The big bang? Or the big *Eureka!*

When you have accomplished the thoughts necessary to digest the above, come back down to earth: nihilism alone is real. Nihilism is the process of removing illusion and staring straight into the world as it is. You cannot will it to be your personal reality; the world is "objective" in that it is consistent regardless of your desires for it. "The world is my representation"[16] does not mean "the world is as I desire it," only that world is known through our thoughts of it. And our thoughts can be misinformed, or inaccurate. The smaller the degree of inaccuracy, the greater our success in manifesting our ideas. Sound familiar? It is similar to the scientific method, but where that is linear, this formulation remains open-ended, because life as we experience it is far from linear. Nihilism is a removal of all human artifacts from thinking. It reduces belief to perception, social pressures to observation, and emotion to assessment.

How can the world be both ideas and physicality, outside of the grim fact that ideas (the product of a electrochemical reaction called a brain) are part of physical reality? One example is biology. We are genetics, but our thoughts influence genetics. If we choose to attempt greater acts, we have a higher chance of losing our lives, but if we succeed, greater influence and wider breeding. If our thoughts lead to higher actions, we play higher stakes, and if our thoughts are disciplined, we might win out. In this way thoughts become not only actions but a genetic heritage by which one's offspring are more likely to behave in similar ways. The crowd would like to believe that at least – at least – 80% of our actions are not determined by genetics, but that's the usual wishful thinking for an equality to obliterate the differences in ability and appearance between us.

---

[16] Cf. Schopenhauer, *The Fourfold Root.*

Life ain't fair, but fair would give it no room to evolve. Intelligent people accept that. Creeping, craven, lying, cognitive dissonance cases and parasites cannot, so they snap back with what they think are convincing arguments. Of course, since most of humanity is brick stupid when it comes to structural argument, most people accept these ideas. However, that in itself is proof of the genetic argument: most people are undifferentiated fools because their ancestors have had little clarity or consistency to their breeding, and thus, are the ones nodding their heads sagely when such foolish lies are presented. Genetics is not "fair" when you compare it on the level of the individual, but it's much better than fair when one looks at history over time. Those who may not have been given the most comfortable place to live or easiest path can advance by making intelligent, disciplined decisions, and this equalizes the natural disparity between someone living in a jungle (easy food, warm) and someone living in an icy forest (hard to find food, freezing). In this light, genetics is not only fair, but it's an ingenious form of long-term RAM:[17] if people's genetics encode decision trees, it enables evolution to over time produce individuals with highly abstracted decision-making skills. DNA reflects design, which is an abstraction, but it is encoded in a firm and tangible method. Thoughts form reality; thoughts form reactions which through natural selection, eventually form this code – closer to thought than anything else – which forms reality.

In the same light, we can look at culture and history and see how these are similar methods of encoding thought into physicality. Culture reflects the shared values of a population as established over many generations. Those within a culture succumb to evolution according to its design. Those who naturally live well within that values system, and find it to help their lives, will breed more than those who do not (at least in healthy times, unlike the present, where any idiot who gets a job can breed as much as he is able to tolerate filling out welfare forms). Values systems come into conflict

[17] Random Access Memory, "computer memory available to the user for creating, loading, or running programs and for the temporary storage and manipulation of data, in which time of access to each item is independent of the storage sequence." Merriam-Webster.

throughout history, and while at first it seems that popularity – lower taxes here, laxer laws about drugs, more whores – will predominate much as climate influences genetics itself, what ultimately determines the difference between a "great" civilization and a merely serviceable one is value systems. Great civilizations push themselves, and push their citizens to act not just for the collective but for an abstract ideal which is more universal than the problems in which it will be applied. These civilizations develop more thoroughly and thus, while they're always susceptible to being outnumbered and slaughtered, when it comes to achievement and leadership they dominate. Thoughts become value systems become culture, which is then used to shape genetics, and thus exists as a physical pattern alongside another physical pattern, which is the course of history, in which those with more stringent value systems rise above others. Thoughts compete in a form of evolution like that we encounter in reality. They are then transferred into pattern design – the migration of informational structures between thought, energy and matter – which influences reality, and eventually, becomes part of it.

The third form in which it is imperative to study thoughts becoming reality is intellect itself. Our thoughts do not occur in a vacuum, but are built upon other thoughts. In order to reach this state, through time we approach any question or problem by attacking its biggest questions first, and drawing conclusions from them, then building conclusions onto those conclusions until we finally have a tower of logical relations. Since we manage not a few thousand details but millions, when one considers the actual likely number of factors in any multilayered contemplation, it soon becomes necessary to re-assess one's entire concept of the world according to this pyramid of related ideas. In that impulse, these ideas switch from being observations to being valuations, and at that point, the pyramid reflects a method of assessing and analyzing reality as whole; by the very nature of our minds, in which methods of analysis occur before the subject being analyzed, it is thus that thoughts about something become more real than the thing itself, since our perceptions, after all, are only thoughts themselves. Our active thoughts become our assumptions, which then become the mental image of the world (how one knows, without direct experiment, how to predict the response of reality toward any given action). We act upon this image, and thus our thoughts become reality.

If thoughts dictate reality, and reality represents thoughts, then clarity of thinking is of the ultimate importance (hence some of us being zenlike nihilists). This leads us to the question of why most of our species is in complete denial of both reality and the need for organized, logical thought. This returns to us *the* human question which adaptation to our environment, which unlike other species is more of civilization than natural forces, after the advent of technology. We have such blazingly precise minds; what went wrong?

To my mind, what has happened with humanity is no different than what happens to an untended garden: weeds crop up, order is lost, and thus there's no efficient breeding. Unlike a forest, it was never good for this kind of order, therefore is a mess. If the land is forest, it is okay. If it is garden, it is okay. In a state in-between, there is nothing but breakdown. Such is the occurrence of humanity now. All of its problems relate back to a lack of order. We are ruled by the crowd, and through their need for competition, consumerism, and thus our values decay. But what caused this crowd rule? A lack of agreement on leadership and, simply put, the weeds outnumbering the gardeners. That is also why "nothing has been done" about persistent problems in human civilization. If two people out of a thousand can understand the problem, they face 998 people they either have to manipulate, murder or drug before they can make any positive change. The six thousand people who can figure it out in the USA, for example, have no desire to take on a losing battle. They're going to live the good life if they can, and get ready to abandon the rest of these morons the instant the Chinese attack or third-world conditions break out.

They hate those morons because morons enforce upon us a collective version of reality, based in artificial anthropocentric values and perceptions, as only that makes them feel temporarily immune to death and to the inequality of nature. When the immunity wears off, the morons feel the soft touch of the abyss and fight it back with more nonsense, which means that no one is ever free from moronism. We call these morons Undermen, for their inability to grasp reality, and the philosophy by which through utilitarianism their beliefs predominate, Crowdism.

People love the artificial human reality because it is equalizing and it is safe. No reason for complicated thinking or doubt; it eliminates ambiguity and makes mortal questions (real reality) secondary to our shared worldview and values system. God, money, products, dogma: these are tangible and yet universal, as we see them. They are safer than death. The Crowdist is one who is unstable without this ambiguity crusher, thus one who is dependent on the Crowd for a vision of reality. This is the source of Underman philosophy: a fear of the real world, and therefore, a retreat into a world of what we all agree are comfortable, easily digestible, non-threatening "truths." The more radically reality threatens to intervene, the more extreme the Crowd becomes about imposing this "truth" upon its world; it is classic cognitive dissonance at work. Ambiguity is the dark side of the infinite, and the Underman values fear more than ambition, and therefore would suppress the Infinite so that the Safe can prevail.

These Undermen form a vicious little community which is, in fact, the majority, because it appeals to those with no skillsets beyond the immediate. Undermen can be rich or poor; undermanness is determined by spiritual attitudes. They can often be found referring to movies as if they're something important you should know about, or talking knowingly about different restaurants and amusements in town. They feel that participation in an event like a rock concert or election imparts to each of them the power of the event, when the converse is true. They'll discuss ideas they consider important and imply you should, too. Their single weapon: "the rest of us know this," and it's not that they make it as a promise, more of a passing reference which you are expected to obey or, in passive-aggressive logic, be considered an attacker. Guilt. Passivity. Parasitism. Conformity. "Authority." Commerce. Bureaucracy. These are all weapons of the Undermen, as they are weapons which are not even considered by those of leadership capacity; leaders are too busy trying to change reality to use a fake reality to manipulate people radically dumber than themselves. Undermen, however, need a place to hide.

192

There is no doctrine to which you can run to escape Undermen, nor any doctrine which encompasses Undermandom. Most Christians are Undermen, but many are also not; it depends on how you interpret Christianity. If you're an Underman, you'll interpret *any belief system* as Underman dogma, where a healthy person will view it from the standpoint of healthy person dogma, and thus see it as a subset of that outlook. Some things are clearly tools of Undermen – democracy – but this does not mean their creation was designed to empower Undermen. It was probably a benevolent gesture which was blind to the depravity of most people, something which arises from their fundamental ability to make long-term decisions. The only doctrine which explains Undermen is the psychology of Undermen itself. Where the rest of us explore the idea that thoughts influence physical reality, Undermen look for a "safe" form of this and translate it into the idea that socially-acceptable fantasies are equal to reality. That is illusion, and as illusion always leads to failure, a diseased mental state. Next time you look up at the night sky, and reflect on the poetry of life, resolve to pursue the healthy mental state of realism – even with all of its horrors and beauties, the contrast forming poetry – instead of succumbing to the brain-numbing, soul-killing, logic-ablating virus of Underman dogma.

October 23, 2005

THE ETERNAL CIRCLE

People in modern times are conditioned by buying products. First, you invest nothing in the product but your money; you are not required to thrust forth energy into understanding it or comprehending its context. You need a vacuum cleaner – locate; buy; read instructions. Second, they are accustomed to selecting from interchangeable philosophies. A vacuum cleaner does not demand that you re-interpret your other philosophies of cleansing, or that you find a broader framework of understanding why to clear. You match problem (dirty carpet) to solution (cleaning machine) and plunk down the credit card, ready to go.

For this reason, when people schooled in a modern way of life attempt to approach philosophy, they almost always make a mess of it by falling into a kneejerk pattern of trying to match "issues" to solutions that are disconnected from a systemic approach and therefore, as philosophy, fail. In fact, most of what people would call "philosophy" is a grab-bag of caveats, self-conceptions and homilies; there is nothing that unites metaphysics and epistemology and ethics within it, for example. It is this type of person who approaches the writings here and, not wanting to admit the logical connections are lost to them, declares them to be "ranting" or "incoherent" or that old standby of the embittered, "it's just a bunch of big words to make you seem smart." Crowdism, indeed.

However, if one is willing to not read between the lines, but look at these philosophies as logical tools much in the same way different pieces of software make up an operating system, it reveals the function behind what otherwise seem as rootless pronouncements coming out of the void. In this article, we look at four major components of the beliefs expressed here, and illustrate how they are connected and thus what implications for the whole can be drawn from their presence.

Idealism

The initial confusion here is that idealism in the populist vernacular means any kind of belief in a progressive or utopian sense, and when we speak of "idealism" we generally refer to someone who screws up reality for some starry-eyed optimal ideal. In the philosophical sense, "idealism" means a belief system in which the cosmic order is composed of, or acts as if it is composed of, thoughts. A good working definition:

> The philosophical doctrine that reality is somehow mind-correlative or mind-coordinated – that the real objects constituting the 'external world' are not independent of cognizing minds, but exist only as in some way correlative to mental operations.[18]

There are two components to this belief. First, we understand the world only through the process of thought. Second, the world acts much as our thoughts do, and because all of our actions thus affect the design of the external world, our actions are like thoughts: a series of reasonings which are by process of elimination filtered into an answer. This answer is the working hypothesis upon which the next level of thought is built.

Idealism is important because it navigates a path between materialism (belief only in material value) and symbolic-literal thinking, in which individual thoughts are more important than reality. Idealism joins human thought and the working of the world by pointing out they have a common mechanism, and thus a common end. It is not dualistic, nor is it solipsistic; idealism is like a highest-level abstraction that explains the motivations of both humankind in world in evolving the design of their thoughts to greater levels of discipline, clarity, and interconnectedness.

Realism

In other words, for the world to think, it is required that we act; our actions, by changing reality, change whatever thoughts correlate to

---

[18] Nicholas Rescher, "Idealism," *Cambridge Dictionary of Philosophy*, Second Edition, Cambridge University Press (1995).

or cause changes in our physical environment. In this sense, much like an inventor with a blowtorch, our actions are the process of designing or redesigning our world, and the reason we act is to achieve change in the design of external reality, or an abstraction of its function. The design may actually exist, like DNA does, or it may merely be our method of understanding how the world can be predicted through consistent tendencies inherent to its operation (frequently called "natural laws"). By altering reality through our actions, we alter the design of our world and if we do so in accordance with natural laws, enhance its function or our position within it.

What is essential for perceiving this design and its changes is a sense of "realism," or a taking of changes in our physical world to be the totally of existence. This separates our thoughts and feelings from our recognition of changes in our external world, and allows us to point clearly at something known as "reality," even if we later interpret it as a process of thought which we change with our deliberate actions. Since this later interpretation will be exacting, and will require us to perceive patterns in our world and then anticipate them with our actions, we call this belief in the primacy and consistency of the external world "realism."

Nihilism

If we are to act on our world and change its design, we must do so with a clear understanding of how it works, and not act on thoughts which are solely confined to our internal design, and are not shared by the external. This requires that we clear our minds of illusion and tighten the correspondence between our perception of events and the actuality of what occurs, so that we might predict as exactly as possible our actions to manipulate our world. Nihilism is the process of clearing away all belief and preconception from the process of perception, so that we see simply *what is* and do not encumber ourselves with illusion, or emotionalism, or other pitfalls of consciousness.

Nihilism is controversial for many as they confuse it with an utter lack of belief in anything, or in the effectiveness of anything. This highlights the difference between a belief that colors interpretation, and a *belief in value*, in that values beliefs do not affect how we see the world but they influence the choices we make as to how we change it. A nihilist may hold deeply-felt beliefs, but will cease to be a nihilist the minute he or she allows these beliefs to intrude upon a realistic perception of the cosmic order. Values are not to be used to interpret the world, but are something that we act upon it so that in the changing of its design we bring them closer to manifestation.

Integralism

These philosophies imply a framework that embraces all of them. Nihilism allows for perception of reality, and realism means that we accurate see its design, while translating that into a thought process of the cosmos through idealism. All of this so far has been operational, in that it describes the workings of the world and our means of interpretative it; none of it has been prescriptive, or instructive of a values system which suggests what we should do with this system. To address this need we have integralism.

Integralism posits a unity of human and external events and thoughts. From comparison of our own intentions to the operations of this cosmic order, we determine how well-adapted our ideals are. This allows us to understand what a higher value might be: a more elegant, greater adaptation which increases the quality of our lives in harmony with the order of the cosmos. It is the achievement of these higher values that is the core belief of integralism, and its prescriptive goal as passed on to any adherents: discover your world, get a clear picture of its design, and work to complement that design, as the same language which describes external design also describes internal adaptation, e.g. the beauty found in thoughts and imagination.

Continuity

William Blake once said that "If the doors of perception were cleansed everything would appear to man as it is, infinite."[19] When

---

[19] William Blake, "The Marriage of Heaven and Hell" (1793).

we unite our imaginations to the process of the universe, as is found in the belief system of idealism, we have opened up that continuity and are now closer to accepting our mortality as part of that larger plan. In this we have found perhaps the one bliss that exists for thinking creatures, and we have done it by entangling ourselves with that which we fear most (nothingness) and finding a sense of order not within it but that includes it. It is this inclusion that forms the basis for our belief in turn in continuity, as we see that all dark things lead to light, and vice versa.

Philosophy does not succumb well to a product-oriented outlook. It is something that does not mix and match well. Regardless of the point of entry chosen, the beliefs of the individual must eventually resolve into a comprehensive worldview, or be seen for what they are: scattered borrowings with no unity. While this makes it difficult to initially comprehend the worldview espoused in these writings, it makes it far easier, once one has accepted its genesis in ideas, to explore its breath and find from it an explanation of and response to our world.

September 19, 2005

VOODOO DOLL

When I was young, I rapidly learned to hate conservatives. They were bloated people of rigid minds who devoted their lives to earning money and owning things, and they had a little list of what was OK and they lashed out against anything that was not visibly on it. In fact, what bothered me the most was their categorical mindset. They had no flexibility of thought. You either taught Creationism, or you were a devil; never mind that evolution could be proof of the infinite genius of their God. You were either married, or a slut; you were either Christian, or a heathen. Not to imply that they should have seen middle ground – after all, that is in itself a complete fabrication in matters of ideals – but that they did not see the whole of the order of the universe. They had an invariant, one-size-fits-all outlook that was convenient for condemning others. It was like a sick little clubhouse.

Fast forward some years. I've now learned to apply the same standard to liberals. They are not bad people, as conservatives aren't bad people, but like your average mass-culture conservative, the average mass-culture liberal is terminally misinformed. Even worse, they are motivated by emotion and not holistic thought, and their responses are as kneejerk as those of the conservatives. Either a certain belief is on their whitelist of accepted ideas, or they lash out against it. They cannot see how traditional lifestyles fulfil much of the liberal dream: local communities, ruled by leaders selected for wisdom and not popularity with the crowd, and a furtherance of culture, justice, knowledge and art. In fact, liberals are willing more than anything else to destroy, even destroy all hope, so long as their one precious hot-button issue is preserved: revenge against those who have more than others through equalization and subsidization of the less-capable. They want to even out humanity into a race of clones so that none are above others.

This leaves me even more of a misfit than before, and unlike those who see politics as their personal identity (most people from New York or London), I don't want a political identity, least of all as a misfit. I am not concerned with the label of ideas, but the ideas themselves, and more importantly, the structure of belief systems into which these ideas fit. There is no place for such thinking except in philosophy, and it like all other aspects of Western culture, is steadily being absorbed by those who have the disease liberals and conservatives have in common: rigid categorical thinking, based mostly in a desire to justify their own lifestyles and empower their own self-image, e.g. "I am right for thinking this, and everyone else is wrong, so whatever I want to do to them is justified."

I have more in common with the average people of the West than most politicians in that I seek not power, not identity, but a practical lifestyle. Those of us with enough experience and mental focus to think through the questions of life have long known that the flashy lifestyles of the city and entertainment culture are meaningless; what matters in life are the intangibles, like friends, family and personal experience, especially in achieving triumph over that which we fear and through that, ascendancy to a higher state of mind. They used to call this transcendent thought, and all the writers and thinkers I've ever loved have idealized this state of mind. Interestingly, so did the knights of medieval Europe as well as the Zen monks of ancient Asia.

When we think in practical terms, it no longer makes sense to passively look for a side to join and hope that They will figure it all out through some mechanistic process. Wouldn't it be nice if life came down to selecting one of two choices, and everything got basically peachy after that? Root for your team, and all of you are good guys, and boo on the other team, who must all be bad guys. Reality is more complicated: both right and left are rotted like a gangrenous limb, and there is nothing we can do to redeem ourselves by blindly supporting them. The only path is to pick the values we find meaningful, to envision a better society, and to support that through any and all agencies that make themselves compatible to its aims. With this in mind, it's hard to want to be a conservative, or a liberal.

Brent Scowcroft, national security adviser to Ronald Reagan, recently took aim at the war in Iraq. "We ought to make it our duty to help make the world friendlier for the growth of liberal regimes," he said.[20] What he's referring to is the same thing Francis Fukuyama referenced in his book *The End of History and the Last Man*, in which he suggests that the final state of human history is one of liberal democracy, human and civil rights, and free economic enterprise and personal economic competition for all. Fukuyama and Scowcroft (and Bush and Reagan and Clinton and Carter) repeat basically the same doctrine: we have found a Utopian "progressive" design, and that is the society driven by equality of individuals and their competition in open markets, open social situations, and other linear challenges. Like the conservative Christian moralists, they see one way to redemption, and anything not on that holy ordained list is "bad" or "evil" and must be crushed. This is the crux of modern Western thought, which combines the idealism of the past with a focus on the individual and material comfort derived from Judaism, coming up with a belief system that is anything but holistic. When we're feeling nice, we call it "anthropocentric." When we're not, we say it's a kingdom of individual pretense that has no leadership, but is a circle of sheep chasing each other in an attempt to manipulate popularity for personal profit.

History tells us that this revolution has been ongoing for two thousand years in the West, and that identical breakdowns have happened in every great society, most notably that of the ancient Athenians, who collapsed shortly after discovering populist democracy and international trade. The individual – all individuals – became kings, and thus, there was no consensus, and shortly, the mechanisms of society broke down and the weakened civilization degraded itself to the point where it was quick work for foreign conquerors to destroy it. This revolution has gained momentum since World War II, when superpowers competed on the basis of which was morally more"progressive" than the other, and conservatism comprises one half of its pincer attack. Like a wrestling match, the outcome is fixed, and the "competitors" bought, but they make

---

[20] Jeffrey Goldberg, "Breaking Ranks," *The New Yorker*, October 31, 2005.

a good show of it because, win or lose, they'll take home a ton of money from keeping the proles distracted, entertained and amused.

Now we get into difficult territory: liberals allege that recent conservative electoral wins (George W. Bush) have made some kind of vast difference. They haven't. Bush and Clinton are brothers in advancing the agenda of worldwide liberalism, even if George W. Bush cloaks his agenda behind mumblings to the evangelicals and traditionalists, and Clinton hides his own impetus behind platitudes to civil rights and "freedoms." They're the same animal in different skins because they've been produced by the same system and the same assumptions which are necessary for personal success, and therefore are not independent thinkers/leaders but those who fulfil a role. Their job is to make money for themselves and their allies, and whatever window-dressing they use to obscure their actual intention is fine, as long as it is popular. As a consequence, they've neatly paralyzed the electorate by dividing it into two camps who form personal identities based on their political orientation, and forget the underlying values and lapse in keeping their leaders accountable for upholding those values. (It's redundant to point out that populist democracy, which hands the vote to any unqualified person over a certain age, is destined mathematically to failure by the inability of that group to make decisions of the complexity required. It's for this reason that history shows that every populist democracy ever created has rapidly collapsed into selfishness, infighting, bickering, theft, graft and deception, then been conquered by more literal minded – did I say Asiatics like the Mongols, Persians, Russians and Chinese? – neighbors).

How could such a system take place – is it a vast conspiracy? I'll say, firmly, it is not. People can collaborate unconsciously if they work toward the same ends, or uphold the same basic outlook. For example, there was no conspiracy to build housing, yet every early human group figured out how to do it. There is similarly, no conspiracy here; what we are seeing is an emotional reaction that is inherent to any human group, and its triumph over the past two millennia has been a product more of its simplistic, lowest common denominator message – and swelling numbers of people who can live well within civilization, but lack the discipline to survive in the wild, a product of civilization's strength in increasing ease of access to food, shelter, medicine, and "learning" – than any grand plan. In fact, we could call it the "anti-plan." Instead of providing an ideology for the future, or a holistic vision of how we could live better, its impetus is a gesture as old as humanity: dividing up the spoils in such a way that every member of the crowd is satisfied. It is pacification.

The disorganized, anti-plan, anti-conspiracy movement has triumphed through something I call the voodoo doll approach. When you are faced with an enemy that unifies its constituents through a belief system, there is one way to take it down that works every time. You build a replica of that belief system, but you change a few things so that like a Trojan horse it slips into the population and like a virus, begins infecting others with the changed outlook. It may take centuries, but gradually it will gain power, because most people cannot tell the difference between it and the real belief that enabled the society to prosper. Even better, sweeten it a bit and appeal to cognitive dissonance – tell people that they've been wronged, and they deserve something for nothing, and they will rapidly fall in line behind the new belief. One can only imagine that cancers in the human body act the same way, appearing to be normal cells but having an agenda of reckless growth (the "anti-plan") which is not discovered until too late. Yet no one calls cancer a conspiracy.

Conservatism is the voodoo doll that emulates traditional beliefs, but sells them out at its core. It is not radically different except that its philosophy incorporates a different scope, and thus creates a changed motive in those who uphold it. Where traditional societies were idealistic and holistic, meaning that people did what was right by the whole of the society and its environment, instead of trying to do right by the individual, modern societies are individualistic: their goal is to gain wealth and political equality for the individual above all else, including all holistic concerns. The individual does what benefits him or her, and lets someone else worry about the consequences. Conveniently, no one is worrying about the consequences – where's the personal profit in that? – which makes it a perfect system for those who wish to accumulate wealth, especially through means that while not illegal are, in a holistic sense, unethical. I include pornographers, politicians and sellers of plastic garbage alike in that indictment.

Where tradition proposed a complete design of civilization, conservatism is a rider to the general agenda of mass empowerment that is the revolution described above that has been consuming the west for two thousand years (the West has died hard; it has taken a long time for this concept to have any momentum; luckily for those who push it, they have no other options, and thus will attempt it perpetually). Conservatism says, yes, let's go forward with the liberal society, but let's make our personal list of what is approved include only things that sound like traditional values. But, of course, in a society of mass revolt, the list needs to be something even an idiot can understand. So it is dumbed down, and then made even dumber, until it reaches the point of being a list of categorical knee-jerk responses. At this point, it makes perfect fodder for the wrestling match of politics, in that its categorical responses are blind to reality, and therefore it constantly fails and gives its twin, liberalism, a chance to get in a few shots. The "voters" – a term that implies that they make actual choices when casting votes – are bewildered and baffled, and thus become increasingly Balkanized, clinging to political symbols and emotions with which they can identify. (It's only fair to mention again that populist democracy casts the responsibility of rule on those who are inherently unable to do it; while they are fine people in everyday life, and it is not a character defect of theirs, they are as out of luck as a car mechanic attempting to perform brain surgery. It's an entirely different task from everyday life to lead a nation, or to pick a belief and political system which benefits it holistically. Thus the voters do not even attempt it, and vote selfishly, casting their society into an early grave through the resulting internal division, graft, etc. that this engenders.).

The Neoconservatives have formalized this membership. Conservatism is liberalism. Like mint iced tea, it's still liberalism, just flavored with a sprig of token traditional values. If you don't believe this, ask what conservatism has done for traditional values lately. Abortion? Banning abortion has not stopped the problem of desperate people, trashy casual sex, and thus unwanted babies. Drugs? People are miserable and bored and find their lives pointless, thus take drugs excessively. Conservatism hasn't addressed that issue at all. What about crime? Depending on which way the wind blows, the statistics claim it's up or down, but that does not change the base reality that it's out of control and impacts our lives negatively. What about corporate power? A decline in culture? Lack of shared cultural values? Conservatism has failed on all of these issues, and always will, because conservatism does not take the stance necessary to control these issues: we need some form of society other than the mass individualized kleptocracy of liberal democracy.

Consider another issue: women. We are divided, permanently and inextricably, between feminists and conservatives. Feminists want women and men to share a role in equality, have abortions and lifestyle flexibility, and generally, to treat each other like commercial products in a jockeying for power. Conservatives lash out with a doctrine that translates similarly into ownership of women, but this time, in theory, women are given to men, who must then serve them and their corporate overlords alike in tedious, conservative jobs. It's clear that feminism is deleterious to women, in that in the name of avoiding a minority of marriages that were abusive and unhappy, it has converted women into a zombie army of faceless single dropouts in their 30s and 40s, burned out sexually and emotionally and romantically by a series of failed relationships in which both parties fought to keep power and, in the grand tradition of crowds, shouted each other down and obliterated any possible direction. Feminism is crowd revenge – equality – for women. It's not really any different than "White Supremacy," which supposes that if one is mostly white one is entitled to rule over the other races of earth, except that it addresses only women.

Feminism has destroyed what made women unique, and what gave ancient cultures the ability to see them as having a unique and invaluable role, and has made them more grist for the mill of commerce, throwing them into careers like men and thus keeping both sexes in competition. Who benefits? Those who use them for labor, of course. Did women benefit? There are all these rules about equality now, and a literal smorgasbord of rhetoric, but in the end, what has happened now is that most of them are ending up in unhappy relationships and the graces of femininity and its unique place in the universe are destroyed. Once again, the crowd clamors for equality and thus destroys quality, dragging us all down to the lowest common denominator. But when the choice is seemingly between blockhead conservative ownership, and blockhead liberal ownership, are women given much of a choice? Not bloody likely.

Tradition saw no one-size-fits-all role for anyone. Women were not equal to men, but men were not equal to men; each person was seen as having unique strengths and weaknesses, and thus a permanent position in a social hierarchy. There was not economic competition, but this meant that people worked less and spent more time developing themselves. There were unhappy marriages and abusive husbands, but those were in the minority (and, amusingly, they still exist, showing us the complete failure of liberal feminist rhetoric). Women had a role which was granted to them by nature and which could never conform to the demands of ownership. It was not a function; it was not based on external traits alone; it did not assign them a linear value through "competition." It granted them something that has been so wholly taken away few now would even recognize it.

In the traditional worldview, one must look at the world as whole. All of us, and all of the elements of our environment, work together to provide a singular reality which is seen as the greatest form of holiness possible. It transcends the difference between gods and humans, as it includes both, and it is more than mere ideas or mere physical reality, but an order which encompasses both. In this context, you did not own a woman, nor did you compete with her as an "equal" as fodder for the capital machine. Men and women together created something holy, which was the family and continuation of the species, and were not obligated to each other but paired as a matter of opportunity (note to feminists: there have always been single women and lesbians living out quiet lives, through all of history, and for the most part, they were unmolested). A woman was something that graced one's life, and a partner in a lifelong quest to continue that which made a life that not only created both partners but had treated them well. A woman and man were the basis of a family. You did not "own" your woman, nor did you serve her, nor did she serve you; it was an attitude of mutual worship grounded in worship of the whole, which was seen as greater than the individual. Women had a unique place and were respected for what made them different, not what made them workers like everyone else who could be owned by some dollars-and-cents business. What we've lost in modern times is this reverence for life, and this mutuality, whereby a man and woman could see each other as gifts to each other from the gods. Contrast that to *Sex and the City* and you'll see how shallow modernity really is.

I call the mass revolt, the equalization, the pity culture, and individualism by a more rightful name: Crowdism. It is giving power to the crowd, and excluding the individual, most specifically an individual who wishes to live on his or her own terms and be valuable for achievements, having beaten fears and conquered doubt, and having sculpted out of raw existence a life which is rewarding. Crowdism fears those who might be satisfied, and its solution is that we all – "equally" – are dissatisfied, and forever snapping at each other and competing in trivial ways. The only people it makes happy are those who do not and cannot think about the consequences of their actions, as they are simply glad to have revenge over those more gifted by nature, and feel that this compensates somehow for their failings. Crowdism is cowardice, because it denies to all of us the need to assert ourselves as individuals, conquer our demons, and create in ourselves and our communities a sense of benevolence and higher order. Not everyone can do that, and out of deference to those few (and a need to use them as foot soldiers in the revolution), Crowdism wishes to drag us all to that unsatisfied, self-doubting, paranoiac level.

There are multitudinous other examples of why conservatism is garbage. It denies that the environment is part of our whole existence, and wishes to sell it, also, to the machine. It denies the differences between individuals and the fact that it's a stark choice between raising up the lowest, or promoting the highest; with the latter, a civilization always has new mountains to climb, but with the former, the mountain is reduced to a foothill so that everyone can climb and thus feel good about themselves. It's an illusion within the human mind, an anthropocentricism so crass that it motivates people to treat their world and each other with a subtly disguised form of scorn. Conservatism even fails in Iraq, where under the guise of bringing "progress," we bring mechanized death and Coca-Cola, and absorb an ancient culture into our economic machine whereby we all serve the low-brow interests of the Crowd. But hey, at least their women have "equality," so they can now be single and bitter in their 30s and 40s while patting themselves on the back for having been handed their new "rights."

The Crowd reminds me of an unstable family, where regardless of the consequences, it is felt that if everyone is doing the same thing, "control" is in place and therefore, it'll all work out okay, somehow, sometime, somewhere. The Crowd therefore has as its first tenet equality and the enforcement of one-size-fits-all logic, and for that reason justifies that logic as "progressive," even if these people under freedom seem more neurotic, single, desperate, sad and lonely than ever before. The Crowd doesn't care; it is motivated by fear, not a desire for higher things. Those who have not been infected with the dogma of the crowd think in a holistic sense, and realize that "One law for the ox and the raven is tyranny,"[21] and that, much as there are many different species in nature, there will be many different types of humanity. It is entirely OK for the women of Iraq to live as they have according to their tradition, and for some parts of humanity to live according to the liberal-consmopolitan rhetoric that liberalism endorses. The holistic doctrine suggests that in different places, different orders will prevail, but the corollary to that is that they will achieve different results. The Crowdists want a lowest common denominator, and the conservatives want a form of that Crowdist logic, but me, I want it all. I want a society that constantly rises to higher orders, based on reverence and mutual rhetoric, and I both desire and work toward that end. For this reason, I'm a traditionalist.

---

[21] Originally, "One Law for the Lion & Ox is Oppression." From William Blake, "The Marriage of Heaven and Hell" (1793).

Conservatism is a subset of liberalism and I want nothing to do with either of those revengeful, petty, blockhead doctrines.

November 5, 2005

CICADA KILLERS AND CHRIST

Lamentations should be reserved for great loss, and the best lamentations are those for a hero, where it is not the mourners feeling their own loss in the person gone, nor assuming that the life lacked meaning because it ended and thus wailing for the hero, but those where the cries go to the heavens for the loss of the world of such a perfect object, one of its creatures and the fulfilment of its design. Today I have a lamentation, and an enduring charge, for you and your soul.

The cicada killers are gone. I can still see solitary ones, sometimes, but they are small and furtive, hiding away from the gaze of humans. It's as if they know their time is over, and the open fields over which they once hunted in the suspension of air from diaphanous wings that gives the greatest levity, darting quickly like a hummingbird and fixing on their target with lethal temerity. They're gone because people spray pesticides, killing prey and predator alike, and because people run them over in cars or suck them into air conditioners where they turn into high-speed paste. But those are only the secondary reasons; the primary reason they're gone is that the open fields to the west of here have been turned into more subdivisions and apartments, and therefore, there's not enough prey for good hunting. Maybe they still exist somewhere else, but I have my doubts, since all the land seems to go to feed our new populations.

Cicada killers are a metaphor for nature at large. They are like large wasps with barrel-shaped bodies, and they survive by stinging cicadas (large buzzing bugs) into submission, then laying eggs in them and stashing them in treetops. They're zombie creators who are remarkably successful when there are enough cicadas – and those aren't nearly as loud or plentiful as they should be this time of year – to make for good meals. You don't want to get stung by one. Their stings are like those of the little scorpions that used to be around here but have all but disappeared. It'll really hurt for a few days, then go away slowly, leaving a nasty bulge of traumatized tissue. For this reason, when cicada killers are around, you're careful not to get too near. If you have a BB gun, they're easy to hit, since they're the size of small birds, but don't miss – no amount of prayer can save you from a vengeful cicada killer.

This, to my mind, is a lot like nature at large. It doesn't cooperate on the level of language and other absolutes, so there are rarely warning signs like "Caution: Hidden Crevice Ahead" or "Beware of Sudden Predators." Not even a blinking light near the thickets where strange diseases lurk, or a detailed guidebook telling which streams will give you dysentery and which are safe to drink during your long hike, as you must drink from some of them or you'll die. Poison ivy warns you like a wasp warns you – its coloring and shape are threatening to those who know a bit of nature's internal language. That warning however is an artifact of its desire to create a deterrent; poison ivy doesn't want to be eaten, and wasps don't want to be touched, so it's in their best interest to communicate *stay away* if they can. Other predators camouflage themselves because they have come not to scare, but to eat. There is a language and structure to nature that only becomes clear after some time in contemplating it.

Seeing a cicada killer destroy a cicada is an exercise in mixed emotions. I like cicadas. They're cool creatures that give music to the summer with their songs rising and falling in treetop crescendos. It would never occur to me, emotionally, to kill one. Nonetheless, there's something impressive about watching a cicada killer take one out, however, just like when watching a UFC or street fight there's something beautiful about an efficient, effective move. They're a microcosm of nature in this, predator and prey, in that from the constant struggle between the two, many good things emerge. First, the slowest of the cicadas are removed; the remaining cicadas, over time, are becoming healthier. Next, the cicada killer population is maintained, giving nature another weapon in its arsenal.

Nature is not cuddly. There is no consistent, absolute, singular emotion one can derive from the process itself; the only real emotion comes from considering the meaning of the process, which is that the world keeps turning and living and thus there's a space and time for consciousness, like that which I possess (that word is used deliberately; consciousness didn't originate in me, and if I existed in a vacuum, my consciousness would not exist). For this reason, despite having mixed revulsion and delight in the process of predation, I can appreciate it in context for what it symbolizes, namely the continuation of life. This is the root of the philosophical term "idealism," which means believing more in the significance of things than in their physicality. Idealism comes in several forms, but the most comprehensive is called "cosmic idealism," in which one believes there is a design to the cosmos and we all play a part by being what we are. (From this come systems of karma: do well, and do right, and you rise in the level of the design at which you interact, in this life or a reincarnation.).

When we look at the current situation in the West, this lesson becomes vital, because there's a tendency to Balkanize and thus identify with a political outlook, or symbol, and not to see into the depth of the equation. A more eternal view would hold that each of us does as is natural given their position in the karmic level, and there are predatory views and parasitic views and then independent views, in which the motivation is to be independent of other motions so that internal evolution can occur. When one holds this view, it's no longer necessary to "fight" leftists or rightists, but to see them as part of an order that balances itself and perpetuates the state of confusion. This order is overloaded with confusion arising from the tendency to sort things into "self" and "not-self," roughly corresponding to "good" and "evil" in the absolute view of the herd that is also the psychological underpinning of leftist and mass culture "conservatism," if we even take that seriously.

The highest cycle of karma is this kind of independence, which liberates itself from being dependent on enemies, on good and evil. In this view, one does what must be done, and pays no attention to the labels, feelings or fears. As our society continues to have deep-seated problems and our elected officials of all stripes fail to address them, these labels will become less important. Currently, people derive an identity from them; if you're a liberal, you buy Apple computers, attend certain types of social functions and buy certain kinds of products, and there's a conservative equivalent as well. Most of this is social behavior and has zero effect on anything of import, but it makes people feel like they "belong" to a group and that they can justify their existence with the concept that they're doing the "right" thing. Greens hang out and talking about unplugging appliances at night, recycling cigarette butts and using dog poop in their gardens; anarchists discuss "safe" alternate media sources, and endless reams of theory that seem designed to "prove" their point. In the end, they and the conservatives happily pack off to jobs and keep working to support the system they mutually despise.

The view I'd like to propose here is one in which we simply do what is necessary, and worry less about what original form of the belief is presented to us. There are smart Christians; they've dropped the pity and the anti-nature stance, and have accepted "God" and "good" as related but separate ideals toward which they work, leaving the rest to nature. There are smart liberals; their basic idea is to make life better for the average person, and they're less inclined to get sidetracked on civil rights issues. Also, there are smart Greens, who leave the "10,000 ways to recycle toilet paper" trends to others and focus on restructuring society to be less destructive (including limiting population). Even among Republicans, amazingly, there are a number of intelligent people who care about fixing the situation in which humanity finds itself. All of these people are allies of the truth, even if the position from which they come is something we're trained to reject and hate.

Of all the factors in this equation, the most important is that truth, which is derived from an understanding of human psychology and how it translates into action, is not universal and thus cannot be realistically made into dogma. When we see class warfare and economic elitism alike as reactionary, defensive revenge, it doesn't matter from what source they come; similarly, when we recognize pity as egoism in all of its forms, its brand doesn't matter. What matters is finding a smarter design, and enforcing the higher-karma ideas over the lower. Those who have psychological problems, or are of a fundamentally lower intelligence, will embrace any number of ineffective or destructive ideas, but there is only one path toward higher design – a better adaptation for humanity. This design will never change because humans do not fundamentally change, no matter whether you put them in caves or in front of computers, or dress them up in suits or bearskins. They are still the same animal, and within that animal group, there is great variance, with only a few capable of the kind of thought that is needed to lead.

I can see a better form of Christianity, for example, where we use nihilism like a scrub-brush and scrape away all the irrelevant crufth clogging up the path toward seeing its actual truth, which is a restatement of the ancient Indo-European belief in divinity through fearlessness regarding mortality. Heaven is a state of mind. In this light, all the concepts of pity and guilt and unquestioning democratic love that have clustered around Christianity fade away. Similarly, if we look at the core belief of leftism, it is that society should be designed in a way that benefits its citizens, instead of being an open market where predators are left to tear apart those who fall into their clutches. Greenism is environmental preservation; all the garbage about human rights, civil rights and peaceful revolution makes no sense. And when we bleach away the confusion around conservatism, it becomes simply this: those who have their act together should be able to live normal lives according to traditional values without being forced to subsidize others. None of this is anything more than common sense, and when we pare these beliefs down this way, we can see that they're actually compatible, but that compatibility would require a new belief-container based in realism and not ideology.

In my view, we've gotten so far off the track from reality that at this point, humanity hampers itself as a matter of reactionary defensiveness and identity politics, which are what happens when one takes the symbol of the belief over the actual beliefs. Laws are essentially predators that restrict justice; if there's some idiot out there doing something stupid, and I'd otherwise run him through with a sword, now I'm restrained from doing that. However, to those who have no brains to plan ahead, the laws aren't even a factor, so he'll still attack me and my widow will receive apologies from the State. That's insanity. We have tried to program a design for ourselves that relies on threats and encouragements, and the end result is a giant neurotic mess that like an octopus in cesspool can never get ahold of anything solid enough to escape.

Morons take away your "rights" because idiots abuse whatever is given them. If we say tomorrow that people can smoke all the marijuana they want, smart people will generally have few problems. Idiots on the other hand will promptly smoke up a ton of weed, fail at life, and become a drag on the system. The problem isn't the marijuana exclusively; it's idiots. William S. Burroughs wrote great books while constantly smoking weed because he was William S. Burroughs and he would have done so anyway. By the same token, idiots commit idiocy while smoking marijuana because they are idiots. The same applies to technology, guns, sex, etc. Not all people are equal, and some are defective; while all of us have some problems somewhere, most of these are manageable, but for some, their problems outweigh their balance and positive direction, and thus they become destructive. If we simply enacted planetary eugenics tomorrow, we would rise to a higher design even within our current political systems, *because smarter people will interpret them in a higher karmic order than dumb people can.* Take an idiot and give him Christianity, and you get destructive guilt, but in the hands of someone smarter, the same religion could be enlightening.

By idiots I don't strictly mean droolers, those generally impoverished shufflers of under 100 IQ points who are doomed to living in a fog from which there is no escape. I mean people without long term vision, which I call moral character, and generally comes matched to a certain degree of beauty and strength and intelligence. Thanks to caste mixing, there are plenty of people with high functional intelligence and no moral intelligence; these become salesman of the sleazy variety, porn producers, Hollywood movie moguls, and the like. They are lower karmic orders in positions that should be reserved for people of a higher karmic (moral character/native intelligence) inclination. Much as an 85 IQ pointer will wreak destruction from such a position, someone with an IQ of 140 and a moral IQ of 85 will be destructive, but they will be more competent about being destructive. It is these sorts of people that have aided greatly in Balkanizing our belief systems.

At this point in my life, I have such a high degree of confidence in my belief that I don't debate it. I talk about it, with an intent to amuse and explain, not "inform" or "educate" or some other pompous nonsense. If people want to know where I am with beliefs, I'll tell them, and let them go home to sort it out. If they're smart, those seeds will take root on their own, and they may incorporate part of what I've told them into their beliefs in a form that originates in them. You cannot "educate" people; education does not improve moral character and congenital intelligence. You can show them things, and if they can find meaning in them, they'll adapt them to their own lifestyle and purpose. It's like eating: you take in food, break it down, and it becomes part of you where you can use it. The rest goes into the carrot patch, and might feed something else.

I seek anyone who is willing to follow truth, meaning a design of a higher karmic order, regardless of their political stance. I may troll them, or lure them into seeing the paradox of their own stated values, or alternately discuss these ideas with them, but either way, I'll leave them with something to think about. If they're of a higher karmic order, they'll understand, and their belief system will slowly convert itself to one compatible with the one truth in existence: reality. Adaptation to reality is the basis of the karmic order. Zionists, Black Panthers, Greenpeace, Republicans, Nazis are all welcome in my worldview, if they're willing to take that step. We all live on the same world, and serve the same ultimate interest, which is the continuation of life as a whole. That is served best, of course, by an intelligent design of a higher karmic order.

In this is the final transcendence of "good" and "evil." To me, Christianity is not "evil," but it's not "good" either; there is only one truth, and where it can be found in Christianity, I will speak it. Any belief can be interpreted according to this truth and made sensible, although the same belief can be utterly ruined by fools who interpret it poorly. Like the cicada killer, belief is a matter of function, and it's hard to have one absolute view of it such as "Satanism is evil," because that is a symbolic and not realistic view. If Satanists and Christians alike think hard on a higher karmic order, they will find the truth is shared between their religions, much as Nazis and

Zionists and Greenpeacers would. Function is the basis of idealism, and arranging our human function into a better design is a way of moving up the evolutionary ladder, and is a form of evolution in itself – and for any organism, this is the highest goal in survival.

June 24, 2005

PERFECTION

When people talk about perfection, they often fall into the trap of assuming a linear world: a place like the mythical Heaven where there is no bad, only good, and good of the purest sense. While as symbol that sounds appealing, when one goes through the process of plotting out life, it sounds terrible, because it would rapidly lead to repetition. If there's one right answer to every question, and every activity turns out excellently, is there any enough contrast to claim one has actually had an experience? Without danger, adventures would become tourist play; without the possibility of failure, success would have no greatness. Without death, there would be no reason to make one decision over another in life, as all experiences would be exactly equal thanks to infinite days and thus zero consequences. Screw up your life? Live another lifetime, within your lifetime. Boundaries give meaning to what lies within them, in other words.

Much as in an equation, we can cancel out elements in common between items being added, or can arbitrarily multiply or add any number to one side of the equals sign so long as it is also done to the other, when we think about life we must recognize that it is the difference between experiences that gives them meaning; the same experience, like the reduced factors of the number cancelled, have no impact on the overall direction of the equation. They are extraneous in part because they are tautological: a known thing requires no activity.

Some of us have identified ourselves as gnostics after the ancient sect of that name because we have grasped the concept of relativity as expressed in such spiritual ideas, which is not properly "dualism" in that it does not assert duality for the sake of having two things. It is better described as "contrast" or "opposition," because if one analyzes any single thing in a closed system, it is clear that all other things relate to it and often counterpoint it, much in the way that mice are balanced by hawks and foxes. The contrast between two things is what separates them, for our consciousness; a lighter object appears closer, a slower sound farther, a mission statement the principle around which the rest of a speech is organized. It is this contrast that redefines perfection from "100% good" to "balanced." Every dark thing permits a light thing, and vice versa. For each good that exists, there is also a negative, although those terms describe human perfections and not the balance in nature.

This opposition can be seen as a manifestation of the perfection of nature. Instead of creating a pure world, which would rapidly cycle into repetition and therefore lose all benefit to making one decision over another, soon drawing itself into a mathematical nothing-state where no change or transfer of energy would exist, our world of positive and negative sustains itself by balance, ensuring that the system as a whole retains energy even if its parts are constantly created and destroyed.

A system of a single part would do transfer energy exactly, and have one will between a singular part ("God") and all else, but this would become entropic as described above. Our system maintains a constant balance between spaces where nothing exists, and things that exist seeking to consume those spaces; it is a universe where even nothing is a meal for something. To a gnostic, this opposition is superior to dualism, where a perfect world (one god, one will, everything right the first time) commands or balances a physical world that might even be seen as evil; to a gnostic, good and evil are not opposed in this moral sense, but contribute to a "meta-good" or good of the whole. This is why in most gnostic mysticisms, nothingness existed first, and because of an implied contrast, somethingness arose; then to keep from dominating itself into tedium, somethingness elected to produce its own form of nothingness, that which lives yet asserts the void, where in the void there was no life – this is what most people call evil.

Modern people are too accustomed to sorting out life as if it were the objects on sale at a mall. Keep the good, throw out the evil; then you have what is pure. We figure that people are the same way, and that good people never make mistakes, and bad people never do good things. We deny that life is a learning process, and prefer to refer to ourselves in the constant present, as if aging does not change us and learning does not make us grow. This is a philosophy of personal instability, a fear of being prey to the void, and therefore, it seeks to deny the void by looking only at positive and negative. It forgets that much as there is a meta-good, there is a form of "meta-bad," which is a return of the void; nothingness is less of a consignment to a hell of torture than a relegation to non-existence, where there is not even consciousness to feel pain (in this sense, Hell is a promise against the fear of death: to those who fear death more than anything else, living on in eternal torment is preferable to nonexistence). Our modern view denies the gnostic and pagan view of the universe as something which created itself and maintains its order through the cycles of creation and destruction which we try to sort into, respectively, "good" and "evil."

If you look at any scene, your mind will try to understand it, and will thus select some feature of it on which to center. When you look at that object, everything else in the scene becomes background, and your mind orders it according to the dominant object perceived: in relations of distance, or flow of action, or physical connection. This is not an artifact of humans, or of being conscious, but the way that all complex information systems are organized. This is relativity at its most basic: for there to be somethingness, there had to be nothingness first, and when somewhere in nothingness stirred an awareness of the possibility of somethingness, it was created by the process of inverting background and foreground focus in this way. Similarly, we do not know destruction unless something has been created first, although we might classify the void as being entirely destruction except for the lack of preexisting things to destroy. Gnostics divided the world similarly into an unconscious will, which could not be quantified, and a conscious aspect, which takes the form of what we describe now as "data." Thoughts, numbers, items, words, recognitions – these are data. They are derived from the actions of the formless, which manifests itself in forms recognizable by consciousness.

The ancients therefore did not remove their thoughts from reality entirely, as they recognized that our brains are part of physical reality and therefore interact with it in ways not requiring physical action – this is the basic of gnostic occult warfare, called by some "magic." Like the modern cosmic idealists, most importantly Kant and Schopenhauer, they believed that humans were entirely of the conscious side of life, except when they tapped into the unconscious and were thus able to see (and manipulate!) the cosmic order. Yet in that view to understand the cosmic order enough to manipulate it was to acquiesce to its wisdom and act within its precepts; even the evil sorcerers of old were players in a metaphysical drama, acting out a role not dissimilar to that of the wolf or another predator. Same with the parasites. The reason for this balance, in the gnostic view, was to keep the people who would be neither predator or parasite from becoming repetitive and cyclic and thus weak. Evil was the province of unconscious will, where consciousness was its counterbalance and yet just as much dependent upon it.

There is a tendency among us moderns to wonder at the imperfection of the world, evidence of which we see in its many evils. The gnostic view is ultimately more positive in that in it we see evils not as a cosmic negative but as empty spaces into which more creation can expand, if it is strong enough, and we see the challenges to creation not as imperfection but as part of a perfect order that keeps good strong. It is a sad fact of history that while the ancients did not have our technology, unlike us they had a population which could understand this "double negative" logic and thus look beyond good and evil to see their role as creative agents in a perpetual nature of immaculate goodness and perfection.

March 5, 2006

LEARNING TO FLY

In ancient literature, a common motif was that in order to find the truth of a complex situation, one had to visit the land of the dead and ask a spirit. The spirit – someone who is not living, and does not have human desires and emotions – then reveals the truth of the situation. It is as if life itself is an addition to the structure of events, and that the dead can see structure, because it takes a mind dead of emotions and fears to reveal structure, which roughly corresponds to an enlightened Platonism, or a view that there are ideal forms upon which reality is roughly patterned.

What is structure? The function and underlying shapes of transaction of energy in a situation. The structure of a forest involves trees trapping sunlight and converting it into products that feed other life forms; then still other forms harvest varying parts of plant and animal life, creating a complex ecosystem. We can diagram said ecosystem, draw it in language, or film its parts and associated numbers (28% of all squirrels are eaten by homosexual bears). These representations of structure do not diminish the fact that, whether or not it "exists," structure is the only accurate way of mapping events and objects.

Some people, and some religions, take Platonism too far. They assume that structure is somehow a pure, dualistic world, and that we live in an inferior world of rendering (structure is the blueprint, rendering is what is created from it in physical reality). This is not what Plato was suggesting, in the view of this author. He was saying that our consciousnesses become ensnared on the details of physical and tangible objects and events, while forgetting the relationship between them, the flow of energy, the actual transaction of significance; the structure and the underlying pattern-based order. He was saying that we get caught up in our senses and lose sight of the way things interact to form our world, and thus we become materialistic, or confined to the physical world and unaware of the world of structure.

Where this gets tricky is that structure does not, for all practical purposes, "exist." The closest we get are encoded blueprints like DNA; show me the structure of a chair, for example, as it exists. You can point out the design of the chair, outline its structural points, and summarize in abstract language or mathematical formulae what a chair is. But the structure of chair, something which would have to be inherent to all chairs, doesn't "exist" – it is an abstraction of our minds. This does not change the fact that it is a vital part of chairness, and that without some idea of that structure, one cannot create a chair. In this we see that the only dualism in Plato is a division between mind (structure) and body (physical reality). Even in those, there is overlap; Plato is clearly not suggesting a dualistic system in the Judeo-Christian sense, where Heaven "exists" somewhere in a purer world than this half-evil, half-good one.

(Side note: every intelligent Christian I've ever met has overcome dualism as a concept by recognizing that God is the world, and the world is God, and that when we speak of God, we're speaking of something like structure that is inherent but does not "exist" discretely in the same way a blueprint or shotgun might. All religions, if meditated on enough, become something like the Hindu or Greco-Roman religions, where gods represent parts of our psychology and the psychology of nature as a joined force of a similar nature, and nothing is promised, and heaven is a state of mind and not a place. Encouraging those Christians who have the brains to understand it toward this state is a more sensible goal than "fighting" Christianity. This places them at a higher level than those stuck in the materialistic Abrahamic faiths, which assert personal power as more important than principle, or the "self-negating" Buddhism that affirms the ego by using it to disclaim the ego, much as liberals advance themselves in social importance by criticizing their societies.).

For the ancients, the dichotomy between design (structure) and manifestation (form, physicality) was profoundly drawn, because they were idealists in the philosophical sense: to them, nature behaved in the same way that governs the creation and nurturing of thoughts, so they saw the world as a system that worked like a mind. To them, this meant that thoughts (creatures, individuals) were created on an ad hoc basis for the purpose of testing hypotheses, and what matters at the end of the day is that those creatures bearing important hypotheses survive and the insane hypotheses do not. Each of us is a test design, in the view of the ancients, and may the best prevail! What matters is not our suffering, not our deaths, not our wealth, not our social importance, but the prevalence of better ideas and designs through heroism. For them, the universe was empty of manifest gods, but it was far from empty, in that it was a living thing in which we like thoughts attempt to rejoin its infinite wisdom by fighting it out. When one warrior stands over the bloodied corpse of another, the ancients surmised, a better design or concept has won. It is for this reason that they had, like most of us have bred into us, a rigid concept of fairness. With fairness, heroism was possible. When cheating became the norm, heroism took a back seat toward self-preservation – who wants to die for a rigged contest, which decides nothing? – and thus society drifted toward materialism. Sad day, that was.

This form of idealistic belief was more realistic than any of the "moral" belief systems that countered it, because it fit in with the organic systems that operated around it. It did not try to impose square, rigid, materialistic moral concepts onto an unruly nature, but sought to understand nature's design (and came closer than anyone else has, to this day). It did not pretend it could make things better with "right" and "wrong," but developed a flexible morality based not on survival (murder = wrong) but fairness (a just fight is the will of the gods). Its core concept was explaining how nature and human thought were alike, and thus, how a higher state of mind could be found that showed why this world, with all of its goods and evils, ultimately makes sense and leads toward a positive goal. This is idealism, but it cannot occur without a counterpart, which is what is symbolized by a visit to the land of the dead: a stilling of the mind that removes the drama and trauma of living, and looks only at structure, not at tangibility. This is transcendental meditation or 40 days in the forest or seven days under the Bodhi tree or Odin hanging himself. In idealism, a hamburger is no longer a hamburger you can taste, but nutrition that empowers you to do certain things; it is no longer a sensual experience as much as it is a step toward a goal; it is no longer a material value of fixed nature ($8.95) but a flexible value placed on being able to get to the next stage of the process, and if it requires a hamburger? – it is possible no cost is too high, or too low.

Realizing this moral flexibility, and land-of-the-dead style mental state, is essential to moving beyond the human condition to accept the place of humans in the entirety of things, and thus to derive an idealism which sees possible higher states. One cannot live until one has died, so to speak, because one has not yet recognized the value of *living*. And what might a modern call this state of mind, this pessimistic Zen, this clarity of deathlike thought? Some time ago, a modern thinker of no fame called it "nihilism." His point was that when one strips aside all but physical, immediate reality, it is possible to derive the structure of things and thus their actual value. In this view, nihilism is not the lack of belief, faith and caring about all things; we refer to that, more accurately, as "fatalism," or in the vernacular, giving up and running home crying to Mommy with your testicles in a lunch sack. Nihilism is a clarity of mind that removes illusion and specifically, human illusion, including emotions, desires, anthropocentric projections and self-interest.

Many people now are so cynical they assume what is written about nihilism is boilerplate marketing with the real product lurking below as a form of anarchic self-gratification, and go elsewhere for definitions of nihilism, coming up with "belief in no value" or variants thereof, and immediately begin considering themselves superior for finding the truth of no truth, and start hassling others for believing in anything. They have, of course, forgotten that belief in no value is belief in something ("no value") and thus that their criticisms are, of course, impotent and pointless. Such people do not care about philosophical truth; they care about finding some mental system to use as a shield and form of self-identification, a way of saying "I figured it out this way" in the same way that others use Christ, drugs, money, sex, belongings, the Army, etc. These people should be seen for the aphilosophical future middle managers that they truly are.)

So nihilism...is not a total lack of belief? It's a total lack of inherent belief, yes; one clears the mind of all preconceptions, then analyzes the situation, then makes a choice of action. Nihilism is a meditative state, a warrior state, of having cleared aside all but structure so that when one acts, it is in concert with the way things naturally turn out, and thus will have success of the longest-lasting and most profound variety. Those who have too much of the illusion of life in their minds act according to the interests of creatures, and thus often miss the point, the structure, the ideal of a situation... to be a nihilist is to clear your mind so that you can always see past the form of a scenario to its organizing principles, and thus to effectively change is however you see fit. Nihilism is not a belief system for those who want to believe in nothing, because of all things, it assaults such emotional reactions ("I'm taking my toys and going home, if you don't make metaphysical value obvious to me now, Life!") first and demolishes them utterly. Nihilism is not an end state, but an initial state, and a discipline that grows as one explores thought. Nihilism is learning to fly.

When one wants to learn to fly, one must first negate all one has learned about living on the ground. Gravity is not absolute, and it can be bent. The wind isn't weak, but strong, and you don't resist it like a stolid building, but find the right way to cut it, and it's like getting energy from the gods. The sky isn't blue, but degrees of blue and black depending on how far you go. Clouds aren't solid, or soft, but are like ghosts in the air, and they're always moving. So is everything, but you can tell more when you're flying. Learning to fly requires that you forget and destroy everything you knew about being a two-footed, meaty land creature. Your bones too can be hollow, and your fingers grow wings, if you see the path before you is not a path at all, but a compass of a very advanced sort. Flying, one moves in three dimensions; on earth, one generally moves in two, mapped to the surface, with rare exceptions for tree climbing and astronomical flatulence. But when one flies? Up and down join forward and back and left and right, and each must suddenly have not only degrees, but some point of reference. Everything is relative, including relativity itself, which is relative to all things, much as nihilism reduces "nihilism" itself. Learning to fly requires the discipline of a clear mind.

(Interestingly, those who resist this doctrine the most are those who complain the most about Christians, liberals, other races, etc. yet fail to realize that while they're not supporting the same groups, they're supporting the same conditions that got us to the state where these groups are in conflict. Individualism is a dead-end street, because it places the individual before all else, and is basically a radicalized form of materialism. Follow this path and you out-Christian the Christians, and are well on the way to heading back down the evolutionary ladder and becoming a crass materialist. Most kiddie "nihilists" fall into this category. They want to come up with one good reason why they shouldn't do anything but complain, and keep goofing off with video games and drugs and plastic garbage mainstream music. They think "nihilism" will do it; if you don't believe in anything, you just keep goofing off. Little do they know that true nihilism of that sort wouldn't allow them to even enjoy their *GTA III* and bong hits, and that nihilism for a thinking person – a non-trivialized, non-anthropocentric one – is something else entirely.)

My advice to any who wish to pursue the truths in the world, or to change the world: for you to alter the state of existence, you must first know exactly – and not in vague college-esque we can creatively type a theory for whatever you want the paper to be about ma'am terms – the changes you would make to its structure. You might not be able to do this, inherently; if the gods did not grant you with the brains, or the moral will, or the judgment, you will fail. No one can educate you into a higher state of mind. Even if you are of the ability, there is no guarantee you can pull this off. You must first discipline your mind, or it will be like standing on a boat in a storm trying to shoot an arrow at a floating target. You now know the basics of the esoteric discipline of nihilism, which will lead you first to realism and next to idealism and finally, to transcendence. Are you ready for this path? If so, my best faith and wishes for you. And one more thing – to fly, you must lighten the load you carry, and infuse joy into your soul so that it rises playfully, without care for its own dead, toward the sun spinning above in an infinite cycle of energy exchange.

October 28, 2005

THE INHERENT

The inherent, in my view, is two things: first, it is reality in the physical sense, and second, it is the set of eternal wisdoms which deal with the recognition of that inherent. The second meaning comes into play in the sense of Jung and mystic (hermetic/alchemical) tradition, at least. It's hard to define it as "fixed" but since the conditions of life in the most universal sense will never change, it is to some degree constant.

When I speak of the inherent, I mean reality as it is defined when one overcomes mind/body dualism, which also translates into spiritual dualism (earth versus the world of Gods/heaven), and other subjective/objective splits in perception. Over enough experience, one realizes that natural laws are consistent and thus a few simple instructions allows the universe to create itself from nothing, or the pattern of a fern leaf to grow from a single basic shape. This is the genius of the universe, in my view; it's a clean cascading hierarchy of concepts which produces reality as we know it, a supremely simple and logical organization. Human conceptions rarely approach this form of design.

You can find this hinted to in many places. Nietzsche's "Will to Power," Burroughs' "Algebra of Need," and the source of the ancient mystical writings, the Vedas (Sanskrit is the parent tongue of German, and India the original proving ground of Indo-European philosophy; the Vedas predate both Hinduism and Buddhism, and are echoed in mystic/hermetic traditions because, after the rise of Christianity, it became a fatal error to speak such beliefs in public, and even those who adapted them to Christianity in slight degrees, such as Eckhart and Luther, faced public confrontation). Life is a *mechanism*, and what's brilliant about it is that it doesn't create a predefined direction where everything is either all well or all bad; it's up to us, as agents of life, to determine our own future. Nature gives us a blank canvas, and a powerful role model.

Interestingly, this philosophy remains relatively consistent throughout the ancients. In the Iliad, Greek heroes have a sense of destiny being shaped by their own hands without succumbing to the fatalism of their enemies, which is hinted as having an Asian origin – it is likely that Asia found its own form of Christianity, or a fatalistic and dualistic mystical-devotional tradition, thousands of years before the West, and this produced the characteristic fatalism of the Asian spirit as well as consuming the ancient kingdoms of China and Japan, although the latter took far longer to fall. The *Aeneid*, the Roman continuation of the *Iliad-Odyssey* tradition of Homer, states:

> *First, then, the sky and lands and sheets of water,*
> *The bright moon's globe, the Titan sun and stars,*
> *Are fed within by Spirit, and a Mind*
> *Infused through all the members of the world*
> *Makes one great living body of the mass.*
> *From Spirit come the races of man and beast,*
> *The life of birds, odd creatures the deep sea*
> *Contains beneath her sparkling surfaces,*
> *And fiery energy from a heavenly source*
> *Belongs to the generative seeds of these,*
> *So far as they are not poisoned or clogged*
> *By mortal bodies, their free essence dimmed*
> *by earthiness and deathliness of flesh.*
> *This makes them fear and crave, rejoice and grieve.*
> *Imprisoned in the darkness of the body*
> *They cannot clearly see heaven's air; in fact*
> *Even when life departs on the last day*
> *Not all the scourges of the body pass*
>
> *From the poor souls, not all distress of life.*
> *Inevitably, many malformations,*
> *Growing together in mysterious ways,*
> *Become inveterate. Therefore they undergo*
> *The discipline of punishments and pay*
> *In penance for old sins: some hang full length*
> *To the empty winds, for some the stain of wrong*
> *Is washed by floods or burned away by fire.*

We suffer each his own shade. We are sent
Through wide Elysium, where a few abide
In happy lands, till the long day, the round
Of Time fulfilled, has worn our stains away,
Leaving the soul's heaven-sent perception clear,
The fire from heaven pure. These other souls,
When they have turned Time's wheel a thousand years,
The god calls in a crowd to Lethe stream,
That there unmemoried they may see again
The heavens and wish re-entry into bodies.[22]

Some years after the Vedas, which were preserved orally to avoid corruption, as it keeps people from referred to a flawed transcription as "absolute proof," the *Bhagavad-Gita* was written, and it, many years before the *Odyssey* or *Aeneid*, describes the same spiritual tradition:

Some say this Atman (Godhead that is within every being),
Is slain, and others
Call it the slayer:
They know nothing.
How can it slay
Or who shall slay it?
Know this Atman
Unborn, Undying
Never ceasing,
Never beginning,
Deathless, birthless,
Unchanging for ever.
How can it die
The death of the body?

Worn-out garments
Are shed by the body:
Worn-out bodies

Are shed by the dweller

---

[22] Virgil, *Aeneid*, trans. Robert Fitzgerald, Vintage (1990), p. 186.

Within the body.

New bodies are donned

By the dweller, like garments.

Not wounded by weapons,
Not burned by fire,
Not dried by the wind,
Not wetted by water:
Such is the Atman.
Innermost element,
Everywhere, always,
Being of beings,
Changeless, eternal,

For ever and ever.

...Death is certain for the born. Rebirth is certain for the dead. You should not grieve for what is unavoidable. Before birth, beings are not manifest to our human senses. In the interim between birth and death, they are manifest. At death they return to the unmanifest again. What is there in all this to grieve over?

...Realize that pleasure and pain, gain and loss, victory and defeat, are all one and the same: then go into battle.[23]

You can see in these an adualistic sense of "Heaven" and "godhead" as a ground of reality that is built in the same world as this; it is a mechanism of this world, and not a contrary world. It seems like a semantic split from the Christian "Heaven" and single God as a pure force in contrast to this world of sin, but note the absence of good/ evil rhetoric and of Heaven being a contrary stage to life; rather, Heaven is the *ground* of life and an element from which it is formed. This is the root of the ancient philosophy which was converted into a fantasy fairytale by pop culture mystics!

---

[23] *Bhagavad-Gita: The Song of God*, trans. Swami Prabhavananda and Christopher Isherwood, Signet (2002), p. 10.

If one is mean-spirited, and believes modern "science" to be absolute, this can be seen as a simple description of consciousness and life being properties beyond the individual, which never originated in the individual; thus, when the individual dies, these same forces are manifested in new life forms. This leads to the question, is the individual consciousness reincarnated, or a new individual produced with the same consciousness that was originally granted to the first individual? It doesn't matter, at least until we face death, as the basic theorem is sounder than anything offered by modern "science" or Christianity.

This, in my view, is a spiritual-mystical translation of the inherent: consciousness and life itself are not originating in the individual, but properties of the universe of which each individual has a share. When one sees life this way, one is not only "beyond good and evil" but beyond worry for the individual spirit, as it is shown as connected to the heavens in the same way trees are connected to earth, water and sun.

December 21, 2004

THE FAILURE OF LIBERAL DEMOCRATIC STATES

Philosophy covers two basic questions, *What is real?* and *What should we do?* These come in to play on an individual level as well as a political one, with the latter including all that it commands, especially social, economic and leadership factors.

The problem humans face is that our big brains are echo chambers and, as individuals, we fear Darwinian predation or its social equivalent, which is being judged inferior. This problem intensifies in a society without hierarchy, where we are constantly being judged to see where we end up, and therefore to be merely equal is to be mediocre, but to have a life worth living requires rising above that base level. Our big echo chamber brains convince us that we can manipulate others into suspending that social judgment through universal acceptance, or egalitarianism. This requires us to engage in social fictions, and use social or peer pressure to control others through manipulation, in order to avoid seeing the truth behind the illusion.

In this way, individualism or selfishness and herd conformity unite toward the same end, which is preached as universal acceptance but is in fact a removal of any obligation toward realistic thinking. This liberates societies to grow recklessly, and to grow powerful, at which point they reach an apex and their lack of internal cohesion – all those individualists pulling in their own directions, subsidized by the group – and they begin the process of collapse. And yet because of their assumption that individualism creates the best possible form of existence, and that denial of reality is not a problem because its consequences have not yet materialized, liberal democracies of the sort created by this individualism-conformity nexus see themselves as the ultimate evolution of all human societies.

The triumph of the West, of the Western idea, is evident first of all in the total exhaustion of viable systematic alternatives to Western liberalism. In the past decade, there have been unmistakable changes in the intellectual climate of the world's two largest communist countries, and the beginnings of significant reform movements in both. But this phenomenon extends beyond high politics and it can be seen also in the ineluctable spread of consumerist Western culture in such diverse contexts as the peasants' markets and color television sets now omnipresent throughout China, the cooperative restaurants and clothing stores opened in the past year in Moscow, the Beethoven piped into Japanese department stores, and the rock music enjoyed alike in Prague, Rangoon, and Tehran.

What we may be witnessing is not just the end of the Cold War, or the passing of a particular period of postwar history, but the end of history as such: that is, the end point of mankind's ideological evolution and the universalization of Western liberal democracy as the final form of human government. This is not to say that there will no longer be events to fill the pages of Foreign Affair's yearly summaries of international relations, for the victory of liberalism has occurred primarily in the realm of ideas or consciousness and is as yet incomplete in. the real or material world. But there are powerful reasons for believing that it is the ideal that will govern the material world in the long run.[24]

The fundamental mistake in the above emerges when we consider that since social control is the goal of individualism, Fukuyama and others may have confused "best system of control" with "best form of government." From the individualistic, reality-denying perspective, liberal democracy serves as the best means of controlling the rest of society so the individual denial of reality cannot be publicly noticed and the individual shamed. A control system works best when it appears benevolent and uses public humiliation, or fear of the group and not the isolated force of government, as a means of inducing compliance. Group individualism derives its power from its ability to hold off the herd in defense of the individual, but the flip side of this bargain is that all must conform to the demands of the group, which because it does not see particularized circumstances demands compliance to universal standards of a bureaucratic nature.

---

[24] Francis Fukuyama, "The End of History?", The National Interest, Summer 1989.

I have not seen Benway since his precipitate departure from Annexia, where his assignment had been T.D. – Total Demoralization. Benway's first act was to abolish concentration camps, mass arrest and, except under certain limited and special circumstances, the use of torture.

"I deplore brutality," he said. "It's not efficient. On the other hand, prolonged mistreatment, short of physical violence, gives rise, when skillfully applied, to anxiety and a feeling of special guilt. A few rules or rather guiding principles are to be borne in mind. The subject must not realize that the mistreatment is a deliberate attack of an anti-human enemy on his personal identity. He must be made to feel that he deserves any treatment he receives because there is something (never specified) horribly wrong with him. The naked need of the control addicts must be decently covered by an arbitrary and intricate bureaucracy so that the subject cannot contact his enemy direct."

Every citizen of Annexia was required to apply for and carry on his person at all times a whole portfolio of documents. Citizens were subject to be stopped in the street at any time; and the Examiner, who might be in plain clothes, in various uniforms, often in a bathing suit or pyjamas, sometimes stark naked except for a badge pinned to his left nipple, after checking each paper, would stamp it. On subsequent inspection the citizen was required to show the properly entered stamps of the last inspection. The Examiner, when he stopped a large group, would only examine and stamp the cards of a few. The others were then subject to arrest because their cards were not properly stamped...After a few months of this the citizens cowered in corners like neurotic cats. Of course the Annexia police processed suspected agents, saboteurs and political deviants on an assembly line basis.[25]

This control mechanism achieves perfection before it acts by coercing its citizens into compliance out of fear of being seen as aberrant and then being attacked by the others. While the instrument of enforcement may be government itself, the unity of the rest of

---

[25] William S. Burroughs, *Naked Lunch*, Grove Press (1992), p 17.

the group in both reporting infringers and allowing punishment to occur without protest, by the nature of being more inescapable than totalitarian police forces who lack the support of every citizen, provides the actual basis of the terror necessary for control. Under liberal democracy, every citizen is an informant who gladly fingers anti-individualists (including realists) so that he can gain the esteem of the crowd, and so that he too is not caught up in the dragnet of public acrimony which resembles the Two Minutes Hate, a lynch mob, a witch hunt and an angry crowd throwing tomatoes. With this, a perfect control mechanism supervises its citizens not by punishing dangerous behavior, but by pre-emptively forcing compliance with a narrative so that undesired behavior cannot occur.

The manager of a fruit-and-vegetable shop places in his window, among the onions and carrots, the slogan: "Workers of the world, unite!" Why does he do it? What is he trying to communicate to the world? Is he genuinely enthusiastic about the idea of unity among the workers of the world? Is his enthusiasm so great that he feels an irrepressible impulse to acquaint the public with his ideals? Has he really given more than a moment's thought to how such a unification might occur and what it would mean?

I think it can safely be assumed that the overwhelming majority of shopkeepers never think about the slogans they put in their windows, nor do they use them to express their real opinions. That poster was delivered to our greengrocer from the enterprise headquarters along with the onions and carrots. He put them all into the window simply because it has been done that way for years, because everyone does it, and because that is the way it has to be. If he were to refuse, there could be trouble. He could be reproached for not having the proper decoration in his window; someone might even accuse him of disloyalty. He does it because these things must be done if one is to get along in life. It is one of the thousands of details that guarantee him a relatively tranquil life "in harmony with society," as they say.

... Ideology is a specious way of relating to the world. It offers human beings the illusion of an identity, of dignity, and of morality while making it easier for them to part with them. As

the repository of something suprapersonal and objective, it enables people to deceive their conscience and conceal their true position and their inglorious modus vivendi, both from the world and from themselves. It is a very pragmatic but, at the same time, an apparently dignified way of legitimizing what is above, below, and on either side. It is directed toward people and toward God. It is a veil behind which human beings can hide their own fallen existence, their trivialization, and their adaptation to the status quo. It is an excuse that everyone can use, from the greengrocer, who conceals his fear of losing his job behind an alleged interest in the unification of the workers of the world, to the highest functionary, whose interest in staying in power can be cloaked in phrases about service to the working class. The primary excusatory function of ideology, therefore, is to provide people, both as victims and pillars of the post-totalitarian system, with the illusion that the system is in harmony with the human order and the order of the universe.[26]

Conformity becomes a method of success, not merely of avoiding punishment, and citizens wish to demonstrate this compliance for the sake of their own futures, leading to a condition where reporting others for non-compliance is seen as a career-positive move. The crowd leads itself by the nose: that which is accepted becomes the basis of all future decisions, and dissenters are removed, so that when the election comes around, the crowd votes for more of the same, because to do otherwise would be to remove themselves from the possibility of success. Like individualism itself, the society has become a closed-circuit feedback loop where reality is cut out of the equation.

A nihilist places no faith in ideology or popular opinion, and least of all in "systems" of economic, political or social rules. Nihilists deny inherent truth and with them any idea of an innate network of universal rules, and instead look at particular decisions. The question is not how someone comes into power, but the results of their decisions – the quality of their leadership – and what those set

---

[26] Vaclav Havel, *The Power of the Powerless*, trans. Paul Wilson, retrieved from http://vaclavhavel.cz/showtrans.php?cat=eseje&val=2_aj_eseje.html&typ=HTML.

up as the next set of decisions which determine the future of that society. To a nihilist, results in reality matter more than what people can convince themselves into thinking is right, or what they do in the small bubble-world of their own self-interest at the expense of larger concerns in reality like consequences, past, future and the type of social order they are creating. For this reason, a nihilist is agnostic to the type of system and looks instead to the outcome of decisions. In liberal democracy, there is no accountability for decisions, because they are decided by "the vote" and then left intact as if public opinion were an inherent truth. In the nihilist mind, this herd decision-making is a substitute for reality itself.

Democracy is a Lie

I offer that suffering and death are inevitable parts of life. Even more, they're necessary; conflict shapes the world. My idea is that suffering should mean something, and some ideal should be achieved by it. Unnecessary suffering is pointless and annoying.

However, I don't believe we have "liberty" in the West. We have the freedom to get some stupid job, commute to work and spend most of our money on health insurance, property insurance, life insurance, etc. to pay for the constant instability of modern society and the pollution that is steadily giving us all cancers. I don't believe we have liberty of thought, as clearly some things are so taboo you'll lose your job and your house and be forced to live in the tumor of the open streets. I also don't believe our society offers the "liberty" of thinking about any social order but its own. So, in short, "liberty" is a word, and it can mean something or mean nothing, or be simply ambiguous, which benefits the person using the word but not the person reacting to it.

To all you defenders of democracy, I'd like one answer: all of us acknowledge that there are hordes of stupid people out there. Why do you want to give them political power? Shouldn't we measure power by its results, and concentrate power in the hands of those who prove the most able to make the *best* decisions, instead of merely the *most popular* (individualistic) ones? I'm not sure I care about having a "democratic" society, either; I'd rather have a society of shared culture and values, so we don't have to create a vast governmental bureaucracy to force some kind of abstract values upon us all. The healthiest society needs the fewest rules and least government because its citizens are mentally competent and do the right thing, and enforce that on one another through the softer means of culture, which rewards citizens for acting according to the values of that society.

It's possible that we've all been misled regarding this "freedom" and "liberty" and "democracy" thing. Under these ideals, have we had fewer wars? No, we've had more destructive wars, although they may be less frequent. Have we had a better life? We have better technology, including medicine, but it still screws up all the time and brings us side effects like pollution and cancer. It also seems that technology is cumulative, and the roots of it lie in a former age, and its increase would have come under any type of society that supported it. Are people smarter and braver now? Consensus says no. Is life more meaningful? Etc.

Democracy is passive, and it forces compromise. One person can make up his mind; two people have a harder time; three harder still; from there it rises to an exponential state of difficulty. People are naturally diverse. The problem is that decision-making requires clarity and a single course of action, which is the *antithesis* of diversity. So somehow we must get one decision out of thousands or millions of viewpoints; we must do what is right for the whole, even if many people can think of things that would benefit them more personally (for example, I'd like us to go to war with China so my Mandarin lessons start earning me money). Democracy is opposed to finding an answer. Democracies are good at constant discourse, never-ending debate, and replacing leadership every four years. They are counterproductive for decision-making, and encourage the citizens to become involved with government *only* through the voting booth. Democracy is to government as television is to life. It's a sick pornography of existence, distilling the wide range of experience into a few pre-prepared options, with people engaging in the process more to feel important about themselves than to get anything done. When it's time to really find a survey about something unimportant, like what color we paint city hall, by all means take a vote – who cares what the outcome is.

When you need real decisions made, find the smartest people in your society, get them to discuss the issue until they're using the same language, and then hash out an agreement. This type of debate requires far more effort than taking a vote, which is what you do when no one can agree and you're tired and you want the usual compromise on the lowest common denominator. A society of realistic reasoning is far better than Democracy, even when the decision reached is wrong, as this process responds more quickly to change and can take a bad idea quickly and evolve it into a good one, where Democracy will become enmired in infighting and personal drama. Democracy is a popularity contest. Democracy is the selection of the most popular product, sometimes called consumerism. Democracy is wishful thinking for personal gain over looking at the whole situation and doing what is right. I know almost everyone you respect has told you Democracy is *just great*, but think of it this way: they could be misinformed.

All they have to do in order to fool us is to get us asking the wrong questions. While we're all kvetching around about liberty, freedom, and other promises of a salesperson, our inner life and our culture life – what holds our society together – is disintegrating. Therefore, there's always an enemy, and always a war on to eliminate the enemies of "freedom." Wouldn't you feel silly if you got manipulated by this rhetoric?

December 21, 2004

The Controversy of Realism

Many of the most controversial aspects of nihilism begin at the point of accepting responsibility for results in reality and rejecting mass opinion, which is calibrated to compromise and mental laziness (sorry, "convenience") instead of looking at the options presented when one knows how the world works! That acceptance effects traversal of the abyss created by the lack of inherent meaning, mainly because unlike modern passive views these controversial views are heroic, and give meaning to life through unitive bonding between the inner self and the design of nature. They advocate an order similar to the one observed existing, and cease to wish to change its fundamental tendencies.

Some big points where nihilism transforms our official narrative are:

- *Race.* People freak out about this topic because since 1945, the prevailing dogma in the United States has been that all people are equal in ability and temperament and should exist in a "multicultural" society. Astute observers notice that this means all of our many diverse races get combined into one average, destroying each, or remain Balkanized forever as independent groups working against the idea of a social norm; either way, no cultural or values standard can survive it, which is convenient for government which is content to impose its own standards to replace those organic ones. A nihilist might support the concept of "localization," which means that when one has ancestral connection to a land and a culture that culture survives, but if that chain is broken the culture dies (causing a lack of diversity in a worldwide context). Modern society spouts on about "equality" and "diversity" but what they really mean is averaging, first between social classes, then sexes, and finally ethnic groups to produce cultureless citizens dependent on government. This gets reality-denialists closer to their actual goal, which is a universal culture and set of values systems that reinforces denial of reality, so that each member of the Herd will never face consequences for having abolished reality in favor of illusion.

- *Environmentalism.* Our attitude is that the basic problem that causes human destruction of the environment is that there are too many of us. Every person must eat, must defecate and have a space to live. There's only so much land we can use before we destroy the ecosystems around us, which although they don't contain people are intricate machines containing parts, all of which need space. Humans should use 25% or less of the land deemed "acceptable" for human use. This requires a world population of under a billion. Since we have nearly seven billion people now, there's an ugly truth coming up: most people on the planet will be either killed or stopped from breeding. If we're going to take such a drastic step, the most important thing is to select the best humans for breeding: the smartest, strongest, and of highest character. Some people would rather we be "fair" by having some kind of lottery instead, but to anyone who sees all life as continuous, this is insane. It's better to pick the best so that the next generation is stronger. With a sane population, humans can live comfortably, but here is where the other part of our environmental aspect comes into play: we deny the importance of a consumer society. "Need" is too strong a word for luxury items and the endless shelves of plastic at Wal-Mart. We can live more efficiently, and less destructively.

- *Values.* This term is almost impossible to define, but "generalized preferences according to choices available" might be a start. Our society is failing not because the Masons or Jews or Nazis infiltrated it (pick your conspiracy) but because its values rotted from within. This happens when civilization takes a bad turn and it spirals out of control. It isn't a moral judgment from a god in a distant perfect world. As with any error, you pick yourself up, dust off your pride and you *try again.* That's the path a hero takes, and that's the path we advocate. Our values are rotten, and have been for thousands of years. The same excremental values that currently have women warring to be "equal" at the expense of family and home were also behind the laws that allowed men to beat their wives with a stick no thicker than their thumb. The same rotten values that allow giant companies to buy and sell and destroy our world at random are the corrupt values that allowed the Church to burn as much of the knowledge of the ancient world and middle ages as they could get their hands on. Our values have become passive, but passive values don't always express themselves passively; they justify themselves with something passive, like a public moral code, and use that to compel people to force that dogma on others. Passive thought therefore requires absolutes, like "Women must serve" or "Nazis are bad" or "Nature is here for our use, only" – these are a degenerate way of thought. Anytime a society gets to the

243

point where it has to write such kneejerk reactions into public standard, the battle is already going, and it's time to admit it was a failure and start a new war. A creative struggle. We don't need "equality," nor do we need "rights," because these are absolutes that naturally come into paradox, but we need good values so that we can trust our society and work with it.

- *Religion.* You don't have the "right" to believe in whatever you choose; rights are a human construction enforced through fear. Some beliefs are insane, and insanity is destructive when placed in a position of power. Dualistic interpretations of religion tell us that there is an absolute truth outside of the mechanism of this world, and that if we follow that other world's order in this world, we get rewarded. This is a fancy form of mind control, but it's very popular owing to the low quality of biological intelligence in humans as a whole today. In any healthy society, all such beliefs are approached with skepticism, and they're unprovable and thus open the way to dangerous conjecture about subjects for which there is no answer. A universal God *could* be watching over us, but it's just as likely that the universe was started from the guano of a universal Bat who eats dreams like insects. When you get into this silliness, there's no way to objectively disprove it, but there doesn't need to be, because there's no reason to start believing it in the first place unless you're schizophrenic. The intelligent gods come to us from the monist realm where the ideas of religion and observable reality are in sync, and the two support one another. Mystical gods with no relation to the mathematical and informational order of reality as apparent to us generally constitute control mechanisms.

The above are part of the analytical thought process of nihilism as applied with common sense to everyday problems. These solutions are neither Left nor Right, or even in the current political spectrum. It isn't an easy transition for someone steeped in the culture of modern free enterprise populist liberal democracy to accept. But we have to acknowledge that despite the shiny objects we have, and our wealth, our society is failing. Ecocide, internal tension, lack of consensus and general decline in intelligence are killing it.

When you strip aside social illusion, and make the passage through nihilism, both this fact and solutions to it become clear.

November 3, 2004

Multiculturalism is Genocide

The great American melting pot changed – well, do you think this change was sudden, or that it was the product of something waiting to happen? After all, the philosophy of a society decides its outcome. If I set up a civilization based on heroin addiction, it will surprise no one when it collapses because we all die from AIDS, bodily neglect and overdose. Who's to say the "melting pot" is in fact a triumph? Indeed, history – the only form of real "proof" of efficacy we have – shows us that melting pot societies have occurred in the final days of collapsing empires, and have rapidly degenerated to third-world status. You might claim that's unfair, or mean, or amoral to say, but let's get back to reality here: it is what happened, and it is what's happening.

America as a melting pot has become a different place than it once was, both culturally and ethnically, since things like that tend to go together. It was a Western European (Dutch, English, German, Scots, northern French, Scandinavian, Finnish) style country until right before the Civil War, when it admitted larger numbers of non-Western Europeans. Then, around 1900, it began gaining the bulk of its population from Eastern European countries and the South of Europe. Not to say any of these are "bad" in their own right, but we know from history that mixing tribes of the same race produces people without any clear culture, and with a confused mental evolution. England's in the same boat. Note that both England and America are exhibiting classic signs of the decline: loss of political consensus, loss of cultural consensus, pleasure seeking replacing achievement. Unlike racists, I don't blame this on the specific racial groups, but on the fact of diversity itself, which destroys the ability to have culture and values outside of government. Note that it's a taboo to express a "racist" opinion (a statement that is not in favor

245

of multiculturalism and the identical abilities and behaviors of all ethnic groups) in America today; is such a taboo a sign of a "healthy" melting pot to you?

We have little to fear from inbreeding, and nothing to gain from mixture. Inbreeding occurs in very small groups, and even the most "homogenous" European populations have vast internal diversity that exists without *any* external admixture. Further, even "homogenous" populations are constantly in evolutionary flux, thus produce favorable mutations to the point where comparing them to inbreeding even on that basis alone is laughable. I've heard the popular line that we must mix races to avoid inbreeding, but when pressed for proof and with historical evidence, every single person bleating out this crowd-pleasing dogma has backed down. I'd like to know what makes you think this way. Note that NASA, the American space agency (I should say "outer space"; our inner space agency is California), determined that were a mission sent to Mars, it would require 200 individuals of the same race to avoid inbreeding, even if it were cut off from earth forever. That's a conservative government estimate. Having a "homogenous" (meaning: ethnic-cultural) population doesn't mean you have to marry your sister. Come on, back to reality here, and stop being silly.

I believe we should affirm the presence of natural selection in producing both (a) better humans, specific to an ethnocultural society, and (b) specialized humans, specific to an ethnocultural society, but I hate crass racism. In fact, I think both racists and anti-racists are the same type of fool looking for a reason to stroke their own deficient egos; the racists want to dominate other races, so they can feel better about their own lives; the anti-racists want to dominate all cultures and replace them with an over-socialized culture that doesn't ever point out the shortcomings of the individual (any time a better way is shown, the previous way is revealed to now have a shortcoming, since we have two options: better or less-better but known, which makes those who supported the previous way look lesser), and thus feel better about their own fears of self-insufficiency. Let me lay those fears to rest: everyone has a place, because what we're fighting for here is the next generation.

246

I know many good people, and some – to the shock of racists – are African-Americans, and I like that term for people of African origin better than certain vernacular words because I believe a gentleman grants respect to all races; part of respect is realizing that they might do things a different way, that way will by nature *never* fit into one's own culture, but it deserves respect nonetheless.

This is similar to a healthy approach to homosexuality; I respect them by not believing they're inferior, and by giving them a place to be homosexual; they respect me by respecting my right to, in the context of myself, be repulsed by such behavior and want to raise my family apart from it. I think, in gay communities, rampant gayness should be the norm, and should be praised; I think in family-oriented communities, sexual behavior should be something discovered and sorted out by each individual adolescent, while being given an example of "normal" sexuality: loving, chaste, families where people are not so mystified by sex that they view it as more important than the goal of sex, namely love, respect and family. When you think about it, quality marijuana is a better rush than sex, and lasts longer to boot (you can have sex for hours, but in most cases, neither partner desires this). People who are obsessed with the feeling of sex are drug addicts of a different form. While Christians divide sex into a linear good/bad, it makes more sense to divide it into realistic and not realistic, and people who are either obsessed with avoiding sex, or with cheapening it, are both insane.

Race is similar. We've all evolved differently, even the different tribes and nations of Europe. Each of us is a history of traits, including mental traits, shaped by our culture. In any given culture, those whose inherent tendencies match the values of that culture succeed; those who don't match are less likely to breed successfully. Over time, this produces a shared cultural values system, which in turn produces philosophical and political consensus, and this is the basis of every great civilization that has ever existed (although most are in decline at this time, and race-mixing is one symptom of this decline). Without consensus, there is no agreement to move upward and become better, so civilizations decline by settling on a pale imitation of that, such as "Social Darwinism" by which we decide those who earn the most money – not those who do the best job at a given task, but those who make the most money from their task, regardless of how well it is done – are the most valued in that society. This is clearly declining, as bad products often make the most money (Apple, American cars, junk food, fast food, cheap heroin), and with this kind of thinking ends the desire of a society to better itself, and it is replaced by a desire to be comfortable during the decline: convenience.

Because we have evolved differently, not only is race-mixing insane, but caste-mixing is insane; if you merge a family of leaders with a family of carpenters, you'll either get a leader who in the role of a carpenter or a carpenter in the role of a leader, but either way, the inclinations of that individual will be mixed between their ostensible task and what they're actually inclined to do. In my desired society, the castes are equally valuable, but their specializations are preserved. It takes a different intelligence to be a carpenter than a leader, and a leader makes a crappy carpenter, but both tasks are necessary for the civilization. Hence caste and not class. Class ranks us linearly by money; caste doesn't rank us, but helps us specialize by task and ensures that each has a respected, honored, necessary place guaranteed to them, unless of course they are grossly incompetent or perverted. Does that help?

I respect members of other races as individuals and respect them in the highest way, which is to say I don't expect them to be like me or to fit into an Indo-European society. You can say that African-Americans are more likely to commit violent crime[27], or that African-Americans are less likely to find social status[28], that there are intelligence differences between the races[29], or even that African-Americans lag behind in intelligence[30], or are products of a different

---

[27] Jared Taylor, *The Color of Crime*, New Century (1999).

[28] Richard Herrnstein and Charles Murray, *The Bell Curve: Intelligence and Class Structure in American Life*, Free Press (1994).

[29] Frank Miele, *Intelligence, Race, And Genetics: Conversations With Arthur R. Jensen*, Basic Books (2002).

[30] J. Phillipe Rushton, *Race, Evolution, and Behavior: A Life History Perspective*,

evolutionary path which valued different forms of intelligence[31], but it doesn't change my love for those I know, or for myself and my own people: I believe I should be able to live in an Indo-European society of my ethnocultural tribe, and be surrounded by only Indo-Europeans, and go visit my African-American friends in their society on weekends, and exile race-mixers from either society to the middle east, which is where race-mixing has traditional had the greatest number of adherents.

In short, I believe the question of "inferior" or "superior" races is an issue for unruly groundlings to debate, and I don't want any part of it; the races are different, and have different types of ethnocultural societies they prefer, and that objectively is clear and thus I prefer a society of my own kind, with shared ethno-cultural values, and I don't view that perspective as insulting to African-Americans or *any other ethnic group*; in fact it's the opposite: the highest respect I can grant to any group is to insist that they be separate and be allowed to do things their own way, since otherwise is to presume that my way is better, and thus to impose it upon them as an "improvement" over what they are. That's crass racism, no matter how much we disguise it as Judeo-Christian liberalism. I don't have any use for racism, but I do believe in eugenics, as it is one of the foundations of a society which is always moving toward higher goals. Eugenics can occur without intervention of the state by simply having a group of similar people with shared cultural values, and allowing them to reward the best among them and downplay the worst, much as Darwin envisioned.

Heredity is more important than inculcated values[32], but this applies not only to races, but to tribes, to castes, to local groups and to *individuals*. One problem I have with the racists is that they believe all individuals are equal, presupposing their origins in a certain general racial group; that's insane to my mind. Not every "white"

Transaction (1994).

[31] Luigi Luca Cavalli-Sforza, *Genes, Peoples, and Languages*, University of California Press (2001).

[32] Stephen Pinker, *The Blank Slate: The Modern Denial of Human Nature*, Viking (2002).

person is someone I'd let survive; in fact, at this point in history, most "white" people are worthless, brainless, spiritless products of industrial existence and have nothing to contribute. My sword is unsheathed for them, because, among my tribe where there is ethnocultural consensus, these people are inferior, simply because: they suck. They're not very smart, they don't have good moral character, and they lack the impetus to do anything but go to do-nothing jobs and boss others around with rules written on sheets of paper. Off with their heads, and let's murder their children too: nothing good comes of such a seed. We have seven billion people on earth, and all but a few million are worthless followers. Fewer people means more forest, more fish, more ecosystem and more animals; what are we waiting for?

Eugenics is very real. One either establishes an ethnocultural consensus and refines every generation toward a better version of this, producing smarter-nobler-healthier people, or one stagnates and because time marches on, devolves, becoming less adapted to the changes in environment that fluctuate in cycles as a means of encouraging evolution. I prefer the heroic outlook, which is to realize the individual is not a world in itself, but a small piece of the whole, and thus to place individual pretense and safety as secondary to having a health and positively-evolving society. Eugenic breeding is not the only question, but it's a necessary tool of civilization to avoid reversing natural selection and breeding itself into domestic docility. Ultimately, everyone benefits, as the children who are born in the future are smarter, healthier and of better character, thus they struggle less with low self-esteem than the bloated products of mixed-caste, Wal-mart shopping, mixed-race, television addicted, pencil-pushing low-achievement breeding. What would you rather do, doom future generations to insufficiency or make sure those children are well-bred and happy? I prefer the latter, and I'm not the only one, but among those who fear their own failure more than they aspire to fulfilling their life's destiny, you find a prevailing opinion: all genetics are okay, all individuals are okay, just don't do anything that might show any of us in a bad light, please!!! – that is the way of the coward, and the undifferentiated crowd, and any type of evolving person has no use for it.

This is just a taste of the philosophies that make life meaningful. Right now, people cower in fear of many necessary things, and as a result, have built a society based on convenience under the pretense of avoiding suffering and making everyone "equal." This is the public veneer, but underneath it, the real motivation is utilitarianism: from fear of our own worth, we hand judgment over to the crowd; the price of this devil's bargain is that we can never again choose a direction, least of all a higher direction than the lowest common denominator, because it will "offend" someone or make them feel inferior. And the effect is manifest: where's the Beethoven for this age? The Nietzsche? The Michelangelo? The Caesar? All we have are sniveling cowards for leaders, and "artists" and "philosophers" who write about trends so they can profit and have houses in the suburbs. The signs of decline are evident, and while diversity isn't the cause, it's a symptom that furthers the decline but one that we can fix. Further, it's important to realize that racial separation is not an issue by itself, but part of a general program of breeding that includes division by tribe, caste, and finally, eugenics applied to individuals themselves.

Dividing by tribe allows each tribe to have its own way of doing things; this is the only way to achieve the consensus necessary for any kind of upward-mobile society. It is this alone, and not some ego-stroking belief in being "superior" or "inferior" for being member of a group, that is the reason for racial separation – not racial antagonism. I'll continue to care about gay, African-American, Hispanic, Asian, and Jewish people, but I will also care first and foremost about myself and my people, for whom separation is required for survival. Don't let the crass racists confuse you – you *can* acknowledge your own preference for your own people without falling into hate, bigotry, and other forms of masturbatory self-image enhancement.

December 21, 2004

SURVIVING MULTICULTURALISM

In the end stages of every great civilization, several things happen. First, impetus is lost: people no longer have an urge to create civilization as, heck, it's already here, let's enjoy it and not think too hard, because the people that made this place, they took life too seriously, man. Second, consensus is lost, in that people accustomed to appreciating the benefits of society no longer have the singular focus on maintaining it that comprises a healthy goal set. Once consensus is lost, what we commonly call "values" cannot exist, since there's no agreement about what is valued. After this, the symptoms set in, namely internal division, loss of learning and culture, and of course, bad breeding, first within the bloodline and then miscegenation.

This is how great civilizations fall, and you can see their ruins today all over the earth. T.S. Eliot was correct to note that it ends with a whimper and not a bang[33], because by the time the ancient structures are falling, there are few left who can actually realize what's happening. Most of the population have already transitioned to the idea of living among the ruins in a more primitive state, and lacking most qualities of discernment in themselves, aren't much concerned about how all finer things are crumbling around them, because they still have their fast food and television and are content with that. There is rarely a sudden appearance by the forces of evil to sweep into the streets and crush a vibrant culture; rather, the collapse of a great civilization is as anticlimactic as the death of a terminal cancer patient.

As always, there is writing on the wall, for those who remember how to read it. Lacking a goal, people become obsessed by novelty and personal conceits, so instead of having hearty, strong people who can create, you have very trendy people who adorn themselves

---

[33] T.S. Eliot, "The Hollow Men" (1925).

excessively and are neurotically obsessed with appearance. This is a natural consequence of having lost consensus, because since there is no longer a goal to the society as a whole and an agreement about how to reach it, people focus on living in a society of disorder. To gain power in such a society, one entertains and flatters, and this requires a decadent but "different" lifestyle in order to distinguish oneself in any way. Bread and circuses for the poor, trinkets and fads for the wealthy.

One can survive such a society, but it requires doing something most free-willed people find abhorrent: dedicating themselves in the largest part toward earning money, and sacrificing most of their time to this goal. Work six day weeks and bring home a fat paycheck, and you can get out into the suburbs where most people are gentler. You can afford the Alta Dena organic dairy milk, the no-pesticide vegetables, the finer clothes; you can drive a nice car, and buy memberships in places where the screaming rabble don't congregate. However, ultimately, such a lifestyle requires increasing amounts of money as the rest of the economy collapses and thus such finer things become aberrations in a consumer environment rewarding goods that above all are cheap; quality becomes second to quantity.

In effect, this destroys the middle class, because it raises the bar on the cost of living outside of the undifferentiated mass. You're either wealthy, and living in a gated community, or you're with the rest living in a technological third-world environment. With the loss of the middle class comes a loss of the ordinary, hardworking decent people in the world, because they are turned into either whores for money or semi-impoverished scatterbrains like the rest. When that occurs, the base of support for the finer things in life – the arts, culture, and learning – falls entirely into the hands of the wealthy, who are not really concerned with getting it right; they're concerned with finding a way to make millions so they can escape the *hoi polloi*. Culture dies; art dies; learning dies.

Of course, the mutant corpses survive. There will be "art" – but it will be little more than decoration, "unique" patterns and styles designed to shock or amuse: the kind of stuff that Hitler, being an artist, had no problem ordered being destroyed. There will be "culture," but it will consist of going to places where you buy things to participate in cultural events will all of the decorum and depth of a Nirvana concert. The institutes of higher learning will continue but will devote most of their time to teaching the ways of the new society, re-interpreting the older knowledge to fit the new rubric and, consequently, destroying it as a system of thought. It, too, will become aesthetics, and although it will exist in reference books (if not burned by the "progressive" newcomers) there will be only a handful who understand it, and none who can add to it.

This is the future that T.S. Eliot and other writers of his generation saw in the 1920s, when America first became obsessed with money and fads, and the first wave of "mostly-white" immigrants rode into the middle of a fair complexioned Northern European stock. Currents in thinking changed, then the population changed, and that cycle begat another. What T.S. Eliot was fortunate enough not to see is the dimension to which modern society has grown. Thanks to industrial technology and greater transportation, this is now a global society, with counter-dependent economies and military alliances. It probably does not pay to wonder if the domino theory will apply in nations falling to decay, but it's clear that most nations are on the same liberal democratic, global industrial society path, and thus will suffer similar fates.

You can't mention any of this in the current time, of course. Since there's no goal, people are concerned with making their own money and "rising above" the undifferentiated masses, thus they are mortified that you might offend someone by pointing out that there *could* be a consensus, because having agreement in values would make some people "better" and "others" worse for the purpose of having citizens who can enact those values. They are also socially concerned; they can't speak out without losing friends and alienating potential mates. Where bravery is called for, sheeplike herdthink prevails instead simply because the immediate personal cost is too high, although the *long-term* personal cost of inaction will be much higher. Most can't handle that so conclude that with personal death their interest in the world ends.

So what is someone concerned about having a *functional* civilization to do?

The first and most important task is to begin sorting the world into yes and no categories. This means finding out what you will support, and what you do not consider part of the fulfillment of your goals. In this, you are escaping some Absolute vision of what is "right," as the conservatives do, and opting for the stronger assertion of will that is "I prefer." It transcends subject and object classifications, and will occur to the degree of which the individual is capable, but this is a more flexible system than some knee-jerk Absolute which rapidly parodies itself and becomes reactionary and preservationist, which is an error because what is needed is not to *save* a society that exists – that one has already fallen, I'm afraid – but to *create* a new society according to the ancient tradition of the Indo-Europeans.

After Friedrich Nietzsche, who asserted a naturalistic and aristocratic social system and derided liberal democracy for its failings, there was Rene Guénon, who gave us a simple logical device for understanding resistance to modern society: all that we saw in the ancients that was functional is part of a set of values that are true in any age because of their fundamental recognition of the problems of reality for those who desire higher civilization, and that is called Tradition; what opposes it is Modernity, and the "progressive" society that believes we can reach some Utopic ideal through egalitarian and utilitarian government. Guénon was correct in dividing current history into these two threads, as Modernity takes many forms, including both Capitalism and Communism, conservatism and liberalism. There is no escape from Modernity once you begin using its divisions.

This split is important in that it allows us to group all aspects of traditional, pre-Christian Indo-European civilization – what is called "ascendant" civilization because it believes in evolving toward a higher state of an eternal ideal, in contrast to "progressive" civilization which advocates a constant change of ideal on a root of progress to Utopic liberalism – into something which can not only be upheld but developed. The only future for Indo-Europeans is to stop trying to finding Absolute reasons to "prove" we are right, and to start building this form of ascendant, Traditional civilization within the train wreck of ideas that is the modern time.

One aspect of Traditional civilization worldwide, regardless of race, is ethnoculture, which is the idea that no culture can exist without its traditional ethnicity to uphold it, because the tens of thousands of generations that produced that culture also shaped the population through selection for those who tended toward upholding its ideal values. Ethnoculture does not designate an Absolute "superior" or "inferior" race. Instead, it asserts an "I prefer": for each culture to exist, it must prefer to have its own ethnic group isolated from all others. This is not inbreeding; there's enough variation in even a small population to avoid inbreeding. It's not "racism," in the sense of wanting to suppress or dominate other ethnic groups who are seen as inferiors, but it's an honest statement of need and will to keep them *out* so that the culture can develop without becoming a mixed-race society like so many remnants of collapsed ancient civilizations.

The only workable way to create a Traditional civilization is to begin working with the declining ruin at hand. Yes, the basic values of society around us are defunct, but like a disciplined wrestler, we can use its oncoming weight against it and thus achieve our own means. For that reason, the first proposition of this article is that we accept "diversity," and take it to its logical extremes.

Diversity means having different groups coexisting; however, in order for them to remain different groups, they can't merge (our media and institutes of higher learning seem to have forgotten this part). As I once put it to a homosexual gentleman, diversity means that I don't think much about what you do in your bedroom, but it also means that you don't begrudge me the right to make gay jokes and be repelled by sodomy, because to a heterosexual, such behavior would be a disastrous submission and loss of masculinity. I respect his "difference," but he has to respect mine. The same applies to different ethnic groups. To acknowledge their difference is to recognize that participation in that group is limited to members of that group, and no matter how much "authentic African art" we buy at Wal-Mart, we're still members of our own tribe with its own identity.

This requires formally defining diversity in the first place, and getting some public agreement on this fact. The definition proposed above benefits all groups, as it keeps them distinct from others and guarantees them the ability to govern themselves culturally. A change of this nature would reverse the current tendency for "diversity" to become an emotional value of a passive nature, translated into "accept everyone regardless of their behavior," which is exactly the opposite mentality of every group that has ever created a civilization with more than mud huts and large rodents roasting on the open fire. Some might call this change "extremist diversity," but every philosophy should be able to be extended to its extremes without becoming paradoxical.

Next, find others who understand this task. Because after culture has fallen the task of restoring culture is an artificial one, meaning imposed externally instead of occurring "naturally" from within, it can't be done with bureaucracy or rules. It has to be done by creating something and drawing those who can appreciate it into the fold, and this can only be achieved by eschewing alienating ideology for a commonsense belief system that does not require them to give up their membership in society or to adhere to any philosophies of a radical or violently emotional nature. The philosophies these people will find meaningful are ones based on "I prefer" which involve action toward a positive goal. They are not interested in bigotry, nor are they interested in Utopic silliness from liberals. They want a better way of life. This is the origin of all civilization-building, from the first caveman who decided having a permanent fire might be a good idea, onward.

We've all read the articles in *National Geographic* talking about the isolated tribe of Whatsitsname "fighting hard to preserve their traditional culture and ways in the face of the onslaught of modernity." You would never guess from public rhetoric in America that Indo-Europeans are fighting the same battle. We can win it by taking our society's mechanisms and adapting them singularly to our own need in the type of scenario described above. If we begin building something new that is an option within the realistic spectrum of choices offered to people in our society, the hardiest among them will consider it and be likely to move. The others are too busy "just doing my thing, man" and we are fortunate for their voluntary exclusion.

This plan would require an Indo-European living space. To get started, it needs some kind of economic base, even if only a single corporation that is willing to hire local people. Once the character of the community is started, the laws of our society must be changed. Anti-discrimination legislation, including the Housing and Urban Development rules, no longer need apply in a modern society, so we can campaign to have them removed, not on the grounds that we "hate" other groups, but on the ethnocultural grounds described above: "white" people are no longer in charge of America, and this group of Indo-Europeans wants the right to preserve itself. Similarly, other affirmative action legislation needs to be repealed. It has served its purpose, and now isn't needed; we want the right to hire only our own kind so we are not forced to alter the makeup of our community to fit racial quotas. This would be a quiet revolution in American law against "one size fits all" legislation to something that would allow actual diversity by giving localized groups the ability to rule themselves, as culturally appropriate, in ways different than those preferred by the undifferentiated masses.

A state such as this, whether located in one place or communities distributed across a continent, will require its own cultural conventions, much as neighborhoods of a longstanding ethnic mix have their own informal ways of governing themselves. It will require its own media: its own television, its own authors, its own artists. It will require its own economic structure that only hires members of that community. Much like successful cultural holdouts such as the Basque or Amish, it must be willing to isolate itself without falling into a passive and hopeless "reservation mentality." In all likelihood, it would be a feudal state organized by breeding into castes, with higher rewards and responsibilities going to those of greater ability and moral character ("nobility"). With only a handful of legal changes, it can happen in modern America and Europe, and can separate those worth saving from those who oblivious go into the same doom that has afflicted all great civilizations.

It may seem like fanciful thinking now, and perhaps this article is only metaphor for the changes needed in society as a whole, but given that society has developed on its current path through 2,000 years of liberal democratic thought, it is unlikely to alter its course without violent collapse and revolution, things which historically have not afforded the birth of a new civilization but have cheerfully destroyed many remnants of the old. Civilizations die like stars, by collapsing inward, and the only way to reverse that is to birth a new star from the ashes of the old. We are in the end stages of what our ancestors built, and the time has passed where we could simply destroy alien elements and consider ourselves saved; we must create something new according to the values which engendered the great Indo-European civilizations. In this new birth is our only future.

January 11, 2005

TRANSCENDENTALISM

Most philosophies focus on quantity, or finding some other alternative to what is. Transcendentalism looks *into* what is to discover its order, the meaning behind it, and the implications of the types of patterns seen there.

Transcendentalism consists of recognizing life as it is, including its terrifying aspects, but seeing a tendency uniting all things that leads to a "meta-good" or overall positive outcome. Including time in the equation, this extends to evolution itself and the conflict it requires. The transcendentals – traditionally "the good, the beautiful and the true" among others – consist of those things which cannot be achieved but always aimed for, and which affirm the fundamental *possibilities* of greatness in this world and our power to do great things within it. Reverence for our world, both awe and love, bonds us to it in a unitive state of mind where we reject our resentments, and look only to what we can achieve within it that furthers its fundamental design of goodness, beauty and truth.

Reverence, not justice, is the virtue that separates leaders from tyrants, as the old Greek poets knew well. In episode after tragic episode, they show how failures of reverence destroy men who are trying to be leaders. Reverence is the capacity to feel respect in the right way toward the right people, and to feel awe toward an object that transcends particular human interests. When leaders are reverent, they are reverent along with their followers, and their common reverence unites them in feelings that overcome personal interests, feelings such as mutual respect. These feelings take the sting from the tools of leadership – from persuasion, from threats of punishment, from manipulation by means of rewards. This is because there are no winners and losers when there is reverence. Success and failure are dwarfed by whatever it is that they hold in awe together.[34]

Unlike mysticism, transcendentalism does not require a metaphysical belief, although it hints at one because a discovery of brilliance in design to our world suggests an underlying force – probably incomprehensible to us – which urges it onward toward the state of order that provokes reverence and transcendental feeling in ourselves. Schopenhauer identifies the universe as being formed of and motivated by a raw, unconditioned Will, lawless like nature itself, which seeks to form in physical reality a type of design which can only make sense to itself. Transcendence is our appreciation of that design.

Nihilism leads to transcendental thought by rejecting human fears and a need to control. Instead, it places us back in our position as voyagers on the ship called reality and our mortal lives within it, showing us not an inherent purpose but grades of options which we can choose and by so doing, rise to be more like the order we see in nature.

---

[34] Paul Woodruff, *Reverence: Renewing a Forgotten Virtue*, Oxford University Press (2001), p. 176.

NATURE IS A BUG-WRECKING FACTORY

In New York, they cannot imagine why someone would choose to live in heathen, dirty, uneducated, Republican Texas. It is simply so un-hip, unglamorous, and the shopping has nothing on fifth avenue. When, as good nihilists, we strip aside all the social pretense and morality and politics, we can see Texas as it actually is, which is a good-sized chunk of land that contains at least five distinct ecosystems, and infinite numbers of wonderfully bizarre bugs.

Specially adapted, these species occupy niches in the environment which are still unknown to science, and their shapes and colors reveal this position. Strange mandibles rise above serrated limbs, and wings come in innumerate shades of translucent color. You can wander through these woods in summer and see a new kind each day without even trying, although you will be trying to swat away the impressively bellicose mosquitoes. Each variety has its own form as inspired by what it eats and what it avoids.

There are moths that you cannot tell from tree bark until they move. Cicadas dwell underground for seventeen years, then emerge as gnarled war machines with razor-like claws, worthy of an underground Japanese monster movie. Worms drop silently from silk enshrouded branches, and multitudinous ants move under a layer of leaves, invisible. Praying mantises like wrought iron stand immobile until their prey is exactly within striking range, and then they obliterate the present tense because suddenly their stillness is past, as is their strike; they dwell patiently in the future, eating or waiting, because their movements are too quick to be captured in current time.

Here there are giant beetles with pincers bigger than any limb, spiders brightly colored as if to warn enemies like children shouting into dark rooms, wasps that hover and paralyze their victims, carrying them off to become zombified food for imminent young. Not only is Texas home to millions of bugs that, once you see how their form mates to a function, are beautiful, it is also a gigantic mixed martial arts competition between bugs. Nature makes them, and out of the eggs they stream, violent and vigilant, ready for war. When they collide, one sees the strength of each design matched against an equally strong will, and that which has the advantage wins. Nature at these moments is an enormous bug-wrecking factory, as if searching through uncountable possible blueprints for the future of each type.

It is not only militant, but playful, because these bugs are without emotion when they grapple. They perform it as a function like eating, seeming to relish every moment of stalking their prey and then sucking out its innards or embalming it in strands, stabbing through its exoskeleton to inject parasitic larvae. It is a dance, when these bugs confront one another, through the detritus of the forest floor or high above on the lichen-speckled branches of ancient trees. They show no fear, or anger, but move toward it like any other fate that waits them, as if more curious to see what happens than concerned about their own mortality. They live, and die, without blinking in the stare of eternity.

This reminds me that whatever force created this universe is present in all things, as if each of us were a device driver or daemon running on a giant UNIX system, and that in its purest gaze, nature is not afraid of death because it does not die, even if its objects are destroyed and consumed. It is eternal, and whatever force engendered and sustains it grants consciousness to its bugs much as to its humans, aware that when they die, consciousness flows back into the whole and then out again to a new set of creatures. Life cannot die (barring ecocide by selfishly individualistic humans) but death is one of the colors of its palette, an unavoidable ochre to stain the canvas so that a watcher might feel an emotion in the contrast as the eye passes over form and vision, a story unfolding.

Like us, the bugs fight it out, neither creating or destroying, but preserving an eternal balance which affords consciousness through *avatars*, or incarnate material forms which conform to cyclic patterns, in which it can exist perpetually. Selfless and fearless, bugs engage in combat knowing that their deaths are meaningless, in that through the massive digital computer of nature their designs are slowly tested in architectonic millions of ways, bettering them at every increment. Through these better designs, the machine of life becomes more efficient, leaking less energy through inexact trade-offs, and pumping life back into its origin so that life can return eternal. There is a massive spiritual peace in war and death as in a sunny day or the birth of a doe, and it is all as natural as our angers and fears and loves.

In the ancient religion of my forefathers, which some call Paganism and others Hinduism, there were many gods but all things came from the same godhead, which was like a great brooding consciousness not outside of the world but present in all of it; it does not exist outside of reality as we know it, but through its will, manifests that reality and thus comes into observable being. It does not judge, and while it makes flamboyantly specialized creatures and thrusts them into never-ending war, it is creating while it destroys, and destroying in order to create. It alone is a perfect balance. When I walk in the woods and see nature's bug-wrecking factory, I am looking into the parentage of the gods and man and nature alike, and it touches my heart with appreciation for the genius of life.

January 4, 2006

DECAY OF ICONS

I noticed something today among the holiday decorations being thrown out. It was a floral arrangement with evergreen and these weird red apples, quite small, on stiff wire. On closer inspection, they turned out to be plastic, and having melted a bit in the heat next to the stove, were in fact losing their outer plastic skin. The red plastic skin had bunched, leaving ugly veins across the surface as if the apples were decaying.

I peeled. Underneath the skin was styrofoam, and a green plastic "leaf" concealing the stiff wire used to stab them into the foam center of the piece. I thought for a moment: this decoration, bought for $0.75 and used for three or four days of holiday "cheer," is now waste that will never compost into fertile soil like a real apple. A real apple will rot, stink, and vanish within weeks, leaving behind either happy plants and animals or those and a new apple tree-in-training.

This plastic object will decompose into toxic byproducts and stick around for a few dozen of my lifetimes, then become some kind of oily sludge staining the ground where it lay. That is assuming it doesn't sit in near perfect stasis in an airless underground landfill for a few thousand years, which is most likely. When I throw this thing out, since no one knows how to recycle it, it gets crushed into junk by a passing garbage truck and thrown into the big landfill north of town, where they're burying trash seventy feet deep and covering it with clay. Should keep it better than a museum for whatever visiting aliens conduct a postmortem on humanity.

Looking at this thing, this fake apple that designed to be appealing but ending up grotesque, brought on that vague form of depression that comes with tolerating broken-ness around oneself. Dysfunction in the self is depressing, but at least the solution is straightforward; if you're fat, stop eating so much and go for a walk. If you're lonely, do something, even casual crime, that helps you meet people. If you're dying, think positive so your last days aren't wasted on feeling bad. But when confronting a piece of trash whose existence is owed to the decisions of those around you? It will depress.

Why do we, as humans, make these disposable ornamental plastic reproductions of natural objects when they have one sorta-good consequence and many bad ones? I suppose it's not fair to say they should be banned, because I will ruin someone's livelihood and possibly shatter their dreams, but when the consequences are this bad *and unnecessary*, maybe it is better to shatter dreams than to tolerate destructive ideas. After all, we take them into our hearts, and we become depressed by the knowledge that we're passing along this destructive buck and powerless to remove it. Their inner ugliness overrides the surface cheer and invades our inner selves, turning us against the possibility of beauty and greatness, and toward a mentality of disposable emotions and a lack of reverence for our natural world.

As I contemplate the object, I see all the reasons for its use: it is cheap, it will never rot, it is brightly-colored, and any idiot can recognize what it is because it's an idealized design, not one marred by worms or misshapen, in the ruby red that screams "This is an apple!" to even the totally braindead. And then I wonder about the one good reason for not having it, which is that it depresses us to know we are so destructive, and leave the world in worse condition than we encountered it. Banning plastic waste would remove some jobs, would shatter some dreams, and might cause inconvenience, but wouldn't it be better to have healthier... souls?

October 11, 2007

TEXAS

One fundamental truth that I encounter as I get older is that we humans are like turtles. We like having our comfortable shells, but we're always craning our necks to get out of them, to see what's on the other side. We suffer for being too clever. We find out what hurts or kills, and we in our big-brained wisdom can keep it away, but then we wonder if we're missing anything, like Rapunzel in a tower made of red plastic-styrofoam apples melting together into impenetrable goo. She can't even let down her hair, because she's not insured against falls.

Our society keeps us apart from nature. I can, if I so choose, live my life so I never have to see a snake or encounter a mosquito. I'll get that downtown apartment, keep the air conditioning running, and when I go on vacation, go to another city where I encounter the outside only when passing between climate-controlled buildings full of sterilized, plastic-wrapped objects. I can structure my life so that I never see more than four trees at once, and my deepest experience of nature is that downtown park that's more landscaping to avoid leaving dark recesses where rapes can happen than it is "nature," whatever that is. It is as if we humans are using external objects to manipulate our internal mentation again, like the man who buys an expensive stationary bicycle to force himself to exercise, by destroying the nature outside as if to banish the nature within: the feral, questing and restless force that demands worlds to conquer and unreachable horizons to chase.

But from inside that plastic electric turtle-shell, unless I'm totally brain-dead (maybe the TV breaks for a week, and my brain freed of propaganda seeks answers), I'm going to wonder about my world. It's natural for any thinking being to wonder, because those thinkers that do not wonder are basically limited to repetition of past impetus. They cannot create a need for a new direction by dreaming

267

and wondering. It is probably the intellectual equivalent of being a kitchen blender or washing machine.

When you go to places far away, and talk to people as best you can, usually because they speak your language because it is associated with commerce (and you blame the Jews for money-culture, when all money speaks English these days), you will see through what lens the world views your homeland. Generally, responses to Americans are hesitant; people are somehow aware that the wrong comment might bring bombers and an army of yahoos hellbent on killing for democracy to their doors. They loosen up a bit when you say "Texas," and then you see it – just for a moment, a fragment of a glimpse – that far-off look in their eyes, like remembering a dream.

They're dreaming of Westerns, and old-time tales. Their minds conjure homesteads in places unexplored, lands without law, and loves so eternal that two people might face the wilderness together. They're dreaming of how Texas used to be, and an image it retains, not through reality but through the power of our wishes. We want Texas, and Australia and other romanticized places, to be this way forever. We want that frontier, that lack of law and safety regulations on every single thing you pick up, that sense of indefinition. We want the adventure. Outside the shell, it might be there – but we're too scientific, too practical and too accustomed to Microsoft Excel spreadsheets to take that trade-off, so it remains a far-off dreamy look, and then is replaced by that normal "snapped back to attention" gaze we use in conversation and staff meetings.

> Evil in the forest in Germany's Green Heart!
> Hateful savages, strong black minds
> Out of the forest, kill the human kind
> Burn the settlements and grow the woods
> Until this romantic place is understood![35]

We all want to live in Texas – that old Texas. At least, some part of us does. It's so *romantic*, human against wilderness, or maybe in concert with it by struggling against it, since everything in nature struggles against nature to survive. Even the lowly fungus would cease to exist

---

[35] Absurd, "Green Heart," *Out of the Dungeon* (1994).

if it didn't thrust back against the forces that from gravity to the trampling feet of mice (herds, when you're .5mm tall) trying to beat it back. And so it is with our vision of Texas: that homestead on the prairie where a wild-haired woman takes the hand of her powder-burned man at the end of the day, and they look out over their meagre homestead, full of dreams of its growth and their own. They know this lawless land will possess them, even kill them, but there's this sense of a power in doing what they do, in thrusting themselves forward against the resistance and making something of it, even not minding its imperfect – like a sense of *meaning* in the lexicon where a struggle returns a feeling of accomplishment.

That's the Texas we want, and that we keep in our hearts, even as it disappears under skyscrapers, shopping centers, and Section 8 housing. It's what is missing from modern society, where we have idealized symbolic apples instead of the real partially-rotted malformed and often blurrily colored thing. It's not nature we want, it's not danger; it's not even the space and "freedom" of that open range. It's the challenge. It's the fear, and the beating it back day after day. It's the conquering of doubt, the whole world against us as we and the beloved head off to the homestead, and restoration of faith in life itself each day we survive. It's the shaking of our fist in those sagely nodded heads and murmured voices under conservative beards that say, "You won't make it removed from civilization – one season, at the outside."

We don't want to fight cougars, but we would. We're not doing it to shoot back at raiding war parties. We're not enamored of outhouses, or sweating through a fever without penicillin. No doubt it's easier the way we do things now. And more comfortable. Less risk. But what's missing, in our lives and in all of modern society, is that we only see the end-product, the tangible and material and human(ist), but we've left out the experience of life. That experience includes taking something on and making it work, or dying in the process, knowing we're not cowards in our turtle-shells. That's what Texas is, as a symbol of our hearts quite different from an idealized plastic apple, and Texas is the antidote to every one of the fears we're too practical to voice.

October 11, 2007

TO REIGN IN HELL

As is known to those who take the time to think on such esoteric topics, it is impossible to know the good without the bad. There is a middle state, without judgment, where nothing much matters, but too much lingering here and one discovers a kind of personal entropy: since all decisions are equally of this middle state, there's no point making any decision. Linger in the stream and let it pass. Of course, in that state, there is also none of the reward of accomplishment.

Making choices after all defines us. From the simplest satisfactions when we choose to clean our homes or organize our lives in a better fashion, to the greatest choices, when we stand our ground for a principle or ideal, choice makes us feel alive because in it we are exercising the capacity of life. This ability is at its simplest level motion, and at its most complex motion through the world of ideas. We feel alive when we encounter a choice and make a good one. We feel dead when we shirk from these choices, even if we're "comfortable" with our warm homes, cars, video games, pornography and serving-size packaged prefabricated foods.

Excepting such a middle state, we live for making choices toward what is good and avoiding what is bad. As with all judgments and categories, these exist in a spectrum from simple goods like a clean house being superior to a filth-hole, to complex ends where we prefer a society that is not failing to one that allows us excess of comfort. Our choices are informed by our knowledge of what is good, or what ends in an order that is beneficial to us, and what is bad, or what results in less organization and less beneficial aspects. Disorder is another form of entropy, one that is fatal to individuals and societies alike.

Our knowledge of good and bad is entirely dependent on experience, although we come pre-programmed with some knowledge. Snakes are for the most part bad, in our genetic heritage, and depending on where our families originated, there may be other primal fears and primal desires. Germans seem to like order and cleanliness over all else, where to an Italian, a warm house full of good food takes precedence. What we all share that is not learned is a knowledge that some things will end well, and others will not. If we are attuned to ourselves, we become uneasy deep in our gut when we are part of a course of action that we suspect will not end well.

We wonder if indeed our universe learned by the same method, since our thoughts and their maturation so resemble the processes we see in nature whether planets forming from circling gases or species adapting general principles to specific environments. Our furthest conjecture might envision a nothingness so absolute it is not even an empty space, only an absence in totality, which at some point through a routine error was able to recognize two parts of itself as distinct, and thus created "space" so both could exist. Is the universe made of thoughts? It certainly seems as if it acts that way.

In John Milton's *Paradise Lost*, the most beautiful of angels so made Error and rebelled against an all-seeing God, and was thus cast into a Hell, dividing existence between Heaven and Hell and their mediate zone, this mortal space of time and body we know as "life on earth." Satan, cast among the wreckage with his fellow rebels, reflects on his fate with the stolidity of a Greek tragic deity: It is better to reign in hell, he surmises, than to serve in heaven. From error comes new life, and from Satan's fall comes what we know on earth as the significance of choice between good and bad. With only heaven, there was no need for such choice, and through error, the universe expanded.

When we return from our spacey conjecture to the reality of our present time, we can see a parallel construction: without certain knowledges, we are unaware of how what transpires will end. A child will not be concerned when people around him or her are taking methamphetamine, because that becomes in that child's experience "normal"; in the same way, a child can be inculcated to live around any population or behavior, but this does not mean such behaviors will end well or poorly. In the same way, we who grow up in a certain society know it as "normal" and must actively assess its tenets and actions as to how they will end.

But our experience limits us, and in this we see the wisdom of hell. Most grow up in the normalcy and do not second-guess it, but accept its failings as a matter of course and do their best to dodge them. Fewer than one percent of all people question the actual direction of society or its future impact. Among those, only a few have either sought or seen hell and remained mentally intact enough to process it.

Of course, hell takes many forms. Some find hell on the battlefield, others in a broken home, and still others in crime or economic desolation. Others find it more subtly in the interactions of people. Win an award, get a promotion, make a work of art, or get famous, and suddenly you find that your friends are retaliating against you. Or sniping, expecting you to pick up the check and not care about the damage they do to your house. In the quiet moments after such events, when the puzzled mind attempts to diagnose the situation... and one realizes that other people can be motivated by revenge, small-minded envy, and even a simple parasitic desire to steal.

Having seen hells created by humans, or even the hell that a solitary human can bring to us, we become more critical of any potential action. Our sphere of good expectations has been violated, but much as Satan in discovering hell found a certain liberation, we find that we are disassociated as a result from an illusion. We no longer believe that all is well no matter what we do. Through the impact of horror, and by seeing the empty and false motivations of others, we realize not only that we are in the driver's seat both of our own lives and of our future as a civilization, but that there is no guarantee things will work out alright on their own – more likely, they'll turn out terribly, since many of the people in command have the same revengeful outlook as the others in whom we discover anew hell.

In the same way an inexperienced Satan could not know the power of his own choice, because he never had the chance to screw up and get thrown into hell, modern people are inexperienced and know not hell. They are virgins of true depression, true fear, and true horror because they have surrogate experiences of pleasure and pain within a system that doesn't vary – although it postpones all of its biggest disasters much like it puts its trash in landfills, criminals in prisons, toxic waste in oceans, incompetents in government. They get excited by a change in job, and get depressed by a broken car. But do they face real horror or victory, the chance for change not in an event within their lives but the form of those lives themselves?

Until one knows hell, one cannot look into the structure of things. Behind the visible, behind the immediate, there is the way elements of a situation interact to perpetuate it. To see hell is to realize how those things bring about negativity. To see hell is to wish to know the only way to avoid it is to tackle these difficult and complex but rewarding invisible structures. Any idiot can bash an attacking wolf on the head, but how many can realize the misdirection of an upstream tributary disrupted a hunting ground and brought on the wolf? Or spotting an error that does not attack like the wolf, but leaves out necessary things, laying the groundwork for future failure. To see hell is to realize, like Satan did, that the visible is only part of what must be considered.

To realize hell is to see that the invisible world must be tackled. We cannot exist in the solely visible world, where tangible concepts are presented to us and we vote upon them or buy them but never change the structure of society. The visible world is what humans create for one another, with words and symbols and flags. The invisible world, more than what they say they mean, is the future results of their actions as designed. The invisible world is what will determine the difference between heaven and hell long before the impact of decisions past makes those states come about.

Critical thinking, or the ability to analyze complex structure where there is no single supporting idea (linearity) but a balance of all points balancing all others (architectonic), is the rarest of abilities in our world. It requires thinkers who dedicate time and energy to understanding, but it also requires a vision of enough hell to desire heaven. It is not surprising that our best thinkers, writers, leaders and artists warn us that our society is a path to hell, and most repeat those words and change nothing of their behavior or political outlook. They haven't seen hell, because hell is invisible until its consequences are felt. For those who can predict those consequences, hell arrives early.

The ancients considered critical thinking to be intelligence. They knew that with enough practice and indoctrination, marginally intelligent people could be made "intelligent" in a narrow field with few tactics that need applying. You can teach almost anyone to be a computer programmer, because most of the "thinking" is responding to variants on already-known scenarios and memory work to find the right matching piece in response. It's like fitting shaped blocks into holes. Our smart people today are singular function linear thinkers, of a partial intelligence that allows them to excel in one area without an ounce of critical thinking, and for this reason they do not recognize hell. They must be shown hell, and this is why our authors and thinkers try increasingly to represent it.

Yet for those who can make the trip from a heaven of ignorant blithe oblivion (modern living) to a realization of not just personal tragedy but the poor design of a civilization leading to inevitable future hell, the experience is life-changing. Small cares fall away. The yawning gap between perception and reality that will swallow us becomes apparent in all that we see. When this wears off, we become accustomed to enduring situations that are so poorly designed it is clear they will end badly, but most people blithely march onward into them. They are ignorant of hell, visible or invisible.

In contrast to our product-oriented media, which tries to make different hells (war, ghetto, sodomy, drugs, AIDS) seem appealing because of their lack of rules, those who have experienced hell have a different look in their eyes. They want to get away from it, because they realize that while the experience of hell is revolutionary, living in hell is not – it is tedious, both in daily endurance and in knowledge of its certain failure. People who have seen hell tend to find wisdom in traditional family roles, in intangible pleasures like creativity and learning, and in removing themselves from the city to contemplate insignificance under a boundless night sky. They have seen hell, and realize that our modern heaven on earth leads to it, and they must escape.

But of course for most it is too late. They don't have the time, and they lack the brainpower at hand, or the learning, to see hell, much less the invisible hell. This is why in our society, 90% of the people are oblivious and 8% are busy profiting from hell while only 2% are actually worried. Hell is easy to avoid, now, because they are worried about visible hells like war and anarchy. Our society of course as an all-inclusive place is bias against genius, because not only do they not need including, but they resist efforts toward norming. It detests those who rise above the crowd as they are both socially and bureaucratically awkward to explain to others. This is why few voices speak out about what hell awaits us, but these tend to be the smartest and most experienced voices.

When one has experienced hell, the world expands most prominently into two options: the choice to continue on a path to hell, or the choice to head elsewhere. For those who have not seen hell, the idea of hell – "freedom" to a teenage self-indulgent Satan in Heaven – seems appealing. But to those who have seen it, hell is not only not appealing but not rare. It is mundane. The freedom of hell and the oblivion of heaven lead to the same place, which is failure, and the determination of the experienced is to avoid both. Much as the universe recognized its own emptiness, and Satan saw his own failing as liberation, we can find liberation in looking unblinkingly into hell, and then steeling our resolve to choose another path.

October 11, 2007

CRUX

The dilemma of being human centers around our ability to turn our shoulder toward any facet of reality we do not like and choose to not include it in our knowledge of the world. Because we have big brains, in which we keep a map of the world in our memories, we can alter our maps without reality changing and so become delusional. Even worse, we can then claim that we've done that for a "higher purpose" and so claim that while it is unrealistic, it is just or moral.

Life thrusts upon us many choices, but each of those choices is made for us by our previous underlying assumptions. For example, if we believe that quality is always more important than quantity, choosing the expensive organic peas over a giant bucket of peas grown in an industrial wasteland is easy. If we believe family is more important than mass media, certain political decisions are already made and await only articulation.

Underneath all of our decisions then, or at the top of a hierarchy of assumptions upon which we base our decisions, is the question of how we should make decisions. We need some kind of pragma that tells us what is important for us to use as the basis for decision-making itself. Whenever a society starts feeling it has no "narrative" or "goal," what is meant is that this highest level of abstraction is missing.

In human affairs, one very basic choice confronts us. We are physical beings with minds that predict more than our immediate state of comfort. Do we use our minds and strive for something more than our physical preservation and state of comfort, or do we zealously defend our physical state?

The latter produces a philosophy akin to both anarchy and consumerism, a kind of atavistic individualism that states we only do what we decide we want to do; we only act for ourselves "in the now"; and any action that offends us, requires us to change what we want to do, or requires sacrifice except for the preservation of ourselves and all other individuals is taboo. It is self-preservation bordering on selfishness, and if we choose it, over time it moves from the former to the latter.

The crux of human decision-making and our highest abstract level of choice can be summarized in this question: do we accept that physical reality is a means to an end, while all ends are abstract, even if they include perpetuation of the means?

Before we've had a chance to think about it, this question seems paradoxical. We, as we know ourselves, are part of the means; we would like ourselves to be the end, so that all things work for our self-preservation. But when we recognize that our survival depends on the order imposed on all of us together and our environment, we have to re-assess the question.

While we can easily group ourselves into a mob that demands atavistic individualism for each and every individual, this leaves many questions unanswered. If society as a whole has no goal, that leaves us with a marketplace and a lack of clear behaviors which reward us outside of our own convenience.

Thinking on that for a moment, we can see how hollow such an existence would be, and how it would lead others into desperation and drag itself down with the weight of many desperate people acting selfishly but still feeling unfulfilled, tempting them toward more consumption, self-importance and other grotesque human traits.

With that in mind, we can see that this crux boils down to acceptance of life itself. We are mortal; we cannot forever preserve ourselves. Furthermore, acting only for ourselves through convenience and material comfort is not rewarding. Acting for the world at large, whether educating bright hopeful children or nurturing an old-growth forest or writing a symphony, is what connects us to reverent, transcendental meaning in life.

This gives us a choice to either accept that life is not absolute and eternally preserving of us, or to demand that it "should be" and deny our mortality and our need for meaning. If we accept life as not absolute, we see that we ourselves are not absolute, and that we should find a goal for which to aim which makes our daily struggles and eventual deaths pale in comparison to the meaning we find in life.

If we demand, instead, that life be absolute like our fear for our own physical presence, and deny the need for an abstract goal which transcends ourselves, we face a path of increasing denial of reality. Even more, we will eventually atomize ourselves, or lock ourselves into worlds of ourselves where by acting for ourselves we shut ourselves off from meaning, creating a cycle of consumption and neurosis where we seek meaning through means that cannot deliver it.

When our ancestors spoke of "good" and "evil", they designed these terms to be used situationally, meaning a bad or good outcome. Similarly, when they spoke of the importance of life, they believed themselves to be means and not ends: hands that labored toward a better society not only for individuals, but for the education of better future generations, nurturing of old-growth forests, and writing of symphonies.

In the modern time, with our rationalist logic encouraging a utilitarian outlook, we have translated "good" and "evil" into absolutes derived from situational fears – fears for our physical selves – and have made absolute a goal of preserving the means, and made it into an end. This closed-circuit outlook on reality starves us of meaning and makes us desperate, but because we've defined the world outside the self as most likely "evil" and threatening, we have no escape from that cycle.

The crux of how we face reality is whether we can accept death and invent meaning, or whether we balk in fear and push back at the knowledge that we are temporary and meaning is outside of ourselves; in effect, that we are means to an end that is far bigger than ourselves. That fear causes us to reject our true salvation, which is not only within ourselves to discover, but if recognized allows us to stop protesting against life, accept it, and make from it a beautiful world of meaning.

February 3, 2009

CPSIA information can be obtained
at www.ICGtesting.com
Printed in the USA
BVHW071333011220
594599BV00002BA/145